Refiguring the Map of Sorrow

Under the Sign of Nature:
Explorations in Ecocriticism

MICHAEL P. BRANCH,
SUEELLEN CAMPBELL,
AND JOHN TALLMADGE,
EDITORS

Refiguring the Map of Sorrow

Nature Writing and Autobiography

MARK ALLISTER

University Press of Virginia
Charlottesville and London

The University Press of Virginia

© 2001 by the Rector and Visitors of the
University of Virginia

Printed in the United States of America
on acid-free paper

First published 2001

9 8 7 6 5 4 3 2 1

LIBRARY OF CONGRESS CATALOGING-IN-PUBLICATION DATA

Allister, Mark Christopher.
    Refiguring the map of sorrow : nature writing and autobiography / Mark Allister.
        p. cm. — (Under the sign of nature)
    Includes bibliographical references and index.
    ISBN 0-8139-2064-7 (alk. paper) — ISBN 0-8139-2065-5 (pbk. : alk. paper)
    1. American prose literature—20th century—History and criticism.
    2. Autobiography.   3. Authors, American—Biography—History and criticism.
    4. Natural history—United States—Historiography.   5. Naturalists—
    Biography—History and criticism.   6. Nature in literature.   I. Title.
    II. Series.

PS366.A88 A4 2001
818'.5409492—dc21   2001023547

Contents

Acknowledgments

Reading and writing about autobiographies has given me great appreciation for the innumerable chain of events necessary to get a person to a particular point in a life, such as acknowledging the debts incurred in the writing of a book. My first such debt, for obvious and less obvious reasons, is to my parents, George and Shirley Allister.

This book was years in the making, and over those years I have been helped by numerous people. Malcolm Griffith, Mark Patterson, and Chris Anderson provided ideas and support at early stages, Carol Holly, John Barbour, and John Eakin at later stages. My sister and brother-in-law, Daphne and Don Rosenblitt, patiently explained psychoanalytic theory to me. Don Scheese turned the direction of the project at a crucial time, helping me to understand better the true subject of this book and encouraging me when I needed it. I am grateful to St. Olaf College for their support in the form of a summer research grant and a sabbatical leave.

Earlier versions of two chapters appeared elsewhere. I would like to thank the editors of Southern Illinois University Press for permission to reprint "Writing Documentary as a Therapeutic Act: Bill Barich's *Laughing in the Hills*," from *Literary Nonfiction: Theory, Criticism, Pedagogy*, edited by Wayne C. Anderson (© by the Board of Trustees, Southern Illinois University); and I would like to thank Dr. James B. M. Schick, editor in chief of the *Midwest Quarterly*, for permission to use "Living the Questions, Writing the Story: Sue Hubbell's *A Country Year*" (vol. 34, no. 4 [1993]: 446–64).

No writer could have a better editor than Boyd Zenner at the University Press of Virginia. She responded promptly at every step of the process, and I appreciate deeply her warmth and goodwill. I owe much thanks to the two readers for the press: John Tallmadge and Scott Slovic gave the manuscript the careful reading a writer can only hope for, and their lengthy critiques helped me immensely. Thanks also to my copy editor, Dennis Marshall, and Sue Oines at St. Olaf College for help with the manuscript.

Creation of this book took years, in part, because my life as a father is more important than my life as a scholar, and I would like to acknowledge my wonderful children, Betsy and Nat, who are and always will be my best creations. And greatest thanks to my wife, Jan, who listens to my ideas, asks me to explain again what isn't clear, and then uses her professional copyediting skills, her knowledge of literature, and her experience to make my writing into something far better than it was.

Refiguring the Map of Sorrow

Introduction

Writing as a way to work through grief is as old as art itself. And ever since romanticism's glorification of reflective individual expression, such writing has often taken the form of autobiography. From Thomas De Quincey's *Confessions of an English Opium Eater*, Henry Adams's *The Education of Henry Adams*, and Edmund Gosse's *Father and Son* to Richard Wright's *Black Boy* and Mary McCarthy's *Memories of a Catholic Girlhood*, autobiographers have constructed narratives to articulate the pain and make sense of it all. In this study I examine a related but distinct form of grief narrative: books in which the writers reframe and work through their grief by focusing on external subjects that absorbed each writer as a replacement for their loss.

All are books of mourning. All begin with the writers recounting a recent trauma and describing their initial despair and subsequent depression. All the books end with the writer announcing that they have moved—tentatively, awkwardly, mysteriously—through the mourning process. By writing of a subject that moves them deeply, by working to understand themselves primarily in relation to the non-human world around them, they learn ways of responding that teach them how to reenvision their own pasts, which helps them temper their disabling grief. These authors—Peter Matthiessen, Gretel Ehrlich, Bill Barich, Terry Tempest Williams, William Least Heat-Moon, and Sue Hubbell—write books about "others," about subjects as diverse as beekeeping, thoroughbred racing, and hiking through the Himalayas to see a snow leopard and meet a Zen lama, books that become, in the process and final product, healing autobiographies.

William Howarth, calling autobiography a literary version of self-portraiture, writes that the autobiographer "artfully defines, restricts, or shapes that life into a self-portrait" (86). Both writing one's life and painting one's portrait, he contends, are "uniquely transactional": the artist as model must both pose and paint; such artists study reversed images in a mirror, familiar to themselves but not to others; the image resists visual analysis, because motion (the painting by hand) changes the image; the image is complete yet superficial, showing bone structure but not bone; the painter, like the writer, works from both memory and sight. The analogy of autobiography to self-portraiture is revealing, but is actually less useful in describing the traditional autobiographies he discusses than the books in my study. Viewing traditional autobiography as self-portraiture obscures the most obvious structural feature: those narratives describe a span of years, "the past." For Saint Augustine, Benjamin Franklin, and Henry Adams, three among many that Howarth discusses, writing autobiography meant describing the events of one's lifetime. But for the self-portraitist, as for the writers discussed in this study, the past is not delineated. Both the self-portrait and these nonfiction texts capture and momentarily freeze a significant time, then metaphorically point that life in a new direction.

All six writers confront issues about how to write one's life, how to translate empirical knowledge of the world into nonfictional text, and how to portray the impact of the nonhuman world on the human. Unique to these books is the way each writer stands explicitly both outside and inside the text: outside in writing exposition about a subject; inside in making that exposition part of the grieving process, part of the writer's re-creation of self. Countless humans have grieved deeply and then slowly moved to a state of being that seemed other than grieving, but these individuals wrote, created a literary text, to help them do their grief work. Their texts are therefore both process and product, and it is as this combination that I wish to explore them. That is, I am interested in the arc of their mourning—the stages and epiphanies that they dramatize along the way, the process by which individually they regain hope or believe in a future, which is one way we might measure the end of mourning. But I am also interested in the intertwining of that arc into their literary act—their style; its relation to their personality as they describe it; the paradoxes and confusions that manifest themselves in the texts, even as the writers emerge into clarity.

I have read, taught, and written about autobiographies for fifteen years. Like so many colleagues who became interested in this field in the 1980s, I have watched with appreciation (and some astonishment) as the importance of autobiography has burgeoned in the academy and in our culture. Literary and general magazines that once relied on the short story—I am thinking here in particular of the *New Yorker* and *Harper's Magazine*—now routinely print portions of memoirs or autobiographical essays as their main feature. And critical studies of autobiographies have multiplied exponentially (a subject I address in chapter 1), as scholars have cast nets wider to enlarge our sense of the genre. This enlarging has been so successful that now the more inclusive term *life-writing,* which then includes forms such as the diary, memoir, and biography, has gained prominence, *autobiography* coming to seem too narrow.

Books that seem sui generis, not quite "autobiography," have long fascinated me. The books I take up in this study have not yet gained the attention of autobiography critics, despite the widening of the field. These books have been largely passed over, I will argue, because they challenge strongly held beliefs about human attachments. As I discuss at length in chapter 1, the recent interest in "relational autobiography" (writing about one's self in relation to someone else) has focused on human attachments, persons connected as parents and children, siblings, friends, co-workers, and so forth.[1] But in the books I will take up here, the writer's connection to the natural world is equally important. Metaphorically, the author's life is written on the land and all its inhabitants, human, animal, plant, and rock, and by turning terrain into text, geography into consciousness, these writers create a new and significant kind of life-writing. Ecology intertwines with culture.

In the past few years I have been teaching a course on environmental literature, and perhaps because of my immersion in such literature (as well as my own life experiences), I have begun noticing, in a way I had not before, the subtle and deep relations between people and land, people and animals. "Tell me the landscape in which you live, and I will tell you who you are," writes José Ortega y Gassett.[2] The contemporary essayist Scott Russell Sanders says it like this: "Nor do I apologize for trying to speak at once about the geography of land and the geography of spirit. They are one terrain" (*Staying Put,* xvi). Writing about one's place, placing oneself carefully in a surrounding ecosystem, both Gassett and Sanders imply, is inseparable from life-writing.

GRIEVING AND GENRE

The books in this study are blends of autobiography, literary nonfiction, and environmental literature. Because distinctions blur at the borders of hybrid genres, the term *ecotone* is useful in thinking about the genre of these texts. Ecologists use *ecotone* to denote an edge or border where two ecosystems merge and plants and animals from both systems mingle. Prairie meeting woodland would be an example. Ecotones often sustain a great diversity and density of life, because plants that need both sunlight and shade, for example, can flourish along borders.

Inhabiting generic edges, the books under investigation here exemplify an ecotone. For all six authors, that is, a nonfictional book about other people and places becomes intimately connected to their own selfhood because something in the nonhuman world teaches them about the human world. Each author begins in depression that shadows grief; each comes to put an end to depression, to move through mourning, by turning observations and stories of the external world into a narrative that heals. The blending of genres is each writer's intuitive response that more conventional ways of presenting the information would not serve their subjects or themselves well.

METHODS OF INQUIRY

Because I emphasize how writing nature is intertwined for these authors into writing the self, and vice versa, my theory and frameworks are essentially those of the literary scholar, though I liberally borrow the tools of psychology, ecocriticism, and autobiography theory.

To further my literary inquiry, I reach into my toolbox for help in discussing grieving. Of particular use is John Bowlby on attachment, separation, and loss; George Pollock and Gilbert Rose on the mourning process and creativity; and Emily Claspell and Larry Cochran on the dramaturgical perspective of grief. Because the writers of this study create dramatic stories, I turn to psychoanalytic narrative theory and to the work of Roy Schafer, Donald Pond Spence, and Meredith Skura. My method, however, differs considerably from the psychologist-researcher who presupposes a theory, interviews people to gather evidence, and finally constructs a model on the basis of that evidence to explain how an emotion such as grief, for instance, works. My method is also a different enterprise from the psychoanalytic model, which stresses free association and the importance of the psychoanalyst's role in transference, because I make the act of writing crucial, which would not be suitable for psychoanalysts who are working in a different setting and without a written text.

To further my inquiry, I again reach into my toolbox for insights from ecocritics such as John Elder, Don Scheese, Scott Slovic, Cheryll Glotfelty, and Peter Fritzell about the relations between humans and the nonhuman world that are described and dramatized in literature. Describing what he calls "the environmental imagination," Lawrence Buell suggests that it is time for literary scholarship and theory to move away from their desire to separate the human from the "natural" world. Human interests are not the only legitimate interests, Buell argues, and human accountability to the environment might be equally important as human accountability to other humans. I am not interested in using an environmental writer's work to springboard into discussions of local or global environmental issues (my book is not about policy or science), but following the lead of Buell and others, I "describe" the environmental imaginations of Hubbell, Ehrlich, Matthiessen, Barich, Heat-Moon, and Williams, and how those ever-imagining minds generate a literary text that, in the making, functions as grief work.

As I explore in this study how the literary act of self-creation can bring an end to grieving, I borrow not just from psychology and ecocriticism but from autobiography theory. When the study of autobiography turned away from its focus on the life lived and toward examination of how the writer creates a selfhood through literary strategies, interest in the genre exploded. While autobiography is certainly not fiction, its connections to fiction have been investigated and articulated, particularly by critics interested in how memory and storytelling, even about one's own past, are guided by fictive structures. Paul John Eakin, one of the most influential autobiography theorists, writes in his book *Fictions in Autobiography:* "Autobiographical truth is not a fixed but an evolving content in an intricate process of self-discovery and self-creation" (3). Eakin's view here helps me interpret these nonfictional, documentary-like books as acts of self-creation, as relational autobiographies that accomplish grief work.

AN OVERVIEW

As a fusion of autobiography, literary nonfiction, and environmental literature, the books in my study pose issues and questions unlike the canonical books in each field, and therefore have floated just out of sight of academic critics specializing in one genre or another. I begin this book, therefore, with a lengthy theoretical chapter that attempts to situate this subgenre historically in the fields of autobiography studies, literary nonfiction studies, and ecocriticism.

In chapter 2 I begin my close readings of the individual books under consideration, examining Sue Hubbell's *A Country Year,* a work that describes the natural history of her farm for a calendar year. Like the other writers, she announces in her opening pages that in her recent past she has been despondent—in her case, over the end of her marriage. The book dramatizes how she discovers, by immersing herself in the natural world, what in particular will help her create a satisfying life. Anchoring herself to a place, running a beekeeping operation, she learns how to build, as she says, "a structure on which a woman can live her life alone, at peace with herself and the world around her." *A Country Year* especially enacts a struggle between two conflicting impulses, paradoxical desires shared to some extent by all the writers. As a botanist, Hubbell has a fondness for naming and describing, for explaining the world in "scientific" language; but as a writer grappling with her own grief, she confronts again and again the mysteries of human existence and desire and, as she sees very clearly, the mysteries of the natural world. The drama of the struggle over how to name or describe intertwines with, becomes nearly indistinguishable from, the drama of her grief work.

In chapter 3 I take up Williams's *Refuge,* a powerful account of her mother's lengthy struggles with and eventual death to cancer. Her mother's slow death proceeds concurrently with the slow but destructive rise of Great Salt Lake that destroys the Bear River Migratory Bird Refuge (and other bird habitats), a refuge dear to Williams personally and professionally. While Williams struggles to accept nature's destructiveness as part of an ever-continuing cycle of life and death, whether it is rising waters or mutating human cells, she learns that she and her mother are part of, to use the book's subtitle, "an unnatural history of family and place." At thirty-four years of age, Williams has become the matriarch of her large extended family, as the women have all died from cancers, women who had been downwind from the testing of atomic bombs in the 1950s. There is no such thing as unnatural history, however, unless we make the common move (and mistake) to place humans outside of nature, and Williams grapples unsuccessfully, I believe, in accepting such a view. But her intense struggles to reconsider all that is "natural" or taken for granted in her life—her gender, family, Mormon religion, or landscape—lead her to find a new "refuge" in her own story, one made of intertwined vignettes of birds and the land, her family's deaths and lives.

In chapter 4, I discuss a second book about a mother dying from cancer. In Bill Barich's *Laughing in the Hills,* however, the author's mother's death is only briefly described, and then largely to give partial explanation for Barich's critique that America, at its heart, is cancerous, and to give impetus to his flight to a thoroughbred racetrack. Barich hopes that the racing world will serve him as a closed, ritualized system wherein he can understand metaphorically the larger world, and himself. And to the extent that his book has often been called the finest documentary on thoroughbred racing ever written, he accomplishes that goal. But the book shows, ironically, that only when Barich sheds his preoccupations with racing and gambling and begins to articulate the mysterious bonds between humans and animals does he come to an insight that helps him move through mourning. Barich's important "other" becomes the horse as totem animal.

In chapter 5 I turn to William Least Heat-Moon's *Blue Highways,* a travel book. Devastated by losing his university job and discovering that his newly estranged wife has a boyfriend, Bill Trogdon (until this point, the author has gone by his given Anglo name) feels compelled to flee, to escape the place that has brought so much pain. He begins a trip, driving his van along America's backroads, journeying through rural America with his books, his cameras, and his notebooks, in a nearly desperate attempt to create a self resistant to being overwhelmed by grief. By meeting people unlike himself and hearing their stories, by seeing and reflecting on unfamiliar landscape, Heat-Moon hopes for wisdom and consolation that will allow him to return "home." As with many of the writers in this study, Heat-Moon begins with a quest that changes as he proceeds, and part of the book's drama becomes the writer's recognition of the changed quest. Why his disabling grief comes to an end remains partly mysterious, and in *Blue Highways* it is connected to the subsequent writing of the book, as Bill Trogdon fashions the persona of William Least Heat-Moon, a "new" American honoring his Native American ancestry and getting to know his country.[3]

In chapter 6 I address Peter Matthiessen's *The Snow Leopard,* a book structurally similar to *Blue Highways* in that Matthiessen chronicles his journey across the Himalayas. Matthiessen hopes that his physical sojourn will spawn a mirror image, a spiritual journey that will put an end to his sadness over his wife's death. The book is filled with lush descriptions of Himalayan animal and plant life, filled with rich images of Tibetan culture. His book, however, aims not to be a travel book, in the usual definition of the genre. He writes primarily about the inner life, both his own and that of people who demonstrate in everyday living the power of Buddhism to center human existence. As moving and beautiful as the book is, paradoxes and questions emerge: What tensions exist between a Zen "seeing" and a Western accounting of that seeing? What emotions and insights can Matthiessen transfer to his "regular" life back in the United States?

All the books demonstrate to some extent how each writer's weavings of the inner life with all the inhabitants (human and not) of a landscape becomes a "spiritual geography" that leads to healing.[4] In Gretel Ehrlich's *The Solace of Open Spaces,* the book at the core of chapter 7, this weaving is at its most dramatic. Born in California, working as a documentary filmmaker in New York City, Ehrlich struggles after her fiancé's death—struggles even to decide where to live. And when she chooses Wyoming, a desolate lunar landscape to her family and friends, she recognizes the need to articulate—first to herself and then to others—her reasons. What is Wyoming? What is Wyoming to her? As she intertwines her own story with descriptions of this unfamiliar territory, Ehrlich pursues answers to these questions, her book coming to dramatize this psycholinguistic and psychobiotic quest. In particular, because of her work as a hired hand and then ranchowner in a traditionally male enterprise, Ehrlich (like Hubbell) wrestles with distinguishing between what she desires and what she thinks others desire for her. And likewise, Ehrlich must conceptualize and describe Wyoming for herself, in metaphors and insights that will make it home for her, will help her move through and out of depression.

In her wise book about inevitable separations, *Necessary Losses,* Judith Viorst details how all of us, beginning in infancy, face the loss of other humans whom we have come to rely on. Such tangible losses, she writes, are accompanied during a lifetime by countless less tangible others: "our conscious and unconscious losses of romantic dreams, impossible expectations, illusions of freedom and power, illusions of safety—and the loss of our own younger self, the self that thought it always would be unwrinkled and invulnerable and immortal" (16). While she does not discount the pain and trouble that such losses bring, Viorst shows how becoming aware of the ways our responses to loss shape our lives "can be the beginning of wisdom and hopeful change" (18). As all six books in this study imply in their closings, the writers have transformed loss into wisdom, which begins the process of change and leads to the living of a different kind of life, one less splintered, less anguished, more centered and interconnected.

In the following chapters I will discuss in more detail the frameworks of narrative, relationality, and loss and recovery that I bring to these books. But while I discuss in some detail six writers who describe carefully the "natural" world of plants, animals, and humans and thereby move through mourning, I am not interested in constructing a model of mourning from their examples, as a psychologist might do. A grieving author of an earlier era, C. S. Lewis, writing in a diary after his wife's death, sets out a metaphor useful to understanding the difference between studies of individual grieving and a model. "I thought I could describe a state," writes Lewis, "make a map of sorrow. Sorrow, however, turns out to be not a state but a process. It needs not a map but a history" (47). Williams, Barich, Ehrlich, Matthiessen, Hubbell, Heat-Moon—their "maps of sorrow" are also descriptions of a process, a history. Though the authors' traumas, personal stories, and subjects differ, as do the ways they interweave grief and recovery into the narrative, central to each book is a dramatic subtext in which the writers search for an appropriate form and language to represent their subjects and, simultaneously, to portray their subsequent healing.

1 Writing the Self through Others

Each of the thirty-six chapter titles of Terry Tempest Williams's *Refuge* focuses on a particular species of bird. A naturalist by profession, Williams fills her book with careful descriptions of the numerous avian species that flock to Great Salt Lake or the Bear River Migratory Bird Refuge for resting or nesting. For example, in her chapter "White Pelicans":

Hundreds of white pelicans stand shoulder to shoulder on an asphalt spit that eventually disappears into Great Salt Lake. They do not look displaced as they engage in head-bobbing, bill-snapping, and panting; their large, orange gular sacs fanning back and forth act as a cooling device. Some preen. Some pump their wings. Others stand, take a few steps forward, tip their bodies down, and then slide into the water, popping up like corks. Their immaculate white forms with carrotlike bills render them surreal in a desert landscape.

. . . The pelicans of Gunnison Island must make daily pilgrimages to freshwater sites to forage on carp or chub. Many pelican colonies fly by day and forage by night, to take advantage of desert thermals. The isolation of Gunnison Island offers protection to young pelicans, because there are no predators aside from heat and relentless gulls. (98–99)

We might call this kind of detailed, elegant writing her "naturalist" talk, grounded in science and Williams's own observations. But because she sees and even interprets the human world in part through bird behaviors and relations, Williams juxtaposes such objective descriptions with a very different kind of writing in which the I supersedes the eye and invites reader interpretation.

In her chapter "Whistling Swan," Williams describes walking the shore of Great Salt Lake after a storm and finding a recently dead swan. Dreading the loss of her mother from cancer, feeling depressed personally and professionally by the enormous loss of Great Salt Lake bird populations, Williams prepares its body as if for burial, an event that, for readers of the book and presumably for Terry herself, anticipates her mother's death. Williams untangles the long neck, straightens the wings, places two black stones over the eyes like coins, washes with her own saliva the swan's black bill and feet until they shine—and then she lies down next to the body and imagines herself a swan:

> I have no idea of the amount of time that passed in the preparation of the swan. What I remember most is lying next to its body and imagining the great white bird in flight.
>
> I imagined the great heart that propelled the bird forward day after day, night after night. Imagined the deep breaths taken as it lifted from the arctic tundra, the camaraderie within the flock. I imagined the stars seen and recognized on clear autumn nights as they navigated south. Imagined their silhouettes passing in front of the full face of the harvest moon. And I imagined the shimmering Great Salt Lake calling the swans down like a mother, the suddenness of the storm, the anguish of its separation.
>
> And I tried to listen to the stillness of its body.
>
> At dusk, I left the swan like a crucifix on the sand. I did not look back. (121–22)

In this passage, the details about swan migrations from the Arctic tundra to Great Salt Lake are certainly accurate, but their significance, I would maintain, is not that Williams is trying to teach us anything or to share biological information, as when she writes about the white pelicans. Instead, she is demonstrating the particulars of her own imaginings. Infusing this passage is the tension between a pastoral nature (camaraderie in the flock, clear nights and navigational stars, the harvest moon, the welcoming breast of the lake as a mother) and what, suddenly, that pastoral nature can become or do—the way, in other words, the pastoral contains destruction and death. The first tension leads to a second, one that Williams points to powerfully but rather enigmatically when she says that she "left the swan like a crucifix on the sand" and then "did not look back." What kind of religious moment is this for her? Does not looking back imply that she has gotten out of this encounter all that is possible, a definiteness? Or does she not look back out of fear, perhaps unacknowledged insight that despite all her desire to have this encounter teach her about accepting death, she cannot really do so when she "returns" to her life that includes her dying mother?

In numerous ways this scene in *Refuge* is a common, though problematic, "figure in the carpet" to all the writers of this study, as they "write" themselves in human and nonhuman "others." On one hand, the external world is available to be known, and each author will find language and structure to turn that world into nonfictional text; on the other hand, who and what each person is, and (in this case) their particular plunges into grieving, dictate how and what can be known of that world. While it is true that all writers of nonfiction face these difficult philosophical relationships between subject and object, mind and world, writer and text, a direct or even indirect examination of these issues rarely appears in nonfiction books. The "documentary" rendering of a nonfictional subject takes precedence over the self-construction. In most autobiographies, the reverse is true, in that the importance of the external world for author and reader lies primarily in how it contributes to evolution of selfhood. The books I discuss here inhabit a middle ground, where the relations between knower (author) and known (external world) in language become the vital subtext that invites reader interpretation.

In the chapters that follow, I focus on books that weave an autobiographical text of loss and recovery into description of and reflections upon an "other" subject. The books can serve readers as revitalizing stories of how absorption into other worlds, and the subsequent writing about it, helps the writer move through mourning, renewed and ready for a different life. By focusing on books structurally similar, I try to turn a sketch of a general pattern into a canvas that reveals details and specifics. But in this chapter I will follow a different impulse, situating these books in a broad conversation about autobiography studies, literary nonfiction studies, and ecocriticism.

AUTOBIOGRAPHY STUDIES

In his wide-ranging article summarizing autobiography studies, "Autobiography and the Cultural Moment" (1980), James Olney argues that autobiography was not considered interesting by critics (and writers) until they began looking more closely at the *autos,* the self, behind the autobiographical act and how that self shapes and is shaped by the act of writing. Attention to the I that half discovers, half creates itself, Olney says, "opened up the subject of autobiography specifically for literary discussion, for behind every work of literature there is an 'I' informing the whole and making its presence felt at every critical point, and without this 'I' stated or implied, the work would collapse into mere insignificance" (21). Interestingly, attention to the *autos* of autobiography created a new interest in *graphe,* because the self is not something there, finished and set in place, ready merely to be described, but something the writer is shaping. That shaping changes, in turn, the self that shapes the writing, in an ever-recursive act until pen is put down or computer turned off.

The last twenty years has seen exponential growth of autobiography studies, and many of literary criticism's insights and beliefs about self and narrative, gender and culture, and the referentiality of language have been shaped by this attention to life-writing, by brilliant readings of texts that at an earlier time would have had no place in the literary canon. But because of their near-exclusive concern with books focusing on individual identity—Augustine's *Confessions,* Rousseau's *Confessions,* Adams's *The Education of Henry Adams,* Richard Wright's *Black Boy,* Frank Conroy's *Stop-Time,* or Mary McCarthy's *Memories of a Catholic Girlhood*—critics attending to the complex act of "self writing life" have produced their own limited canon. The emphasis on texts that are not just autobiographical but that clearly announce themselves as "autobiographies"—focused on the writer's self-growth, on identity—is certainly understandable, in large part because critics have been intent on establishing principles and making categories. Representative titles of seminal early essays and books on autobiography show the emphasis on defining the field and asserting its singularity: Georges Gusdorf's "Conditions and Limits of Autobiography"; William L. Howarth's "Some Principles of Autobiography"; Louis A. Renza's "The Veto of the Imagination: A Theory of Autobiography"; William C. Spengemann's *The Forms of Autobiography: Episodes in the History of a Literary Genre;* and James Olney's *Metaphors of Self: The Meaning of Autobiography* offer but a few examples.[1]

In this, autobiography criticism has followed the path of any emerging field, and the similarities to the evolution of American literature criticism are striking. After World War II, as response, perhaps, to the United States shrugging off its sense of provincialism in cultural matters, ambitious and influential critical studies of American literature appeared, among them F. O. Matthiessen's *American Renaissance,* Charles Feidelson's *Symbolism and American Literature,* Richard Chase's *The American Novel and Its Tradition,* R. W. B. Lewis's *The American Adam,* and Leslie Fiedler's *Love and Death in the American Novel.* Such books both established American literature as worthy and attempted to codify a canon of texts by defining what was particularly "American," New World–like, about them. It was not until the conflicts of the Vietnam War challenged assumptions about whether Americanness was necessarily good, not until the racial conflicts of the 1960s and the beginnings of the women's movement showed that *American* in this literature equated with male and white, that the literary canon opened up.[2] Marxist and feminist theory, in particular, posed different questions about the relation of literature to culture. To find evidence for their theories, such critics often went to texts that had not been understood as American literature, even if they had been written by United States citizens living in the United States.

As with American literature criticism, studies of women's autobiography have provided a useful challenge to assumptions about how identity is textually created and presented, feminist critics showing how the preoccupation with individual identity has been shaped by male models of self-development. Mary G. Mason, in an early essay, "The Other Voice: Autobiographies of Women Writers" (1980), argues that for women, unlike men, "the self-discovery of female identity seems to acknowledge the real presence and recognition of another consciousness, and the disclosure of female self is linked to the identification of some 'other'" (210).

In numerous books and collections of essays that focus on gender in autobiography, feminist critics have elaborated and added to Mason's ideas on relational identity. Sidonie Smith, in *A Poetics of Women's Autobiography,* theorizes about "the ways in which the autobiographer's position as woman inflects the autobiographical project . . . the ways in which the autobiographer establishes the discursive authority to interpret herself publicly in a patriarchal culture and androcentric genre that have written stories of woman for her, thereby fictionalizing and effectively silencing her" (45). Domna Stanton and Susan Stanford Friedman problematize our notion of *bios* by showing the fluidity of "life" portrayed in noncanonical autobi-

ographies of women. Following their leads, Julia Watson, in her essay
"Toward an Anti-Metaphysics of Autobiography," "politicizes" autobiography further by using women writers of color and the German
writer Christa Wolf to destabilize Western, democratic, and middle-
class notions of selfhood in their relation to constructing a life. Betty
Bergland situates her work on autobiography in a matrix of postmodernism, feminism, and ethnic studies, and from the interweaving of these three prisms she argues for the recognition of a multiply
situated subject, a subject socially and historically shaped. What unites
all such inquiries is the strong desire to theorize the subject through
gender, which results in both the broadening of the canon and a loos-
ening up of the genre's principles. Texts such as Gertrude Stein's *The
Autobiography of Alice B. Toklas* or Maxine Hong Kingston's *The
Woman Warrior* become representative of a women's autobiography
that is defined, in large part, by the autobiographer's attempts to find
new forms that subvert the traditional, Western, male narrative of the
self-defining autobiographer-as-hero.[3]

Feminist critics often cite Nancy Chodorow's *The Reproduction of
Mothering* and Carol Gilligan's *In a Different Voice* for their work
showing how women, unlike men, view their lives as relational. As
Gilligan writes:

> Relationships, and particularly issues of dependency, are experienced
> differently by women and men. For boys and men, separation and indi-
> viduation are critically tied to gender identity since separation from the
> mother is essential for the development of masculinity. For girls and
> women, issues of femininity or feminine identity do not depend on the
> achievement of separation from the mother or on the progress of individu-
> ation. Since masculinity is defined through separation while femininity is
> defined through attachment, male gender identity is threatened by inti-
> macy while female gender identity is threatened by separation. Thus males
> tend to have difficulty with relationships, while females tend to have prob-
> lems with individuation (8).

While I agree with the general findings, Chodorow's and Gilligan's
conclusions have often been overstated and oversimplified.[4] The extent to which humans view themselves as having autonomy or being
entwined in a network of relationships is a spectrum (not an either/or
box), and individual men and women fall across this spectrum. The
claim that women write relational autobiographies while men write
autonomous autobiographies is too simplistic, because gender is only

one of many crucial factors that contribute to a book's purpose and design.

At the National Conference on Autobiography in spring of 1994, Paul John Eakin, in his keynote address, argued that all selfhood (for men *and* women) is relational, that narrative "is the mode in which relational identity is transacted" (25), and therefore life-stories about "others"—mostly, for Eakin, other family members—should be a central concern of autobiography critics. Eakin's claims are not radical of course, particularly to feminist critics, as we have seen, but I note the importance of this address because it brought the term *relational autobiography*, unhooked from its sole connection to women's books, into the center of autobiography studies.[5]

This concept of relational identity-making brings into sharp focus the many superb biographies of the late twentieth century in which the writers compose a parent's life: Geoffrey Wolff's *Duke of Deception,* Vivian Gornick's *Fierce Attachments,* Carl Bernstein's *Loyalties,* John Edgar Wideman's *Brothers and Keepers,* Carolyn Kay Steedman's *Landscape for a Good Woman: A Story of Two Lives,* Adam Hochschild's *Half the Way Home,* Philip Roth's *Patrimony,* Art Spiegelman's two *Maus* books, and Kim Chernin's *In My Mother's House: A Daughter's Story.* Biography and its study as a genre is closely tied to autobiography. Like the autobiographical act, in which a "past" narrative is given form by a "present" consciousness, the writing of biography is the self-creation of an other, as we see in this only partial list of biographies that finally become a kind of autobiography, wherein the authors show that telling another life can become a version of telling one's own.

For example, in Wolff's *The Duke of Deception,* Wolff's subject is his father (the father's given name is Duke), and for the son, telling the story of his father accurately means discovering what he did not know as a child and young man: his father's "real" past and therefore his own. In his essay on the craft of biography, "Minor Lives," Wolff said that when he began writing biographies he had written three novels "and had an affection for the novelist's control of his world, the sense of a world poised to be made up whole and shaped" (60). What becomes important in this new try at writing about his father is that he is not writing a novel. He has to discover and then confront, as a biographer, the "facts" of his father's life. That is, he cannot invent, while sitting at his desk, what seems right to invent; instead, he must do research—interview those who had known his father, write schools and companies for information about Duke, look up records in old newspapers.

What makes the research necessary is that at the core of Duke's "life" was deception, and the core of the book must be the untangling of it. What makes *The Duke of Deception* so powerful is that we see, directly in the narrative, the struggles of Geoffrey to "construct" his father and then reshape his own past with that new knowledge. The autobiographical text that weaves through this biography comes to function for Wolff much like psychoanalysis, in that the fusing of his father's biography and his own autobiography demands that he use new knowledge, new beliefs about his father, to reconceive his own past. "Writing," he says in "Minor Lives," "can heal, translating vague, unarticulated pain into narrative" (71). And this is what writing the biography of his father has done, transforming the chaotic feelings and desires of the unconscious, and even the half-shaped memory, into narrative, into stories that show, explain, heal.

If autobiography critics shift the focus from "autonomous selves" to how humans change and grow "relationally," then *autobiography* need not focus on the writer's "life." The "self" of *autos* might well change to "self/others," and the linear narrative of one person's life, as is typical in autobiography, might well be altered to include structures that are more ecological than chronological, figuratively more like an interconnected web. Nevertheless, all three emphases in autobiography studies—the early focus on the solitary self; the feminist critique that shows how culture encodes different models for women's identity formation; or Eakin's claims for relational autobiography—have rendered invisible, in a sense, books such as the ones in my study, for numerous reasons.

First, for Matthiessen, Ehrlich, Barich, Heat-Moon, Williams, and Hubbell there is no particular human "other" that shapes identity (at least in the text): the nonhuman world affects them equally (or more) and it is this world they also "write." Second, these authors do not tell stories of their childhoods, describe a religious conversion experience, or sustain a dramatization of selfhood in a way that makes their books seem comparable to the many solitary-self autobiographies. Third, because these authors embed the act of self-creation in a text primarily about an "outside" subject, their books are classified, for example, as "natural history," "travel," or "sports writing," and therefore are not autobiographies, understandably, for autobiography critics. And fourth, because Hubbell, Ehrlich, and Williams exemplify women who have made a satisfying life of outdoor work and write, in some sense, a version of a "masculine" narrative, their works have not fit well into theorizing about women's autobiography.

The philosopher David W. Hamlyn, in his essay "Self-Knowledge," makes a distinction between knowledge about ourselves and *self-knowledge,* a distinction useful to our considerations about relational autobiography and these texts. Hamlyn calls the first (knowledge about ourselves) self-consciousness, which can prohibit a gaining of self-knowledge: "Someone who has true insight into himself needs to be aware of what he is to others, but he does not need to be looking over his shoulder all the time to see how others are regarding him; to do so would inhibit a concern for and a commitment to what he is engaged in and thus one of the essential conditions of self-knowledge proper would be missing" (174). Crucial for Hamlyn is the idea that self-knowledge requires commitment and involvement; a person cannot stand back, observing actions from afar. One must, as Hamlyn says, "be involved in oneself" (194). But on the other hand, a person must have the capability to reflect, to understand intention and result, both for oneself and as one stands in relation to other people and the world.

If the typical autobiographer is immersed in self-consciousness, as Hamlyn means it, and writing nonfiction about the natural world or other people or places can lead away from reflection on one's own life, the writers in this study blend the two nicely into self-knowledge. *A Country Year* or *The Snow Leopard* or *Refuge* sit happily in the middle of a spectrum where on one end we might find an autobiography of an egoist, who seems interested only in himself, and on the other end a documentary by a writer absent in the work.

Involved in both reexamination of their own lives and other people and places, the writers in this study favor—in their use of verbs as well as in their actions—weaving, twining, meshing. For Barich, Heat-Moon, Matthiessen, Hubbell, Williams, and Ehrlich, connecting is not enough. They need to do more than "only connect." Being bound is not a matter of reducing freedom and limiting life, but one of enlarging life—of intertwining to heal and therefore become more free.

Autobiographers usually demonstrate a different impulse, as the very name of the genre suggests. Traditional autobiographies depict through time and space a single self, undeniably the star of the show, around whom everything revolves. An artist asked to represent the subject of an autobiography would in most cases draw a portrait of the writer. But for the books of this study, what would be drawn? A cowboy or jockey? The Bear River Migratory Bird Refuge? a Himalayan mountain peak? a van equipped to go on the road? Like Copernicus understanding the true nature of the solar system, these writers see themselves not solipsistically but as just one planet spinning around the suns of human, plant, and animal life.

Through metaphors such as the biotic pyramid or the Web of Life, ecology has brought us relational categories to understand our connections to others and to the natural world. The majestic blue whale is dependent on the lowly plankton, and humans can affect plankton in the oceans by what they do on land. All living things (and dead things, too) are interwoven into innumerable ecological communities, a good metaphor for what the books in this study demonstrate.

Though no autobiography critics probably believe, literally or metaphorically, in the Great Chain of Being, they often have written as if they valued most the writers and texts who replaced God at the top with the autonomous self who controls and acts upon a chain of events and does so through the passing of years. The focus on relational identity, on the way writers use other people to understand and explain themselves, has shown how the genre of autobiography can lessen its preoccupation with the self and move metaphorically toward the web of life. But as ecologists and ecocritics have argued, we must now take the next step and extend relationality to include human connections to animals, plants, and the land, connections to nonhuman others that can be just as influential.[6]

As autobiography studies has gained a longer history, as the insights of feminists about nonnormative texts have been applied to lifewriting not only for purposes of gender definitions but to embrace the multiplicity of voices in this enterprise, the scope of autobiography studies has widened, and will continue to do so.[7] For example, one of the most interesting directions in recent autobiography studies concerns the study of "illness narratives," which have been written and published in unprecedented numbers in recent decades. The journal *a/b: Auto/Biography Studies* published a special issue on illness, disability, and autobiography in 1991, and Thomas Couser investigates many forms of *autopathography* in his superb book *Recovering Bodies* (1997). These examinations of *autopathography* are related to my attempts to bring into view a kind of book outside the present range of vision. A second interesting direction in autobiography studies serves not as example but as model. Sidonie Smith, in "Performativity, Autobiographical Practice, Resistance" (1995), focuses not only on how autobiographical storytelling is performative, but how the self is actually created by (and shifts and responds to) the storytelling and the performance. And Leigh Gilmore, in her book *Autobiographics: A Feminist Theory of Women's Self-Representation* (1994), coins the term *autobiographics* for a description of self-representation and a reading practice that is "concerned with interruptions and eruptions, with resistance and contradiction as strategies of self-representation" (42). Because Smith and Gilmore probe the way that social constructions of gender, sexual orientation, and race constrain the "reality" of women's lives and therefore their life-writing, they are not addressing issues or books similar to those I take up. Their method, however, of reading "against" the Augustinian, coherent autobiographical self serves as a useful reminder that a literary act to perform grief work— through writing about human and nonhuman others—is anything but a simple performance of self-creation.

LITERARY NONFICTION STUDIES

Autobiography critics rarely know the books, or even the names, of Matthiessen, Barich, Hubbell, Ehrlich, Williams, and Heat-Moon. These writers are widely known, however, to readers of literary nonfiction and to teachers of writing.[8] Despite this popular and classroom audience, the writers have received almost no critical attention, in large part, I believe, because the books have been "considered" as documentaries of a specific subject. How these writers portray their own consciousness and self in relation to their subjects has yet to be analyzed.

Two books published in the 1940s are landmarks for contemporary American literary nonfiction: John Hersey's *Hiroshima,* a description of six survivors of the atomic bomb blast; and James Agee's *Let Us Now Praise Famous Men,* a study of Alabama tenant families during the Great Depression. Hersey tells the story of the nuclear bombing by following six ordinary Japanese people as they go about their day of August 6, 1945. Using narrative and scene-by-scene construction, Hersey renders in horrific ways the aftermath of the bombing, creating an immediacy in nonfictional prose that caused a sensation when it was published. Hersey, like Truman Capote and John McPhee to follow, is always the arranger, artfully maneuvering the action from behind the scenes, but he is ever absent, calling no attention to himself even as the writer or observer, like Flaubert's transcendent God of the text.

What sharply distinguishes *Let Us Now Praise Famous Men* from *Hiroshima*—and the poles of literary nonfiction—is the direct presence or absence of the writer. Agee, while at times writing himself completely out of the narrative, even to the extent of minimizing the artist's selectivity, at other times makes his own feelings, desires, and reevaluations of self an integral subject of the book. The writers of this study follow Agee's line.

Agee insists that any writer who claims "I have seen and know this" must directly explain how and why he is making that claim. "I would do just as badly," he writes, "to simplify or eliminate myself . . . as to simplify or invent character, places or atmospheres" (240). All documentary that Agee would consider truthful, therefore, becomes autobiography, which is as much discovering and fashioning a life as telling it. The relation between subject and self, and the desirability or necessity of acknowledging it in the text, are vexing though often masked issues in literary nonfiction. Agee, for example, struggles between two presumptions: that the external world is available to be known and has a reality independent of him, and that before he came to Alabama he did not know it as he does now. In other words, who and what he is dictates how and what he can know. "For in the immediate world," he says, "everything is to be discerned, *for him who can discern it*" (my emphasis) (11). Agee, presumably, becomes one who can discern it; being so, his task is to discern "centrally and simply, without either dissection into science or digestion into art, but with the whole of consciousness, seeking to perceive it [the immediate world] as it stands: so that the aspect of a street in sunlight can roar in the heart of itself as a symphony, perhaps as no symphony can: and all consciousness is shifted from the imagined, the revisive, to the effort to perceive simply the cruel radiance of what is" (11). Agee's oxymoronic *cruel radiance* points up his difficulty, however, as a demonstration of the problematic relationship between subject and object, mind and world.

Agee accompanies his prolonged probing of the subject-self relationship with lengthy explorations of what it means to put "real people" into language, into text. Unlike the "fictional" being present in drama, poems, or novels, there is an "actual" being, Agee argues, present in the external world. That actual being has enormous consequence independent of its presentation in literature: "In a novel, a house or a person has his meaning, his existence, entirely through the writer. Here, a house or person has only the most limited of his meaning through me: his true meaning is much huger. It is that he *exists,* in actual being, as you do and as I do, and as no character of the imagination can possibly exist. His great weight, mystery, and dignity are in this fact" (12). Agee decries the impossibility of language to embody, to capture actual being—the tenants' and his own. Words, says Agee, are "the most inevitably inaccurate of all mediums of record and communication" (236). One reason for this inaccuracy is their misuse by politicians, journalists, advertisers—anyone with deceptive motives. But that misuse also extends in general to American mass culture and even to thinking writers. Agee's frustration over the incapacity of language to portray life accurately becomes so great that he wishes for a directly representational artistic medium: "If I could do it, I'd do no writing at all here. It would be photographs; the rest would be fragments of cloth, bits of cotton, lumps of earth, records of speech, pieces of wood and iron, phials of odors, plates of food and of excrement. . . . A piece of the body torn out by the roots might be more to the point" (13).[9] *Let Us Now Praise Famous Men,* because of Agee's need to portray being in the text, becomes a literary manifesto about the capacity (or incapacity) of language in a nonfictional text.

Self-creation, autobiography, nonfiction books about other people—these suggest that there are real people who write real lives. But deconstructionist critics would deny this by arguing that such foundational concepts as truth, reality, knowledge, history, or the self rest on a naively representational theory of language. "History," for example, does not exist except textually; all we can know of the past are texts that attempt to tell us "history." And a writer cannot recreate the self in a text because the writer disappears behind the text of a text. Answering the question "what is an author?" Michel Foucault argues that the author's name on the title page does not refer to a real person—that there is no subjective presence who originates and takes responsibility for a text. Linguistic structures replace the concept of self. Michael Sprinker, taking Foucault's lead to its obvious conclusion, therefore declared "the end" of autobiography. If the self is a fiction (as perhaps the life is, too), then how can the self write its own life truthfully? The challenges of these theorists are instructive about the role of writing in the autobiographical act and a corrective to certain simplistic notions. A literary text cannot reproduce events, conversations, and feelings as they exactly occurred. But writers of literary nonfiction or autobiographers insist on their ability to portray humans living in a real, not just a textual, world.

Though Hersey's *Hiroshima* and Agee's *Let Us Now Praise Famous Men* raise almost all the important issues for writers and readers of literary nonfiction, it is not until the early 1960s that these issues enter a national debate, with arguments over the ethics of the reporting that came to be called the New Journalism.[10] To the reading public at large, the New Journalism broke down the belief that journalism is merely a transcription of events, rather than an artistic interpretation, in large part because the New Journalists discussed the fictional techniques they used to structure their reporting. When Truman Capote called *In Cold Blood* a "nonfiction novel," he initiated countless arguments, in and out of print, about whether or not the two "concepts" were antithetical, each dealing with their own kind of "truth." The New Journalists also made familiar the nonfictional text with direct authorial presence, as they often included themselves in their narratives, in part to shatter the illusion of "objective" reporting.

Much literary nonfiction blends self and subject on the text's surface. Tom Wolfe compares his role as a New Journalist to that of a method actor, one who gets inside the emotions and passions of people, but stays the actor. "It is a matter," he maintains (as quoted in Zavarzadeh [126]), "not of projecting your emotions into the story but of getting inside the emotions, inside the subjective reality of the people you are writing about." Such a view is obviously incompatible with the aims of the writers in this study, whose primary focus is to weave tightly their own emotions and stories directly into the narrative in order to show how their writing helps them re-see their own grieving.

By choosing to write about books that blend autobiography with writing about human and nonhuman others, I am moving in a direction somewhat different than the critics who have written scholarly studies of New Journalism or the broader category of literary nonfiction. John Hollowell in *Fact and Fiction* (1977), Mas'ud Zavarzadeh in *The Mythopoeic Reality* (1976), Ronald Weber in *The Literature of Fact* (1980), John Hellman in *Fables of Fact* (1981)—all generally address books that have engaged great cultural and political issues: the march on the Pentagon in 1967, the space program, the California drug counterculture, the Vietnam War. Such books as Norman Mailer's *The Armies of the Night* or Truman Capote's *In Cold Blood* enable these critics, who are primarily interested in New Journalism and the nonfiction novel, to place large genre questions about fiction and nonfiction, literature and journalism, within a historical or cultural framework.[11] Hollowell, in a representative statement, claims that his study "properly begins with the pervasive social changes in America during the 1960s and the responses of novelists and journalists to those dislocations. A most interesting response has been a form of nonfiction that relies upon the narrative techniques and intuitive insights of the novelist to chronicle contemporary events" (ix). "Reality" had by then become so bizarre, the line goes—following Philip Roth's argument in his oft-cited *Commentary* essay—that one could no longer write realistic fiction.[12] Writers could turn toward fabulism or metafiction or, if they wished not to leave the "world," toward nonfiction forms based on verifiable facts and records. Counterpointing fact and fiction—New Journalism or the nonfiction novel—became the most authentic way of dealing with the reality of society.

The apocalyptic belief during the 1960s that society was about to change, and radically, perhaps spawned the book-length studies of Hollowell, Zavarzadeh, Weber, and Hellman, written during the 1970s, when the outcome of social upheavals was still undecided. But since 1980, when American politics and culture of the Reagan-Bush-Clinton era have suggested the impossibility of large-scale change, studies of literary nonfiction have likewise altered. Though there has been more *writing* of literary nonfiction (its market has grown tremendously), the scope of criticism has shrunk, critical essays replacing books, and those essays generally moving away from historical and social issues toward more sophisticated theoretical arguments of genre, responding to the influence of poststructuralist theory.[13]

Because it has become a commonplace—in literary study as well as in fields as diverse as history and anthropology—to presume that all factual narratives are versions, "constructed," in Barbara Herrnstein Smith's words, "as *all* versions are, by someone in particular, on some occasion, for some purpose, and in accord with some relevant set of principles" (218), critics interested in nonfictional texts have shifted the emphasis toward explaining how readers use textual clues to take a position regarding the status of fact, the objectivity of the author, and so forth. Though deconstructionists argue generally that the boundaries between nonfiction and fiction have become effaced—all texts are "fictions," no language is purely "referential," and "facts" are dependent solely on individual perception—those critics who wish to maintain some distinction between a *reading* of a novel and a nonfictional text have looked toward understanding the ways that readers and communities of readers make meaning, which leads away from the deconstructionist impasse.[14] Critics of literary nonfiction, attempting to show more precisely how readers create truths out of factual works, have demonstrated that a reader's constructions are influenced by notions of what constitutes the "literary" or the "political," crucial categories for assessing the impact on the reader of much literary nonfiction.

Whether critics are arguing about contemporary American nonfiction for historical or theoretical purposes, one of the primary (overt and usually stated) aims is to persuade other critics to take literary nonfiction seriously—to grant it the status of poetry, drama, and fiction. The publication of Chris Anderson's book *Style as Argument: Contemporary American Nonfiction* (1987) began a new direction for the study of literary nonfiction. Anderson, like most nonfiction critics before him, addresses the texts of Wolfe, Capote, Mailer, and Didion (arguably *the* canonical American nonfiction writers), but his goal was "to take the next step in the study of nonfiction discourse, not arguing in the abstract for the value of the genre but dramatizing that value through concrete, inductive readings of actual texts" (4). Anderson states that as his analysis unfolds, he wants "not only to explain the central strategies and forms of contemporary American nonfiction but also to demonstrate how its rhetorical self-consciousness prepares us to regard style itself as argument" (5–6). A collection of essays edited by Anderson in 1989, *Literary Nonfiction: Theory, Criticism, Pedagogy,* continued the effort to create a practical criticism.

Unlike Anderson, my attention on prose style will be to show how Hubbell, Ehrlich, Matthiessen, Barich, Williams, and Heat-Moon use various structures and styles to do their grief work, but like Anderson, I will not, in *Refiguring the Map of Sorrow,* try to place the genre of literary nonfiction in a particular historical context or rehearse arguments about fact and fiction. Likewise, I will not argue in the abstract for the value of nonfiction but rather will dramatize that value through close readings of books, though of a particular kind. The drive in the last decade of literary nonfiction is to the particular and specialized, away from the books that grandly conceptualize and comment on American cultural events. The more-specialized "line" that interests me here is, of course, nature writing, which is often a kind of literary nonfiction, but one usually unacknowledged because the primary focus is the nonhuman world, and New Journalism and literary nonfiction in general are preoccupied with people—individual people, humans in groups, and human culture.

NATURE WRITING AND ECOCRITICISM

Most academics are, by demographic definition, urban or suburban residents. Moreover, they live constantly in a world of human language: newspapers, magazines, books, conversations. Literary scholars have a bias for the techniques and languages of poetry, fiction, and drama, for the human world over the nonhuman world, for *culture*, a human construct. The writers who write human-centered autobiographies and literary nonfiction that, in structure and language, are most like poetry or fiction are the ones who receive the greatest attention. Because autobiography critics emphasize in general the "textual world," they conflict with writers who insist on another, not-textual world, who insist that inherent in the land is a stubborn force ultimately primary and dominant. The mystery of that land, these writers believe, is finally unfathomable, and the force and mystery can only partially be articulated in language.

Henry David Thoreau (in the *Journals*), John Burroughs, John Muir, Mary Austin, William Beebe, Henry Beston, Edwin Way Teale, Roger Tory Peterson, Rachel Carson, Joseph Wood Krutch, Loren Eiseley: even a short roll call suggests the long and distinguished tradition of natural-history writing in America.[15] Beginning with such texts as Thomas Jefferson's *Notes on the State of Virginia* and William Bartram's *Travels,* the descriptions of the American landscape (and all of the plants and animals in it) have often been useful to those, like Emerson, seeking to create an "American" literature, one not dependent on the British Isles, but looking to this land for its subjects and inspiration. As scientists or natural historians with the novelist's gifts of language and narrative, many of this country's greatest environmental writers have described what in nature disturbs them or gives them profound joy.[16]

One line of recent American environmental literature has continued in the vein of the literary naturalist, and these writers, among them Ann Zwinger, John McPhee, John Hay, and Gary Paul Nabhan, make biology or geology (science) their primary orientation. The authors, though present in their books, distrust making epiphanies about the psychology of human lives and seem reluctant to create metaphors that bridge the natural and human worlds. But for a second major line of contemporary nature writing, writers such as Annie Dillard, Edward Abbey, Kathleen Norris, Brenda Peterson, Scott Russell Sanders, Barry Lopez, William Kittredge, John Elder, and Linda Hasselstrom, observations of nature are inseparable with their observations of human lives, particularly their own. The writers of this study follow this line. As Sanders writes in *Staying Put,* "I have been thinking about stories of place in an effort to understand how the geography of mind adheres to the geography of earth" (150).

In a famous passage from "The Ponds" in *Walden,* Thoreau shows how writing self and writing nature are intertwined for him:

These experiences were very memorable and valuable to me,—anchored in forty feet of water, and twenty or thirty rods from the shore, surrounded sometimes by thousands of small perch and shiners, dimpling the surface with their tail in the moonlight, and communicating by a long flaxen line with mysterious nocturnal fishes which had their dwelling forty feet below, or sometimes dragging sixty feet of line about the pond as I drifted in the gentle night breeze, now and then feeling a slight vibration along it, indicative of some life prowling about its extremity, of dull uncertain blundering purpose there, and slow to make up its mind. At length you slowly raise, pulling hand over hand, some horned pout squeaking and squirming to the upper air. It was very queer, especially in dark nights, when your thoughts had wandered to vast and cosmogonal themes in other spheres, to feel this faint jerk, which came to interrupt your dreams and link you to Nature again. It seemed as if I might next cast my line upward into the air, as well as downward into this element, which was scarcely more dense. (120–21)

Thoreau here gives much concrete, literal description, then presents himself acting in that scene, and finally draws a large metaphor from the event. As befitting description and narration, the first sentence is cumulative, continuing on and on with coordinate modifiers. *And* is the most important conjunction; *as* and *at length* suggest how this style depicts something happening in linear time, as opposed to the back-and-forth of argument. The passage is immensely poetic, the rhythms enacting the description. For example, in the sentence "At length you slowly raise, pulling hand over hand, some horned pout squeaking and squirming to the upper air," the embedded adjectival modifier slows down the action of the sentence and the repetition of *hand* creates the effect of hand-over-hand. Or, in the phrase of the next sentence, "to feel this faint jerk," the spondee *faint jerk* in a generally iambic rhythm makes the reader take up, feel like a fish has just bitten. The description and poetry build to an epiphany when Thoreau unites heaven and earth, dreams and nature, his body with his transcendental self, in that final metaphor. His "line" can go up into the air or down into the water, the two having merged to give him a spiritual at-oneness with his world. And in the constant interchange of *I* and *you,* he unites himself to the reader.

For Thoreau and other contemporary nature writers, attachment to the land and its inhabitants is equally important as attachment to humans. In a prophetic remark that seems truer for people in our period of history than in ancient Greece, Socrates says in Plato's *Phaedrus:* "I'm a lover of learning, and trees and open country won't teach me anything, whereas men in the town do."[17] In countless ways, from school curriculums to disparate salaries for work, Socrates' belief is one thread that stitches our culture together.[18] Our minds are little attuned to anything but the human-made world or, if to the day's weather, how it affects our choice of clothing. Work and leisure for nearly all Americans are fundamentally *human* activities; likewise, most autobiographies and works of literary nonfiction are absorbed in the author's or subject's encounters with other humans or our surrogates: books, school, work, ideas, or writing. This human-centeredness powerfully influences what we see and categorize. And because we value the human bond over the bonds between humans and animals or humans and plants, books about animals and plants are considered of lesser importance.

When Odysseus returned to Troy he hanged a dozen female slaves of his household whom he suspected of misbehavior. In *A Sand County Almanac,* Aldo Leopold uses this example to demonstrate that in Odysseus's time the women were merely property, to be treated as Odysseus saw fit, without any of the rights that in today's United

States we would accord all humans. But we still do not accord rights to animals or the land, Leopold says, because "there is as yet no ethic dealing with man's relation to land and to the animals and plants which grow upon it. Land, like Odysseus's slave-girls, is still property. The land-relation is still strictly economic, entailing privileges but not obligations" (238). And what results for humans when there is no land ethic, when, indeed, there is disconnection in everyday life from land, animals, and plants? What results from hundreds of years of increasing dependence on technology and human-controlled environments?

In his intriguing meditation on "perception and language in a more-than-human world," the subtitle to his book *The Spell of the Sensuous,* David Abram has reflected on what this disconnection of human to land means, wondering, he writes, "if my culture's assumptions regarding the lack of awareness in other animals and in the land itself was less a product of careful and judicious reasoning than of a strange inability to clearly perceive other animals—a real inability to clearly see, or focus upon, anything outside the realm of human technology, or to hear as meaningful anything other than human speech" (27). What nature writers do is listen to nature, and then try to turn that listening into text. As Norman Maclean writes in the famous conclusion to *A River Runs Through It:*

Like many fly fishermen in western Montana where the summer days are almost Arctic in length, I often do not start fishing until the cool of the evening. Then in the Arctic half-light of the canyon, all existence fades to a being with my soul and memories and the sounds of the Big Blackfoot River and a four-count rhythm and the hope that a fish will rise.

Eventually, all things merge into one, and a river runs through it. The river was cut by the world's great flood and runs over rocks from the basement of time. On some of the rocks are timeless raindrops. Under the rocks are the words, and some of the words are theirs.

I am haunted by waters. (104)

If we know how to listen, the novel suggests, we can hear the words of the rocks. Nature speaks. But in our discourse nature is silent, a symbolic presence only, a mute object.[19]

Our society's efforts to lessen discrimination and to be tolerant are reflected in how obvious it seems for literary critics to discuss literature in terms of race, gender, class, or sexual orientation. But the environmental movement, a social force for forty years, has only recently spawned literary criticism to accompany it. As Lawrence Buell puts it: "To investigate literature's capacity for articulating the nonhuman environment is not one of the things that modern professional readers of literature have been trained to do or for the most part wish to do. Our training conditions us, on the contrary, to stress the distinction between text and referent" (10). Few teachers and scholars focus on ecological concerns; few attempt, that is, to change *ego*-consciousness to *eco*-consciousness, in Glen Love's phrase.[20]

Ecocriticism takes as its cornerstone the desire to articulate the intricate webs of relations in the natural world. Humans, who are animals and just as "natural" as mountain lions, oaks, or rocks, are an important part of such relations, but nonhuman "others" are given attention, both for themselves and for their relationality to humans. Cheryll Glotfelty, an editor of *The Ecocriticism Reader,* suggests that as a critical stance ecocriticism "has one foot in literature and the other on land; as a theoretical discourse, it negotiates between the human and non-human" (xix).

In subsequent chapters I take up in more depth subjects particular to environmental literature, such as the debate about anthropomorphizing or how books that are romantic and pastoral can also embrace postmodern relationality. But I will conclude this section by showing briefly how the act of nature writing and autobiography can become linked, and what that linkage means to autobiography studies. Authors who "write nature" confront issues familiar to autobiographers and writers of literary nonfiction: issues about the self and subject, about the autobiographical hidden in but shaping the nonpersonal; about representation of the external world into language.[21] One aim of my study is to show that how we tell about the land around us, the ways we reveal its various and complex meanings, says implicitly much about who we are; for example, Terry Tempest Williams's passages on the white pelicans and the dead swan demonstrate how these subjects become intertwined. Barry Lopez, in "The American Geographies," writes that "it is through the power of observation, the gifts of eye and ear, of tongue and nose and finger, that a place first rises up in our mind; afterwards it is memory that carries the place, that allows it to grow in depth and complexity" (131). Memory brings stories, and the stories connect memory to the land, and this connection prods us to look again, in an act combining both fieldwork and imagination. The writers whose books I discuss in this study counter our usual ways of thinking about autobiography: *my-*

self, *my* life, *my* writing. Change the familiar terms of autobiography studies *(self, life, writing)* only slightly to *land, memory, stories* and the writing about other places and landscape may become an autobiographical act.[22]

I am not the first critic to note this connection, of course. Peter A. Fritzell, in his important early work of ecocriticism, *Nature Writing and America: Essays upon a Cultural Type* (1990), argues that "the best" American nature writing "arose from an uneasy, inherently unstable, and especially American attempt to meld or blend the traditions and forms of Aristotle's *Historia Animalium,* on the one hand, and Saint Augustine's *Confessions,* on the other" (3). In discussing in depth Thoreau's *Walden,* Leopold's *A Sand County Almanac,* and Dillard's *Pilgrim at Tinker Creek,* and referring to books by Eiseley, Abbey, Lopez, and John Janovy, Fritzell is most interested in writers who enact in their texts epistemological doubts and metaphysical despairs, even while they concretely describe the nonhuman world around them. Fritzell's thesis, though rather wide-ranging, is usefully suggestive. And in a broad way my study attempts to refine that thesis, though I am less interested than Fritzell in naming "the best," and in my attempts to describe this literary act of doing grief work I include books that he would not call nature writing. His desire to create a distinctively American genre leads him to emphasize exclusively the Thoreauvian tradition, and so he mistakenly places Hubbell's *A Country Year,* for example, into the category of "rural literature." Fritzell is not able to see, perhaps because of the book's style and because the self-creation is less obviously "confessional," that Hubbell, likewise, blends natural history writing with autobiography.

One of the most astute and persuasive of autobiography critics, Julia Watson, helps us inadvertently discern what books such as *The Snow Leopard* or *A Country Year* accomplish, even while they remain invisible to her and to autobiography studies in general. In her important essay "Toward an Anti-Metaphysics of Autobiography," Watson uses two sets of writers to attack the privileging of *bios* and a Western metaphysics of self. A group of "troublingly self-reflexive narratives," the autobiographical writings of Montaigne, De Quincey, and Rilke, "can be read as transgressive boundary texts that disrupt the genre's *bios*-based self-definition and reveal the shifting instability inscribed within the representation of any Western self" (61). A second group of writings, by women of color who are marginalized in multiple ways, "argue for resituating autobiography as an inescapably collective and oppositional form" (72).

I agree in both cases with Watson's analysis, and I will add a third set, nature writers, who critique our usual notions of selfhood by arguing in essence for a relational view of humans within the physical world at large; and, moreover, who emphasize the shaping of human emotions by that physical world, thus undermining the importance placed in autobiography studies on a life's events performed by a solitary actor, the autobiographer, with an audience of other humans. But I also want to go a step farther. The books I discuss here—*Laughing in the Hills, Blue Highways, The Snow Leopard, A Country Year, The Solace of Open Spaces,* and *Refuge*—show that most theorizing about relational autobiography, in its privileging of race or gender, its privileging of particular forms such as the "conversion" narrative or the "friendship" narrative, needs altering as well as enlarging. And simultaneously, most theorizing about nature writing, because of its preoccupation with "environmental issues" or science and its desire to keep humans completely away as one defining characteristic, needs altering as well as enlarging. As Matthiessen, Williams, Barich, Hubbell, Ehrlich, and Heat-Moon do their grief work by carefully turning "others" into text, whether other humans or the nonhuman world, they can help teach us about "writing the self," and their writing of the self can teach us about the "other" world.

2 Living the Questions, Writing the Story

Sue Hubbell's *A Country Year*

In her essays "Bad Government and Silly Literature" and "The Edge of Town, Duluth, Minnesota," Carol Bly, a long-time farmer, writer, and teacher from rural Minnesota, decries the lack of ethical consciousness in most American writing and sees the act of "nature-describing" as an avoidance of naming that which is evil, wrong, or immoral in our society. Bly sharpens her criticism in words quoted on the back cover of a collection of poems by Joe Paddock: "When a poet wants to avoid pain, he or she sometimes settles for sharp imagery that excites readers but leaves them free to work for the CIA during the daytime"; a person living in the country who wants to avoid pain, Bly adds, "sometimes becomes a regional nature-describer."[1] Bly criticizes nature-describing as stories written by the financially secure and privileged, read by those who like only a light repast before going to sleep untroubled.

Though Bly sees only hordes of "nature-describers," there is an equally long tradition of American writers who have used the natural world to re-see the human-made world, who have gathered ethical and moral insights by temporarily distancing themselves from human activity. Henry David Thoreau's observations of society from the vantage point of Walden Pond—and his caustic utterances do outnumber the actual descriptions of nature—have been prophetic to later generations. For contemporary writers from Annie Dillard to Paul Gruchow, *Walden* has served as a model of how to create personal and social epiphanies from experiences in nature. Many of our visionaries and prophets (as well as ordinary people) have gone to the "woods" in order to live deliberately, to front the essential facts of life, to learn from nature.

If, on one pole, nature-describing avoids ethics and even reflection, as Bly suggests, and on the other pole, nature writing leads to transcendentalist truths and to testimony of ecstatic experiences, Hubbell's *A Country Year* resides nicely in the middle ground. Her social commentary is implicit, understated. Hers is a quiet book, filled with descriptions of the animal and plant life around her, with descriptions of her daily activities. Hubbell exemplifies the belief that to turn place into home we must understand how, as Sanders says in *Staying Put*, "the geography of land and the geography of spirit are one terrain" (xvi).[2] Though much in American culture, particularly the powers of capitalism and advertising, urges us to be discontented and to wander, to desire the new and the different, Hubbell shows how slowly gained but deeply felt knowledge of where she lives helps her understand how to live. She turns her gaze outward, toward how she fits into the natural world of her farm, hoping to see more clearly what is inside. When she comes to know how intimately she is tied to the network of nonhuman relationships, she gains understanding that not only lessens the pain of the human link that failed (her marriage) but gives her a framework to reevaluate her own desires and needs. Writing her farm's natural history for one year leads her to reframe her present life-story in similar terms—in a narrative of ecological balance, self-sufficient and self-sustaining.

As we read Hubbell's literary act, the writing of *A Country Year*, a book that dramatizes how grief work and recovery can be interwoven into a book of animal and plant biology, questions emerge: How does nonhuman relationality serve Hubbell's act of self-creation? Can and even should a human life be comparable to an ecosystem and have ecological balance? How do the living on and writing about her farm help her compensate for loss and move through mourning? How do two opposed actions of the mind—trying to pin the thing down, luxuriating in mystery and the irreconcilable—work in both science and art? Responses to these questions are not only crucial to reading *A Country Year* in its deserving complexity, but their variations serve as the informing questions for all the books here, as I will show in subsequent chapters.

Hubbell begins the natural history of her farm in a rather unexpected way, with a discussion of boundaries and claims. The river that bounds her property east and north is "claimed" by the U.S. Park Service, the creek to the south by the Missouri State Conservation Department. Hubbell's deed to the land says she owns 105 acres, but the farm is really only about 90 acres, she believes, because the last survey, done in the mid 1800s, was inaccurate. No one is sure where the farm's boundary to the west really lies.

These are typical economic claims about land, human claims of course, though their placement here is ironic because inaccurate surveys, the impossibility of owning water, and the possibility of shifting river banks make difficult the kinds of economics usually necessary for buying and selling. But there is another kind of human claim about land, Hubbell goes on to say, an emotional (not economic) one. She calls her farm "prime land," though not because of its fertility or its availability to be "developed," two of the common ways we measure a land's worth. The farm is prime land to her because it is beautiful and she lives there.

Hubbell questions human ownership by introducing others who have similar kinds of claims: animals and insects. She describes, in this opening, the indigo buntings who eat and sing, acting like "they own the place." Her census of the farm includes buzzards, goldfinches, phoebes, whippoorwills, cardinals; coyotes, bees, snakes, turtles, raccoons, skunks, deer, bobcats; and insects beyond number. "All of them," Hubbell writes, "seem to have certain claims to the place that are every bit as good as and perhaps better than mine" (7). Human boundary arguments ignore such claims. Some of her neighbors, for example, are in a dispute because one wants to bulldoze and develop—wants, in other words, to make a claim that ignores the census of animals and plants, and the desires of human neighbors.

When Hubbell begins her next chapter with a discussion of her failed marriage, she introduces, again, boundary questions. She gives only a few details, and these in a matter-of-fact tone: "I met Paul, the boy who was to become my husband, when he was sixteen and I was fifteen. We were married some years later, and the legal arrangement that is called marriage worked well enough while we were children and while we had a child. But we grew older, and the son went off to school, and marriage did not serve as a structure for our lives as well as it once had. Still, he was the man in my life for all those years.

There was no other. So when the legal arrangement was ended, I had a difficult time sifting through the emotional debris that was left after the framework of an intimate, thirty-year association had broken" (8). Boundaries, we often believe, are restricting, but they also structure, create a viewpoint—a reference around which to organize what is seen and known. Hubbell's loss of marriage meant a loss of a known framework, a known way of viewing herself in the world. Her disorientation led, she writes, to "the usual things": depression, a destructive affair, bad decisions about her honey business. Most painful of all, she says, "for a long, long time, my mind didn't work. . . . My attention came unglued when I tried to read anything but the lightest froth. My brain spun in endless, painful loops, and I could neither concentrate nor think with any semblance of order" (8–9).

Hubbell's responses to her failed marriage echo descriptions of researchers who study grieving. In his monumental three-volume series on attachment, separation, and loss, John Bowlby applies his attachment theory of mother and child to grief in general. Bowlby identifies four general phases of mourning, though he suggests that the phases are not clear-cut and an individual may oscillate back and forth between any two of them. As an initial reaction to the loss, the grieving person usually has a short phase of numbing alternated with outbursts of distress and anger, followed by a phase of yearning and searching for the lost person. Phase three, Bowlby suggests, is a phase of disorganization and despair that can last for months or years (and, in pathological mourning, sometimes never be gotten through). The disorganization and despair comes often from the radical and disturbing change in how one imagines a present and future life—that is, that the self's role has become undetermined, the self's script utterly lost. Only by rewriting the script (to continue the metaphor), which requires reexamining selfhood, may the grieving person move, in Bowlby's words, to a final phase of a greater or less degree of reorganization of one's role and life (*Loss*, 85).

What rescues Hubbell's mind and helps her begin the move from disorganization to reorganization is nature in general and botany in particular. Linnaeus's scheme of Latin binomials, she writes, is "a beautiful tool for thinking about diversity in the world," because the first word of a plant's name tells the genus (diverse plants that nevertheless share a commonality) and the second word of the name identifies the species, plants alike enough to interbreed. She "botanized obsessively during that difficult time," because it gave her a frame-work for understanding, "a way to show how pieces of the world fit together" (10). Linneaus leads her back to believing that the world has order, and so Hubbell fills a fat notebook, writing down plant names, their habitats, habits, and dates of blooming. "My brain, unaccustomed to exercise, was now on overload," she writes. Her botanizing extends to careful observation of the surrounding animal life, and one day she realizes that "the world appeared to have been running along quite nicely without my even noticing it. Quietly, gratefully, I discovered that a part of me that had been off somewhere nursing grief and pain had returned" (12). Her divorce had led her to feel that there were no ties, no enduring relations, no self that was not Paul's wife; her botanizing teaches her differently, even if those ties are less to the human world (and certainly a particular human), and more to the animal and plant world.

Hubbell's interweaving of traumatic loss and natural history, dealing as it does with conflict and change, lends itself particularly to psychoanalytic theory. Analysts agree that analysis must teach a patient that his or her disturbed past continues to be, unconsciously, the disturbing and disturbed present. A "cure" becomes dependent, therefore, upon the patient's ability to fashion, after examining the past life, a certain kind of story based on key recollected events. That story must be a history that heals instead of paralyzes. Analysts disagree, however, on the role that the patient must or even can assume, both in "recovering" or understanding the past, and in living the present.

Freud (as usual) lays the foundation of this argument. In order to "resolve the symptoms" of neurotics, he says in his *Introductory Lectures on Psychoanalysis,* "we must go back as far as their origin, we must renew the conflict from which they arose, and, with the help of motive forces which were not at the patient's disposal in the past, we must guide it to a different outcome" (454). In this and many similar passages, Freud implies that patients in analysis can recover the past, heretofore buried under layers of defenses, and then present it to themselves and their analysts for modification. The analyst, as Freud was fond of saying, becomes an archaeologist sifting through memories and desires, careful to keep what is of value.

The "analyst as archaeologist" assumes that patients' memories of their lives always contain "historical truth," always tap into an actual happening of the past.[3] And yet Freud himself demonstrated, in his famous "Wolf Man" case, for example, that if we cannot recover the past, we can create it in order to make sense out of later symptoms. Freud showed, that is, the persuasive power of a coherent narrative. One's personal past does not have to be, cannot be, remembered precisely as it happened, but it can be constructed. Roy Schafer, though a Freudian analyst, simply accepts as a given rule that all life-histories are a fiction. Psychoanalysis, he writes in *Language and Insight*, "consists of the construction of a personal past . . . merely a history of a certain kind" (8). For a "cure," the patient and analyst need to make a "narrative truth" that is coherent and consistent, that satisfies because it makes sense of something confusing. The analyst functions less as archaeologist and more as editor to the patient's novel.

Schafer counters Freud's view that one is helped by recapturing memories and repetitively reworking them. Because patients have been shaped by language and can use it in turn to create new meanings, Schafer argues, they must, in essence, rewrite old events in new terms: rewrite in such a way that the past creates a healthier present. Schafer teaches patients to reinterpret and then "write" their own interpretations of past events and then to recognize their own power in authoring significant future events. With this emphasis in psychoanalytic theory on narrative truth, it is a short—but radical—step to have patients not address directly their present problems, but instead immerse themselves in something else in order to escape the memory's sustained probing of past actions and feelings. The displacement allows the person to move the conflict from the current life into an arena that takes on a metaphorical function. George H. Pollock, a prominent psychoanalyst who studies the relations between creativity and grieving, suggests that persons mourning who feel "dead" inside can do grief work by being creative in any way, not necessarily about their own lives. Though a grieving person seldom has the creative capacity early in the mourning period, when creativity does become possible again it helps the mourner move through the process (270).

These two psychoanalytic versions of how we use the past in order to live a better present are similar to the difference between classic autobiographies and the books I take up in this study. The autobiographer's sustained attention to his or her life through writing corresponds roughly with a psychoanalytic patient's long and involved talking out of the life-story. Hubbell and the other writers in this study, however, are more like persons who recognize that they are depressed but immerse themselves in another subject, hoping that immersion will help them metaphorically to understand their lives. Like the other writers, Hubbell begins by revealing her motives, by telling us of her failed marriage and how that failure led temporarily to a failure of her mind and life. But her personal story of loss is then made the subtext, as she begins writing more directly the natural history of her farm.

This structure is tricky, for both writer and reader. Assuming that her readers want to know more about country life because they are interested in it, Hubbell must keep this at the forefront. But by introducing personal material that creates expectations for development and success, Hubbell must artfully shape this natural history into a narrative of how her initial incomprehension becomes insight, of how she raises herself from depression. To accomplish both of these goals, she structures her book by juxtaposing seemingly unrelated short descriptions of country life and by providing minimal authorial commentary to join the scenes. A reader's interpretive act is to fill in the gaps, make connections, construct a framework to understand the significance of the vignettes.

Like Thoreau in *Walden,* Hubbell in *A Country Year* describes one year passed in a particular place—in her case, her beekeeping farm in the Ozark Mountains. In the afterword to her second book, *A Book of Bees,* Hubbell explained the genesis of *A Country Year:* "I am a beekeeper but I am also a writer, and some years ago I sat down at the typewriter to experiment with words, to try to tease out of the amorphous, chaotic and wordless part of myself the reason why I was staying on this hilltop in the Ozarks after my first husband . . . and I had divorced. I wasn't sure why I was here, and because I am a rational creature and like to know what's going on, I wanted to process what I was doing . . . I traced the natural history of my hilltop from one springtime to the next, discovering by the second spring that I was in a new place and understanding the value of where I was" (175). Hubbell, we might say, is moving from a phase of disorganization and despair to reorganization and hope, but she needs to know with certainty whether this Ozark mountain farm, which she had moved to after years of living in Providence and working as a librarian at Brown University, will become her home. She needs to understand how her caring for it will give her the anchoring she needs.

In his essay "Natural History," in *A Sand County Almanac,* Aldo

Leopold suggests that modern natural history deals only incidentally with the identity of plants and animals, or their habits and behaviors. Such identification and knowledge is a necessary first step, but the natural historian "deals principally with their relations to each other, their relation to the soil and water in which they grew, and their relations to the human beings who sing about 'my country' but see little or nothing of its inner workings" (209–10). This shift in emphasis, as Leopold describes it, mirrors Hubbell's move through the mourning process. Botanizing had helped her mind work again and helped the part of her return that had been grieving. But Hubbell still had to settle down, she writes, "to the work of the afternoon of my life, the work of building a new kind of order, a structure on which a fifty-year-old woman can live her life alone, at peace with herself and the world around her" (12). Building that new kind of order would require two steps for Hubbell: first, to become Leopold's naturalist, coming to understand the relations of animal and plant life, and their claims because of those relations; and second, to write *A Country Year,* in order to understand how the relations and claims of the animal and plant world might create meaning in her life and, furthermore, teach her about her own claims. In this literary act, Hubbell composes narrative truth that gives new meaning to the disturbing past and new hope for the future, thus exemplifying Schafer's belief that a patient and analyst must construct an explanatory life-story that heals.

In *Nature Writing and America,* Peter A. Fritzell argues that the best American nature writers create a "literature of extreme positions: egoistic celebrations of self alternating with various forms of self-deprecation or self-effacement" (6–7). These writers—Thoreau, Leopold, Dillard—believe that one cannot easily know or comprehend The Wild or The Natural, and that the "mind's road to The Muskrat or The Phoebe, if one is truly given to it, is just as difficult as the mind's road to God; and for the best American nature writers the roads have been essentially one, evoking the same fundamental awareness of the limitations of human language and conception" (16). Fritzell goes on to say that the vast majority of America's nature writers, and he would include Hubbell here, turn instead to some form of science and turn away from self. They write books that are undramatic, "works not so much of interrogation or inquiry (and certainly not of introspection) as works of identification, information, and appreciation, works that establish and assert rather than doubt or question, works of explication rather than complication" (17). Fritzell misplaces Hubbell's *A Country Year* into the category of "rural literature," which follows not an American but a British tradition, follows a georgic (not pastoral) impulse, one that rejects urbane civilization in favor of the morality and history of farm or village.

If Fritzell's is one kind of mistake (one kind of misreading) regarding Hubbell's book, a different but equally common one is made by Marilyn Chandler McEntyre, who writes of *A Country Year* that it is the book, more than her others, in which Hubbell "combines autobiography with nature writing. In itself this does not distinguish Hubbell from many other nature writers who routinely include self-reflections in their repertoire of observational habits" (409). McEntyre's essay, published in Elder's *American Nature Writers* series, has delightful insights into Hubbell's writing as a whole, but her simplistic view of autobiography (a text that includes self-reflections in the observations) leads her to devote most of her space to Hubbell's *The Book of Bees* and to describe Hubbell the entomologist, who knows about bees and bugs and can write poetically about science.[4]

To sum up, there are two main views of *A Country Year* that, in my mind, make it far less interesting than it is: one, Fritzell's view, that most American nature writers, including Hubbell, turn toward science to evade difficult issues about the self and knowing, and that Hubbell is a writer of "rural life"; and two, McEntyre's view, that Hubbell is an entomologist who can write elegantly, even poetically, about "nature." Hubbell is, no doubt, an amateur biologist par excellence, one committed to the orderliness of botanical/biological systems, but there is another side of Hubbell not easily reconciled to this "scientific" persona, but equally not reconciled to the poetic writer of nature who adds occasionally some self-reflections. Hubbell suggests with her epigraph to *A Country Year*, a passage from one of Rilke's *Letters to a Young Poet*, that her book will be an unusual kind of natural history: "Be patient toward all that is unsolved in your heart and try to love the questions themselves. . . . Do not . . . seek the answers, which cannot be given you because you would not be able to live them. And the point is to live everything. Live the questions now. Perhaps you will . . . gradually, without noticing it, live along some distant day into the answer." Rilke's questions transferred and translated into Hubbell's text are, I suggest, a critique of the scientific method;

the epigraph argues that one must care about what gets questioned in "life." Hubbell intentionally complicates two divergent stances that humans may take toward the world, and she does so because in this, her first book, she is doing grief work, performing an act of self-creation in a narrative text.[5]

Some readers have argued that Hubbell's sketches, as beautifully constructed as they are, seem almost too tidy. I have taught *A Country Year* several times and know many people outside the academy who have read it. The book is almost universally liked and highly regarded, but the one criticism that I've heard concerns the rather seamless structure of these numerous, finely created vignettes. In large part, such comments come because readers have missed the paradoxes that Hubbell has built into the short narratives, have missed the tension she continually creates between the two kinds of mental activities— pinning the thing down and reveling in mystery.   Science, to speak generally, favors analysis over narration, "facts" over anecdotes. As she relates in describing Linnaeus's system of Latin binomials, "a beautiful tool for thinking about diversity in the world," Hubbell is drawn to the scientific mode: "The first word in his scheme of Latin binomials tells the genus, grouping diverse plants which nevertheless share a commonality; the second word names the species, plants alike enough to regularly interbreed and produce offspring like themselves. It is a framework for understanding, a way to show how pieces of the world fit together" (10). But Hubbell juxtaposes this description with a classification that Jorge Luis Borges devised, claiming that

A certain Chinese encyclopedia divides animals into:
   a. Belonging to the Emperor
   b. Embalmed
   c. Tame
   d. Sucking pigs
   e. Sirens
   f. Fabulous
   g. Stray dogs
   h. Included in the present classification

I have not reproduced the entire list that Hubbell quotes, but one immediately recognizes the "unscientific" nature of Borges's grouping. Hubbell shares allegiance, however, to both these systems of classifications, and one drama of the text is her discovery of ways to put them in productive tension with each other. How does one who is a lover of scientific knowledge not seek the answers? How does one who is mourning live the questions? The autobiographical act to solve such questions encompasses more than self-reflections mingled with observations.

The chapter following the revelations about her divorce serves as an example of Hubbell establishing a ground for her nature writing that incorporates science and mystery. Hubbell describes in wonderful, understated humor an evening in the spring when she was reading a newspaper in her living room and discovered suddenly that hundreds of frogs covered her three floor-to-ceiling windows. Putting down her newspaper, she identified them, noted their name (spring peepers, *Hyla crucifer*), thought that they seemed to be attracted to the light, and then gave her evening up to watching them. The following morning they were gone, never to return; curious behavior, she says. She had been reminded of them because the previous evening a gray tree frog had jumped into her bed, and she then discovered three more under the bed. After carrying them out to her hickory tree, she looked up the story in the book of Exodus of God sending a plague of frogs to convince the pharaoh to let the Jews leave Egypt. She, too, was having a plague of frogs, she writes, but unlike the pharaoh, she liked it.

The subject of frogs leads her to other ruminations, about the previous summer when she allowed a pickerel frog to live in the passageway to her honeyhouse, and how he came to serve as a "tutelary sprite, the guardian of the honey house, the Penate Melissus"; about when she dissected a frog in a high-school class and thought that she had learned all about them; and how before she moved to the Ozarks, she never thought about frogs because she never saw them. She doesn't know as much as she once did, Hubbell writes: "There's nothing like having frogs fill up my windows or share my bed or require my protection to convince me of that." She adds, to conclude her discourse on frogs: "I don't cut up frogs anymore, and I read more poetry than I did when I was twenty. I just read a couplet about the natural world by an anonymous Japanese poet. I copied it out and put it up on the wall above my desk today: *Unknown to me what resideth here / Tears flow from a sense of unworthiness and gratitude*" (18).

Attempting to resolve the tension between knowledge that answers questions and knowledge that leads toward mystery, Hubbell's sketch is both exploratory and shapely, process and product. Recollection interwoven with present events structures the chapter, as Hubbell dramatizes her mind's workings. She is the scientist, observing carefully, naming correctly. But the references to the Bible, her refusal now to dissect creatures, the quoting of poetry whose message undermines the scientist's typical attitudes, and, above all, the anthropomorphizing—these all undercut her scientific stance. And this structure moves toward a literary, "show-don't-tell" conclusion. She desires to dramatize that her thinking about frogs shows her how she is connected to the natural world, reminds her of how she once was not, and demonstrates how that connection leads both to more knowledge and the recognition that she knows very little.

Reasons—conscious and unconscious, artistic or personal—motivate any narrative shaping, but unlike fiction writers, who can create a structure that is completely symbolic or metaphorical, Hubbell (like other writers of nonfiction) is restricted to some extent: restricted to, she says, "trying to express in words what I saw out there on my farm."[6] But she is, of course, trying to do much more, as her text of grief and recovery suggests. These sketches show Hubbell doing far more than advocating for rural life; she is creating a self that can move confidently forward. Hubbell balances two desires: to write natural history, and to endow it with resonance while avoiding a reliance on epiphany.

The writing in *A Country Year* finds this balance by being made up of small parts. Individual sketches assembled chronologically take on greater meaning as scenes and reflections accumulate, showing Hubbell entwined in the life of her farm. Lawrence Buell, writing in *The Environmental Imagination* about Thoreau, distinguishes between a fictionalist and a nonfictionalist (environmentalist) interpretation, a distinction that helps shed light on reading Hubbell:

A fictionalist reading tends to presuppose that the persona is the main subject, that selectivity is suppression, that represented detail is symbolic, that environmental knowledge (in either author or reader) counts for little. A nonfictionalist reading presupposes that the persona's most distinctive trait is environmental proficiency—not the professional scientist's command of data and theory but the working knowledge of someone more knowledgeable than we, who seeks to communicate what he or she knows in a shareable form. It presupposes that the persona's chief rhetorical resource is exposition, that the metaphorical and tonal and meditative complications enriching exposition cannot be distinguished as the sole or even chief ways in which the text becomes artful. (96–97)

By entwining her natural history in an autobiographical framework of loss and recovery, Hubbell invites a dual reading that folds together aspects of Buell's fictionalist and environmentalist readings. The information and knowledge given about her farm's natural history suggest that the teaching of environmental proficiency is most important, but the ways that she carefully structures the vignettes recommend us to pay attention to persona, selectivity, metaphor, and symbol as modes conveying Hubbell's attempts to build the structure on which she can live her life alone and at peace.

Because Hubbell began writing in order to explain to herself why she wanted to stay on the farm, why she wanted to work hard and be poor, she wrote sketches (such as the one about the frogs) without a chronology. Only later, when she realized she was writing a book, did she have to think about structure. In deciding to track her farm's natural history for a year, Hubbell followed many writers who use nature's model of the seasons. And yet, unlike most writers, she added a fifth season, a second spring, in order to dramatize her own change; as she said, "My idea [for the book's structure] was to have a spiral. That's why I included two different springs. The point of it, of course, is that at the end I was in a different place than I was at the beginning."[7]

In *Trauma and Mastery in Life and Art,* Gilbert J. Rose discusses numerous connections between the grieving and artistic processes. Psychoanalysis, he writes, undoes repression, while art counteracts denial. Mastery of past trauma, contemporary reality, and the anticipation of future trauma comes from ongoing attempts of the imagination to split off and repress some parts of the past while elaborating and reintegrating others (x–xi). "The creative work," Rose writes, "is a building up and melting down, again and again, a losing and refinding oneself by proxy, a rapid oscillation between imagination and knowledge of reality. . . . It continues until the work itself takes on a reality and autonomy of its own, whereupon the author also becomes free, or at least freer, to go on to something else" (209–10). This formulation of creative work, as it relates to grieving, helps explain why the literary act of writing *A Country Year* could get Hubbell to that "different place" in the second spring.

"I have travelled much in Concord," said Thoreau, with his characteristic paradox that reveals great insight. One thing he learns by doing so, as Paul Gruchow points out in his essay, "Traveling Much in Concord: Regaining Our Sense of Place," is that he is as deeply attached to the biological community as to the human community and, moreover, that attachment to one lends itself to attachment to the other. Hubbell, too, travels much while staying on her farm, and like Thoreau she becomes deeply aware of how separated these two communities are for most humans and how interwoven they have become for her out of necessity. Her communion extends not only to those parts of the biological community that humans are often attracted to—flowers, certain animals, trees—but to creatures of whom we are often leery.

Hubbell likes to show that many humans react to some creatures—for example, snakes and poisonous spiders—out of ignorance and fear, which makes for poor observation: "It is hard to tell what a snake is up to if you are running away from it or killing it" (53). One pre-dawn morning, as she sits under her oak trees sipping coffee, the mosquitoes discover her, only to be themselves discovered, in turn, by a bat, which swoops down to devour them. After a few moments of silence, Hubbell writes, the mosquitoes return to buzz in her ear, and then the bat swoops by again. Silence; the whine of mosquitoes; the bat. "The arrangement was a pleasant one for both the bat and me. . . . I served as bait to gather the mosquitoes in one rich spot, and the bat ate them before they bit me. . . . All this gives me a fine, friendly feeling toward bats" (35). The episode provides Hubbell an opportunity to discuss bats, matter-of-factly presenting information that dispels harmful myths about them. Because unfamiliarity often breeds fear, Hubbell helps us see why irrational fears not only hurt us psychologically but, when we kill bats, alter a system that is beneficial, in that bats eat mosquitoes and moths, helping to keep them in manageable numbers. She also shows that a bat's arrangements with other creatures are complex: for example, ear mites lay their eggs only in one ear of their hosts—night-flying moths—so as not to damage the moth's hearing, which helps them escape the bats. "We are a text of suitability one for another," Hubbell concludes, "and that text is as good as any I know by which to drink my coffee and watch the dawn" (39).

Hubbell's stance here, her strong desire to see herself in a "text of suitability," contrasts strongly with Annie Dillard, another prominent nature writer fascinated with insects. In his essay "Beyond the Excursion: Initiatory Themes in Annie Dillard and Terry Tempest

Williams," John Tallmadge suggests that Dillard's encounters with
water bugs or beetles are "a religious practice that engages beings in
nature as tokens of God's character and intentions" (199). Dillard,
then, when she's "stunned by the beauty of nature," sees God as "an
extravagant, joyous creator." But when she "is shocked by nature's per-
versity, grotesqueness, or cruelty," her faith "in a humane and loving
God" is challenged (199–200). Hubbell, desiring neither the rapture
nor the despair, sees the creatures themselves straightforwardly, or "ob-
jectively," not symbolically.

While Hubbell likes to dispel myths about animals and insects by
telling what she has learned about them, she also wants to show how
their behavior is often unexplainable to humans, how their actions
often lead only to questions. Sometimes the issues are large ones, such
as how birds find their way when migrating, which humans can only
guess at. Sometimes the questions come from something particular
that Hubbell is doing, as when she collects a swarm of bees, or when
she and a friend watch, amazed, as a caterpillar walks across her table
unerringly toward the milkweed leaves in a vase. When a spider builds
a web near a hive and begins stocking her larder with honeybees,
Hubbell reflects that they are both beekeepers, making a living from
bees. She and the spider are similar in other ways, too: "We are both
animate bundles of the chemicals common to all living things. . . .
Both of us have been presented with a set of problems posed by our
chemistry and quickness, among them how to grow and how to make
a living. Those are big questions, and as is often the case with Big
Questions, we have come up with different answers—answers that in
turn are still different from those of the honeybee" (58). In the care
and reflection that she gives to these relationships with bats and
snakes, bees and spiders, Hubbell exemplifies a human who believes
in a "land ethic," Aldo Leopold's term for the belief that the human
community should extend to soil, water, plants, and animals, and that
when humans see land as a community to which they belong, then
they will begin to use it with love and respect.[8]

Hubbell likes working with bees because they lead her both to answers (explanations for how they communicate, such as the bee dance)
and to unanswerable questions (such as why they swarm). The more
she learns about bees, the more they remain a mystery to her. Working with bees also gives Hubbell joy because it allows her to earn a living in a way that is perhaps most appropriate to her particular farm;

she can work with, not against, the land. Wendell Berry, in his essay "Preserving Wildness," maintains that mistreatment of the land often occurs because the economy practiced on it is not suitable, as, for example, when corn is grown year after year on hilly land, which eventually becomes gullied. Three questions, he says, must be asked with respect to a human economy in any given place: "1. What is here? 2. What will nature permit us to do here? 3. What will nature help us to do here?" (146). When Hubbell (and her husband) fell in love with the farm and then had to decide how to earn a living from it, she chose beekeeping because she could scatter her hives around her neighbors' farms and use the flowers, berries, and clover pastures already there, whereas crop farming or raising pigs and cattle would have been possible only by clearing large areas of her own land and fertilizing the ground heavily.

Like other stewards of the land, Hubbell does not give priority in her work to setting goals and solving problems, the quintessential mode of most capitalist activity, but looks instead to understand in a broad way what might give that work meaning. She makes no attempt to dominate anything, but tries instead to integrate herself almost unnoticeably into what is already in place. Her beekeeping operation allows for a diversity of other creatures—plants, birds, animals—to thrive, which in turn gives her joy, entertainment, and even companionship.

A Country Year, as with *The Solace of Open Spaces, Refuge,* and other books in this study, inhabits the classic pastoral mode only obliquely, if at all.[9] In the most famous of all pastoral poems, "The Passionate Shepherd to His Love," Christopher Marlowe wrote:

Come live with me and be my love,
And we will all the pleasures prove
That valleys, groves, hills, and fields,
Woods, or steepy mountain yields.

And we will sit upon the rocks,
Seeing the shepherds feed their flocks,
By shallow rivers to whose falls
Melodious birds sing madrigals.

The speaker-shepherd is not the working shepherd—he and his love are more like tourists visiting a place of tranquility, of "naturalness," where human feelings can be highly felt and directly spoken. Marlowe's fantasy prompted an equally famous reply, Sir Walter Ralegh's "The Nymph's Reply to the Shepherd," a qualification of the pastoral myth:

> If all the world and love were young,
> And truth in every shepherd's tongue,
> These pretty pleasures might me move
> To live with thee and be thy love.
>
> Time drives the flocks from field to fold
> When rivers rage and rocks grow cold,
> And Philomel becometh dumb;
> The rest complains of cares to come.

As literary "realism" became increasingly dominant, the highly stylized pastoral mode fell into disfavor, either in its idealized version or as object for ironic critique.

Hubbell has no interest in creating an idealized description of rural life set in contrast to city life. She describes matter-of-factly the things her Ozark neighbors must do for money: killing for food or pelts what swims in the river or walks in the woods; killing a bobcat that has frequented Hubbell's farm. Though Hubbell writes occasionally of human companionship—afternoons drinking sherry with her town friends, the annual Beekeepers Pig Roast, her involvement in a town movement to stop the river from being dammed—she is uninterested in giving a sense of small-town, Ozarkian life. She does not minimize the difficulties of earning enough money through beekeeping to stay in business. Her life on the farm is not an attempt to lead the "bucolic Simple Life," which is simple only if one has savings to spend. The people who come from the cities in search of the simple life are misguided: "What they have not yet discovered is that a life is as simple or as complicated as the person living it, and that people who have found life in the city overwhelming will find it even more so here, where it is much harder to make a living" (210–11). She is always, she says, just barely getting by, and the economics is more complicated than for a person earning a salary and paying bills. She raises chickens, for example, giving eggs to the general store in exchange for feed, giving eggs to her neighbor's family in return for his working on her truck, and getting her own eggs for free. Because she earns no large cash crop, she must find ways to cut costs, to live on less money; and so when she goes on the road to sell her honey in the Eastern cities, she sleeps in her truck.

Hubbell's attempts at self-sufficiency sometimes gain her a bonus, because one thing that helps Hubbell with her grief work is learning tasks that lead her away from thinking of herself as a victim and toward thinking of herself as being strong, as having human agency. An example is her cutting of firewood, which serves as the only heat for her cabin. Because she has acres of trees and little money, she cannot afford to have it brought to her. But when Paul was still there, he cut the firewood, she says, "and I, like all Ozark wives, carried the cut wood to the pickup" (45). Doing it herself means that she gains control.

Hubbell tells us that once she was ignorant of tools (tools bought, organized, and used by her husband), which made her feel defeated and stupid. But she patiently teaches herself how to use some of them and creates a system to manage the rest. She becomes so exhilarated by her capacity to make things with the tools that she sides her barn, builds a new pump house, repairs her chicken coop, finishes off her study, and rebuilds her bedroom during the autumn months, when there is little work to do with her bees. By performing these carpentry jobs, usually done by men, Hubbell becomes assured not just that she can be self-sufficient, but that she can thrive on her own. And she also, of course, attaches herself to her house, turns it into "home" by knowing every part of these additions, and being able to see her own labor in them.

At times, doing these tasks becomes dangerous, as on the morning when a large tree she is cutting falls the wrong way and gets hung up in branches of other trees, trapping her saw. But such problems become opportunities, problems to solve. In this instance, she returns to her cabin to get a portable winch known as a come-along, which, she says, "is a cheery, sensible tool for a woman . . . [because] it divides a heavy job up into small manageable bits that require no more than female strength" (47). She eventually gets the big tree ratcheted down to the ground, where she can then saw it up, load the logs into her truck, and stack the wood next to her cabin to await splitting.

Becoming self-sufficient, learning new skills, using her intellect and common sense to solve problems—these are all benefits to Hubbell of running a farm alone. But there are other, less immediate and tangible benefits perhaps, that are equally important to her. "It is satisfying," she writes, "to build up a supply of winter warmth, free except for the labor. But there is also something heady about becoming a part of the forest process . . . deciding which trees should be encouraged and which should be taken." She knows that a great black walnut she is fond of needs space and light, so she cuts competing trees. Dogwoods grow extravagantly in close company, and so she does not need to thin them. A diseased tree needs to be cut to save its neighbors. Dead trees make good firewood because the sap is gone, but if she leaves them, they continue to be a home for woodpeckers, squirrels, and owls. If she leaves a fallen tree, ants, spiders, beetles, and wood roaches will use it for shelter and food, and delicate fungi will grow out of it before it mixes with leaf mold to become a new layer of soil. "One person with a chain saw makes a difference in the woods," she writes, "and by making a difference becomes part of the woodland cycle, a part of the abstraction that is the forest community" (49).

This point, about the place of humans in the natural order, is important to Hubbell in the reconstruction of her life, and separates her from many who write about nature. Bill McKibben in *The End of Nature,* for one, sets himself apart from the natural world when he argues that the hole in the ozone layer makes for an irreparable sadness because we know incontrovertibly that humans have affected nature everywhere. Though most people think of nature as "out there beyond the window," Hubbell says, "this is bad biology." To make this matter simple, she says, just realize "that nature is the air we breathe, the water we drink. We're part of it all the time."[10] She knows that humans alter things, often in dramatic ways, but that does not separate humans from nature.

Hubbell has a wonderful example of human intervention when she describes the consequences of her keeping chickens: first the mice thrive because they eat so much of the corn she feeds the chickens; then the black rat snakes come to the barn and chicken coop to eat the mice; then a snake swallows a pair of baby phoebes, which Hubbell saves by shaking the snake upside down. Her "meddling" comes full circle: chickens, corn, mice, snakes, phoebes, Hubbell, chickens. Such a diagram, she says, only hints at the complexity of the whole, because "each of us is a part of other figures, too, the resulting interconnecting whole faceted, weblike, subtle, flexible, fragile." But the natural world, no matter how idealized we make it, follows similar rules in that a mountain lion entering a new territory changes the web, as does a forest fire. Her fiddling, meddling, altering, she writes, "is neither good nor bad, merely human, in the same way that the snake who eats mice and phoebes is merely serpentish. But being human I have the kind of mind which can recognize that when I fiddle and twitch any part of the circle there are reverberations throughout the whole" (77). There are, of course, irresponsible human acts that do not acknowledge the reverberations, and one measure of human selfishness and ignorance is the refusal to judge such acts. But what we see of Hubbell, as she writes the natural history of her farm with herself as part of the story, is a growing awareness of this role she plays and her desire to play it well. And in this, I would maintain, she models an ethics that refutes Carol Bly's notion of the unethical nature-describer.

Hubbell's communion with the natural world becomes increasingly important to the process of building, in her words, "a structure on which a fifty-year-old woman can live her life alone, at peace with herself and the world around her." Paradoxically, humans have called such communion "solitude" (though Hubbell demonstrates joyfully her numerous "relationships" with nonhuman creatures). As a preparation for struggle, or as an initiation into adulthood, human solitude has a long history. In recent decades when psychologists and the mass media have focused attention heavily on interpersonal relationships, the value of solitude has become diminished.[11] Often we can break habitual ways of thinking only by changing our situations dramatically, by not having human companionship, for example. Our capacity to be alone, and to enjoy it even, goes unrecognized perhaps when we are married or have constant company. For Hubbell, solitude—or, more precisely, companionship with the nonhuman world—is essential for her to complete the extended mental process we call mourning. In solitude she gains insight and begins change; she rethinks herself in different circumstances than the roles that society has created for a woman of her age, education, and so forth. Living on her Ozarks farm demonstrates to her that renewal can come from nature's order, can come from her knowledge of how she is part of an ecosystem that both reflects her own specific actions and yet, by virtue of its grand complexity, is marvelous almost beyond comprehension. She is part of numerous "texts of suitability," part of numerous "interconnecting wholes." She has gained "scientific" knowledge that leads her to mystery, and she has reflected about mystery in ways that lead her to "living the questions."

In her second spring, Hubbell sleeps outdoors, even on cold nights, so that she can see the stars. "I wonder if I am becoming feral," she writes. "Wild things and wild places pull me more strongly than they did a few years ago, and domesticity, dusting and cookery interest me not at all" (195). When she wonders about herself as a single older woman, that in American culture (unlike other cultures and in other times) such a woman has no place compared to men of any age or younger women, Hubbell realizes that she does have advantages. She has independence, she says, and an awareness of time that prompts care and thought in living. Moreover, being marginalized means that she can make up her own role, rather than feeling bound by society's role for her. "It is a good time," she writes, "to be a grown-up woman with individuality, strength and crotchets. We are wonderfully free. We live long. Our children are the independent adults we helped them to become, and though they may still want our love they do not need our care. Social rules are so flexible today that nothing we do is shocking. There are no political barriers to us anymore. Provided we stay healthy and can support ourselves, we can do anything, have anything and spend our talents any way that we please" (196).

Unlike the spring before, when she was searching for a reason to stay on her farm, Hubbell knows a year later what she desires. She wants, she says, to hear wild turkeys gobbling at dawn, wants indigo buntings singing their couplets as she awakens, wants oak leaves and dogwood blossoms and fireflies. "I want," she writes, "to find out what happens to moth-ear mites in the winter. I want to show Liddy and Brian [her son and his wife] the big rocks down in the creek hollow. I want to know much more about grand-daddy-longlegs. I want to write a novel. I want to go swimming naked in the hot sun down at the river" (196). These desires, she knows, have been shaped by the joys she has found living on and writing about her farm. "A house is too small, too confining," she concludes. "I want the whole world, and the stars too."

In her beautiful book *Gift from the Sea,* Anne Morrow Lindbergh suggests that middle age is a time for humans to slough off what they no longer need. In her extended, elegant metaphors, the growing accretion of the oyster-bed shell, which symbolizes an earlier life of family and career commitments, should be shucked layer by layer; middle age is a period to shed "the shell of ambition, the shell of material accumulations and possessions, the shell of the ego" (84). A woman might then be free at last, she continues, for growth of mind, heart, and talent, for spiritual growth. Hubbell, we might say, is one of the few who reaches Lindbergh's next stage, symbolized by the argonauta shell. The mother argonaut, after rearing her young, leaves the shell to begin anew, setting sail for the freedom and adventure of the open seas. Hubbell dramatizes this process in *A Country Year,* metaphorically setting sail and journeying by staying on her farm and writing.

In his essay "Into the Maze," Robert Finch describes his longing to gain entrance into the maze of trees around his house, and to do so not like an outsider, an intruder (a human), but "without a rustle," like the fox, rabbit, deer, hawk, or snake do. "These creatures," he writes, "tease me with their unconscious competence, a sureness that implies not so much prowess as belonging, of knowing where and who they are, of being local inhabitants in a way I am not" (182). In a companion essay, "Scratching," Finch describes the flats of Cape Cod (and his evenings spent digging for clams there), which create a different problem for a human than does a landscape of forest: "In contrast to the maze of woods around my house, the flats pose a problem of orientation rather than one of entry. Out there one finds few or no landmarks to go by; distance and size become notoriously deceptive, and men have been lost and drowned on the far bars when sudden fogs come in with the tide" (186).

Orientation, entrance: these metaphors become leitmotifs for those writers who seek not answers in the natural world but relationships to it. Such metaphors also serve, in Hubbell's book, as markers of psychological well-being, because orientation and entrance shift with every new context; they place importance more on knowing and becoming than having become. It is her ability to thrive in, not master, different roles—as beekeeper, single woman, friend, carpenter, naturalist, and so on—that gives Hubbell such satisfaction. By year's end, she has become that "local inhabitant" with claims to her farm both human and surprisingly similar to those of the indigo buntings or the frogs.

Meredith Skura, in *Literature as Psychoanalytic Process,* suggests that a main goal of psychoanalysts is to encourage patients to change their ways of seeing. She emphasizes that during a successful psychoanalytic process the patient has moments of insight and self-consciousness that organize and integrate the welter of confusing experiences, feelings, and beliefs, and those moments allow the person to interpret his or her symptoms or distress in a new way.[12] Though a metaphor or generalization often emerges out of these moments, however, psychoanalytic "truth" and meaning, Skura says, come out of the entire process.

Skura recognizes that individual and small insights come at various times during analysis, but that substantial truth and meaning come when those insights are added to one another, acted upon, added to, acted upon, and so forth; her description of this process is strikingly similar to the feel of *A Country Year*, as Hubbell piles up the vignettes, all variations on the theme of how she can live productively and happily in the ecosystem of her farm. By book's end, she has shown her life moving from a phase of disorganization and despair to one of reorganization and hope, and the literary act has helped accomplish the grief work, enabled the self-creation.

Hubbell's ending to *A Country Year* testifies to her having moved through mourning, and this pattern is repeated for each of the writers whose books I discuss in this study. Though Hubbell's successful grief work mirrors the other writers', each of them performs a different literary act, has a different style, to do that grief work. They not only raise issues particular to their own lives and loss, but they try out different solutions that have different strengths and different weaknesses. Hubbell, more than any other writer, creates textually a life of sustainability, one in which she is in near-perfect harmony with all living things that surround her. She models Leopold's vision of a human acting ethically toward everything that inhabits the earth. But what we don't see in the text is what happens when such an ethic can't be acted upon, or contrary impulses simply grab her. We do not see, that is, moments such as in *Walden* where Thoreau has a woodchuck cross his path and he writes vehemently how much he would like to seize and devour it raw, a scene that has been problematic for numerous readers of Thoreau who want to construct his beliefs into a neat whole. For some readers, who prefer either more philosophizing in the way of Thoreau or Dillard or more science, Hubbell and her book may finally be too ordered, too quiet, too "in-between" as she walks the tightrope she stretches between natural history and autobiography. But unlike a Thoreau or Dillard, Hubbell is performing grief work, and her tendency to smooth the rough spots is understandable. In *Trauma and Mastery in Life and Art* Gilbert Rose suggests that a viewer of formal line drawings tends to see more regularity, symmetry, and completion than is truly there, and that humans dealing with grief or trauma, working with their troubling pasts, might do something similar in their desires to construct plausible stories (188).

Do we "smooth out the rough spots" of stories as a psychological necessity, thereby creating a "false" version of the past, or do changes in our lives and emotions actually help us recall and construct a more accurate version of those past events? As Hubbell textually places herself repeatedly into interconnected wholes and dramatizes the joy she gains by understanding her role in these interfaceted webs, she manifests the position that self creates language as language creates self, in an endlessly looping process that has no beginning and no end. As Paul John Eakin has written in an oft-cited passage from *Fictions in Autobiography* about the autobiographical act:

Instead of debating the old either/or proposition—whether the self is a transcendental category preceding language in the order of being, or else a construct of language brought into being by it—it is preferable to conceptualize the relation between the self and language as a mutually constituting interdependency . . . I view the rhythms of the autobiographical act as recapitulating the fundamental rhythms of identity formation: in this sense the writing of autobiography emerges as a second acquisition of language, a second coming into being of self, a self-conscious self-consciousness. (8–9)

Unlike with biology, there can be a middle ground with memory and lived or living life—a middle ground with "autobiographical truth." Hubbell's careful descriptions of a particular locale in nature lead to her autobiographical truth, which comes from her ability to fashion from the natural world a structure that makes a complicated web of daily actions, so that the small things she does are meaningful.

3 An Unnatural History Made Natural

Terry Tempest Williams's
Refuge

Refuge and Hubbell's *A Country Year* serve as bookends for this study. Whereas Hubbell sets the "present" of her book near the end of her grieving, as she is moving from disorganization to reorganization of her life, Williams writes from the beginnings of her trauma—when her beloved bird refuges begin to drown, when her mother is diagnosed with cancer—and ends before we see the new directions her life will take. Whereas Hubbell writes an understated, quiet book, filled with scenes where she shows herself weaving and being woven into numerous "texts of suitability," Williams challenges angrily the place of women in Mormon culture and the political decisions of the Utah legislature or the United States military, critiquing the "patriarchy" even as she escapes from its effects at the Great Salt Lake or in the wilds of Utah's canyonlands. Whereas Hubbell's sketches are shapely, elegant, almost effortless, addressed to a seasonal task or situation, Williams focuses each chapter on a bird species and stitches her chapters together with short, journal-like passages, a collage structure. Both authors do grief work through a literary act, but the writing is a contrasting performance of self-creation.

While students in my classes (and adults whom I know) have found *A Country Year* to be quite enjoyable and Hubbell to be quite admirable, they do not discern at first the complex literary feat that Hubbell enacts. But nearly all readers find *Refuge* to be powerful and moving, and though it is the most recently published (1991), it has spawned more literary criticism and is taught more often than the other books in this study.[1] Its power, I contend, comes because at the book's heart is paradox and contradiction. Williams is not ideologically consistent, in the way Thoreau, Leopold, or Hubbell are; her conflicting attitudes and desires make it difficult for a reader to "place" her. Williams is an influential Mormon woman who refused to have children and who challenges Mormon religious and patriarchal beliefs but does not renounce her religion. She is an environmentalist who lives in Utah, a state historically in favor of mining, logging, dams, and "development." She is equally comfortable saying "I am desert. I am mountains. I am Great Salt Lake. . . . When I see ring-billed gulls picking on the flesh of decaying carp, I am less afraid of death" (29) and "We shopped in the finest stores and twirled in front of mirrors. We lived in the museums. Having overspent our allotment of time at the Met in the Caravaggio exhibit, we opted for a quick make-over at Bloomingdale's to revive us for the theatre" (25). Perhaps most importantly, Williams believes intellectually in "natural" processes but can't accept emotionally that heavy rains that flood bird refuges might be similar to cancer in mothers. Such "inconsistency" does make her very human. In part because she is not consoled by rational belief systems, her trauma feels devastating and her grief authentic, which is the source of the book's power.

In her prologue, Williams writes: "I am telling this story in an attempt to heal myself, to confront what I do not know, to create a path for myself with the idea that 'memory is the only way home.' I have been in retreat. This story is my return" (4). The words echo those of the other writers in this study. Just as Barich, Heat-Moon, Matthiessen, Hubbell, and Ehrlich write about "others" in a way that helps them fashion a therapeutic life-story, Williams writes about the Bear River Refuge, Great Salt Lake, and the birds, trying to use the "natural" processes and world to understand what feels to her "unnatural," the cancer of her mother and other women in her family. It takes several years after her mother's death and after the receding of the lake for her to believe she has made peace with the losses of both her mother and the birds. The peace comes in large part by Williams learning what else in her life can serve as refuge, and also her coming to accept that change—for humans as well as lakes and rivers—is inevitable. But though inevitable, she believes that change is not necessarily natural, as her subtitle suggests: "An Unnatural History of Family and Place."

In describing the grief work that she performs with this literary act, I will focus on Williams's developing representation of these two words—*refuge* and *unnatural*—as markers of her psychological state. In an essay placing Williams into the tradition of the "excursion," John Tallmadge notes correctly that although Williams goes to nature "to find peace, hope, and healing for herself," she rarely goes alone: "So her journeys not only teach her about the land in its scientific and spiritual dimensions, but also deepen her relationships with people" (202). Because Williams uses nature's lessons to understand personal problems that she then connects to politically charged issues, *Refuge*, Tallmadge says, moves the excursion form beyond a "self-centered romanticism toward a socially transforming process" (202–3). Most critics have been interested, like Tallmadge, in this direct social critique, in how Williams uses her own grieving to engage social problems. *Refuge* differs from nearly all traditional natural history, Cheryll Glotfelty says, because "Williams wears her gender on her sleeve and remains ever-conscious of how being a woman colors every aspect of her experience" (159). Williams certainly focuses on the women of her family, and the book is often taught in women's studies courses and written about as an ecofeminist text. Even when she writes about her father or brothers, she sets such talk in a larger gendered discourse. But because I am most interested in the arc of her mourning, I take a different view than most critics. The book is less successful, I believe, when Williams makes an examination of "unnatural" into a cause for advocating ideological positions. The book succeeds as grief work when she interrogates what *refuge* means for herself and comes to understand the term more complexly.

Heavier than usual snow and rain hit Utah's Great Salt Lake Basin in 1982, and continued heavy for the next five years. In that shallow basin, the Great Salt Lake rose more than seven feet, flooding hundreds of square miles, destroying businesses, railroads, roads, and homes, even threatening the Salt Lake City International Airport. The lake's rise also flooded the Bear River Migratory Bird Refuge, killing or displacing millions of birds so dear to Williams's professional and personal heart. For the birds that figure so prominently in Williams's book, refuge is a place of safety, where they are protected from hunters and developers, where they can stay for a season and breed or they can rest while on their migrations. While the refuge gives birds the necessary protection from humans, ironically it is nonhuman forces that kill and displace the birds when Great Salt Lake rises.

Williams laments the flooding of the refuge not only on behalf of the birds, but because it has been a place of retreat, safety, and comfort to her, particularly since she had spent numerous days there as a girl with her grandmother Mimi. In Terry's young mind, the birds mediated between heaven and earth, bridging cultures and continents with their wings (18). But now "the birds of Bear River have been displaced; so have I" (97), because her mother's cancer leaves Williams feeling unmoored. She thus intertwines two processes, one seemingly natural, one not, but both destroying that which has comforted her and made her safe. "I could not separate the Bird Refuge from my family," she writes. "The landscape of my childhood and the landscape of my family, the two things I had always regarded as bedrock, were now subject to change. Quicksand" (40).

Change and refuge—when we're scared and we want the world we know to remain, we oppose these two. Refuge becomes the place that change doesn't touch. We "retreat" to some soothing place, literally or in memory; we seek refuge with some soothing person. What is doubly hard for Williams is that both of these refuges are unavailable. She cannot go to her beloved bird refuge without encountering destruction. She cannot go to her mother or even anyone in her family (they remind her of her mother) without encountering imminent death. "How," she asks simply but poignantly, "do you find refuge in change?" (119).

Williams writes the book, in a sense, to answer that question, to do grief work by creating a self that is not devastated by change. As is true for all the writers of this study, who are often using journals or field notes, Williams relies little on memory to perform her act of self-creation, as more traditional autobiographers do. While her mother was gradually dying of cancer and the Great Salt Lake was rising, Williams recorded both situations faithfully in her journals. After her mother dies and Great Salt Lake finally starts to recede, volunteers begin to reconstruct the marshes, she writes, "just as I [was] trying to reconstruct my life." The distinction between background and foreground, text and subtext, is erased as Williams intertwines these stories of family and place. *Refuge* is that reconstruction, her journal entries forged into a devastatingly powerful book that shows her Ferris wheel ride of grieving, when it seemed there was no refuge and only sorrowful change, when it seemed as if she were capable only of spinning in circles, coming round to the same place of sorrow. But in the change from journals to shaped, rewritten narrative, Williams finally does get off that wheel. Her looking back and forward shows her how a new refuge can be constructed. She slowly realizes that refuge exists in her capacity to love, not in a place outside herself. The Great Salt Lake, forbidding wild desert that it is, hospitable home to her beloved birds, symbolizes that capacity, and her narrative closes there with a ritual burial acknowledging acceptance of death.

The belief that "refuge" is not an unchanging place but an emotional act of loving "in place" comes hard to Williams, not easy. For over seven years the road to the Bear River Bird Refuge is closed, a time that roughly marks the beginning of her anger and sadness and the ending of her mourning for her mother's death, her grandmother's death, and the displaced birds. As the water levels go up and down, but mostly up, as the cancer reports are worse and better, but mostly worse, her hopes rise and fall in a seemingly never-ending cycle. Hubbell in *A Country Year* described one year in the life of her farm, a time period after her early emotional difficulties, but Williams describes seven years, from the beginnings of trauma to the end of grieving. As such, she shows herself in the narrative going through all the phases of mourning, from initial numbing to a yearning and searching for the lost figure; from a phase of disorganization and despair to reorganization and hope. She also writes about anticipating sorrows, not just coping with loss but fearing it in the future. Williams witnesses and testifies to suffering—of birds dying from loss of habitat, of her mother's slow death (and the deaths of others in her family), and of her own grieving. The authors of most texts of "autopathography"—life-writing about illness—have the illness themselves; this is not so in Williams's case, but Maia Saj Schmidt places *Refuge* into this category because Williams communicates in two voices, the voice of personal experience and the voice of professional knowledge. She provides, writes Schmidt, an "embodied, situated" account of suffering.

"An individual doesn't get cancer, a family does" (214), writes Williams, and when after two years of treatments the medical tests show that the mother's cancer has not gone away completely, the family feels shock and sorrow, which in turn wounds her mother. She says to Terry: "'You still don't understand, do you? . . . All we have is now. I wish you could all accept that and let go of your projections. Just let me live so I can die. . . . Terry, to keep hoping for life in the midst of letting go is to rob me of the moment I am in'" (161). The words, Williams writes, "cut through me like broken glass," and the scene cuts through a reader almost as cruelly. Is it unreasonable, or even possible, for a person facing her mother's death not to wish for a miracle, for life? Williams sees or talks to her mother most days, takes her to the hospital for radiation treatments, helps her make plans, and nurses her when she has declined greatly. Williams knows firsthand that a "person with cancer dies in increments, and a part of you slowly dies with them" (173). For Williams, at this point in her mother's life, "refuge" is a fantasy that an impending future can be averted, that the figure of death can be converted to life.

Change *can* serve as refuge, if it leads to an act of self-creation, to a "different" self capable of accepting deep grief. As Williams struggles over these seven years to discern what refuge means for her outside of the fantasies that keep death or flood away, she comes slowly to understand what no longer serves her as it once did, what no longer defines her. Her roles as a Mormon and as an environmentalist, tied through her family's prominence in the Mormon Church and their love of nature, shift slowly and in surprising ways.

"As a people and as a family," she writes, "we have a sense of history. And our history is tied to land" (14). Given her experiences and also her professional work as a naturalist, Williams looks to nature not just for solace or escape but for understanding. Her strong beliefs that humans are one link in various and multiple ecosystems leads her to explore how different species of animals organize, how individuals are part of larger communities, and why some human communities are more successful than others in their connections to the land. For example, Williams notes how white pelican colonies cooperate to feed and take care of their young, then compares them to the United Order of the Mormon Church, a utopian community formed in Brigham City in the 1860s as an economic cooperative intended to meet completely the needs of its citizens. Williams interprets the attempt ecologically: "Lorenzo Snow [the founder] was creating a community based on an ecological model: cooperation among individuals within a set of defined interactions. Each person was operating within their own 'ecological niche,' strengthening and sustaining the overall structure or 'ecosystem'" (100). For fifteen years the community flourished; Edward Bellamy, researching his utopian novel *Looking Backward,* came to Brigham City. But eventually townspeople wanting to do business their own way were treated as outcasts, and those who criticized the United Order were asked to leave. The lessons for Williams? Exclusivity undermines creativity, which lies at the heart of adaptive evolution. A self-sustaining system necessitates diversity, and the United Order, unlike the "Infinite Order of Pelicans," could not continue as a closed system.

The Fremont, ancient native peoples who inhabited the Great Salt Lake region a thousand years earlier, appeal to Williams because they constructed a way of living that allowed them to endure rises and falls of lakes. Hunter-gatherers who lived in small bands, who were closely tied to their immediate environment, the Fremont adapted to living conditions by being flexible and diverse. "In many ways," Williams writes, "the Fremont had more options than we have. What do we do when faced with a rising Great Salt Lake? Pump it west. What did the Fremont do? Move. They accommodated change where, so often, we are immobilized by it" (183). Watching her community try to cope with the flooding of Great Salt Lake, trying herself to accommodate change both from that flooding and her mother's illness, Williams seeks guidance from any culture, any species, that demonstrates both rootedness and a capacity for change. But these explorations of alternative living do little for Williams, distant as they are from her life.

Williams's Mormon values and history should be able to contribute to a model of groundedness, given Mormon ties to the land and their emphasis on generational history. Her family roots go back to the Mormon settlement of the region and her extended family is prominent in the Salt Lake City Mormon Church. Williams is particularly attracted to Mormon recognition of a "magical worldview," complete with "divining rods, seer stones, astrology, and visions" (195). For Williams, connections to the occult make Mormonism more human: "To acknowledge that which we cannot see, to give definition to that which we do not know, to create divine order out of chaos, is the religious dance" (196). Moreover, she was "raised to believe in a spirit world, that life exists before the earth and will continue to exist afterward, that each human being, bird, and bulrush, along with all other life forms had a spirit life before it came to dwell physically on the earth. . . . We learned at an early age that God can be found wherever you are, especially outside" (14). Mormon prayer taps into these beliefs and, furthermore, unites generations in their prayer rituals. The Tempest family gathers together to "bless" their mother. When she had an earlier cancer, her name had been entered "among those to be healed" by the prayers of the brethren, or church leaders, in the holy chambers of the Mormon temple; when the family subsequently gathered at home and knelt together, Terry felt "the presence of angels," and their mother was cured (196–97).

Faith, Williams thinks one day when she is helping move her grandmother to a nursing home, "defies logic and propels us beyond hope because it is not attached to our desires" (198). Furthermore, she writes, faith "is the centerpiece of a connected life. It allows us to live by the grace of invisible strands. It is a belief in a wisdom superior to our own. Faith becomes a teacher in the absence of fact" (198). And yet after her mother's death, faith is hard to hold in the same way, and Williams comes to detach it from her Mormon beliefs. In a vignette symbolizing an important change, Williams contrasts two events that take place simultaneously several months after her mother's death: General Conference, when Mormons from all over the world convene to hear the latest counsel and doctrine from the brethren; and her trip out of the city and to the Great Salt Lake, to listen and be still. While Mormons sit inside on wooden pews, implicitly constrained, once out at the lake, she says, she is free. "I am spun, supported, and possessed by the spirit who dwells here. Great Salt Lake is a spiritual magnet that will not let me go. Dogma doesn't hold me. Wildness does" (240). And being at the lake on her own, not in town at the religious gathering, leads her to a profoundly important meditation on her personal religion.

In Mormon theology (as in that of other Christian churches), the Holy Trinity is composed of God the Father, Jesus Christ the Son, and the Holy Ghost. Where, Williams asks, "is the Motherbody?" (240). If, as she believes, the Holy Ghost is female, She has still remained largely hidden, bodiless, less important than the other two. Mormon women, Williams says, "are far too conciliatory." A Mother-in-Heaven should balance the triangle, and prayers should drop their masculine salutation to include both the Mother and Father. Then, Williams writes, "perhaps our inspiration and devotion would no longer be directed to the stars, but our worship could return to the Earth" (241). She concludes by asserting that although her physical mother is gone, her spiritual mother remains: "I am a woman rewriting my genealogy" (241).

Family, cancer, and religion are interwoven again a few months later, when her beloved grandmother Mimi, soon to die, discharges a tumor and tells Terry this story: "'I could only say this to you. But when I looked into the water closet and saw what my body had expelled, the first thought that came into my mind was "Finally, I am rid of the orthodoxy." My advice to you, dear, is do it consciously'" (246). Williams, as well as other women she knows, are critiquing and evaluating all life under these pressures of death, consciously ridding themselves of the orthodoxy, making for themselves a modified religion.

If human communities seem unable to maintain sustainability in adverse circumstances, if her Mormon religion does not acknowledge a female deity that would in return empower individual women in community, then ecology and religion help only partially. What appears to help Williams more is her individual response to others— friends, family, and, in particular, birds. In the introduction to their anthology *Intimate Nature: The Bond between Women and Animals*, Linda Hogan, Deena Metzger, and Brenda Peterson assert that "at the center of empathy and compassionate understanding lies the ability to see the other as true peer, to recognize intelligence and communication in all forms, no matter how unlike ourselves these forms might be" (xiv). The experience of reading *Refuge* is to watch this act of a human seeing the animal as true peer demonstrated repeatedly. The relationality of her autobiographical act—the way she tells her life through the other—is with birds. This bond is highly unusual, particularly in an autopathography, in that Williams rarely looks to childhood or young adulthood to investigate directly the mother-daughter relationship, even though her mother's suffering and dying stands at the center of the book. Her human bonds are certainly strong, but Williams looks outward, to the birds and the nonhuman world, to understand these connections, to give her peace and teach her about refuge.

The birds, that is, teach Williams, who then attempts to use the lessons in her own life. Williams demonstrates her lessons by spotlighting one bird species at a time, each bird focusing one of the thirty-six chapters, which taken together deliver a wealth of information about the region's birdlife. In some chapters the birds seem relatively unimportant to the narrative either in fact or metaphor.[2] In "Yellow-Headed Blackbirds," for example, Williams simply mentions seeing them among other birds at a wildlife refuge she drives four hours to visit. Or, in "Redheads," Williams uses the duck to discuss marshes and wetlands loss, because redheads are hit particularly hard by loss of habitat. But in other chapters the information about the bird species wraps around and through the personal narrative, anchoring it to the land. In "Canada Geese," for example, Williams moves first from describing a vespers service she and her mother attend to discussing Canada geese, which her mother says have always been her favorite birds, then on to asserting what is known and not known about bird migrations, to speculating in general terms about beginnings and endings, and then to depicting mother and daughter feeding the birds.

While the emphasis on bird life certainly provides a natural-history backdrop in *Refuge,* more importantly it shows the intertwining of human and animal. As with the other authors in this study, Williams does not lay out a linear argument or explanatory narrative. Like *Laughing in the Hills, A Country Year,* and *The Solace of Open Spaces, Refuge* has short scenes where readers, like the real-life participants, must figure out things for themselves. Because Williams forsakes explicit connections to tie together these short vignettes, the chapters in themselves and particularly in their relations to each other invite interpretation. The chapter "California Gulls" exemplifies how Williams blends the writing of natural history with autobiography, blends bird life with human life; as such, the chapter serves as example for Williams's literary act that assists grief work. She begins by recounting the day in 1984 when her mother had a biopsy to see if the cancer had gone into remission. The doctor comes in exultant because all the tissue looks pink and healthy; the family rejoices, prematurely. When the lab technicians run their tests, they discover a few microscopic cells in three of the fifteen biopsies. Her mother plunges into depression and Terry and her father and brothers feel guilty because they had "wanted everything back to its original shape . . . wanted a cure for Mother for ourselves, so we could get on with our lives. What we had forgotten was that she was living hers" (68). Williams flees "for Bear River, for the birds, wishing someone would rescue me."

What she sees there are the gulls, all flying in one direction on their daily commute from fishing grounds back to nesting grounds. For the first time in her life, gulls "seize her imagination." In a story echoing the starving time and rescue story of the Pilgrims at Plymouth Rock, she tells us the familiar Mormon origin (and rescue) story, how in a time of great need the gulls saved the Mormons' crops by eating the locusts. Wanting rescue, she remembers what had rescued humans before. Feeling grateful, she tells us all about this common bird, including its history at Great Salt Lake. Because she goes to the lake to orient herself in the midst of change, she is soothed that the gulls are always there, gliding through the sky. Williams closes the chapter by thinking again of how her mother, unlike the gulls, won't always be there; moreover, that the denial of that truth is stopping (and may continue to stop) Terry from listening to her mother, from letting her mother live out her life knowing she will die. Such fusing of personal and scientific information, narrative and exposition, field observation and book knowledge, runs through many chapters. The collage structure, the almost dizzying shifts of style and subject, replicates Williams's personal response to such intense moments, even as it makes demands on the reader like those made by poetry or fiction.

Unable to separate the Bear River Migratory Bird Refuge from her family, Williams creates numerous examples that show her linking birds to her life. In her early chapter "Burrowing Owls," Williams tells us she gauges her life by these particular owls (8). In "Whimbrels," she writes that the bird refuge is a landscape so familiar to her that she and the birds share a natural history: "It is a matter of rootedness, of living inside a place for so long that the mind and imagination fuse" (21). On a day when she needs solitude, she finds open space and sky and long-billed curlews, a species that similarly requires solitude (147).

Not only does Williams identify with particular bird species, their needs or adaptations, but she sees birds as religious beings, mediating between heaven and earth. She prays to birds, explaining, "I believe they will carry the messages of my heart upward . . . because I believe in their existence, the way their songs begin and end each day—the invocations and benedictions of Earth . . . because they remind me of what I love rather that what I fear. And at the end of my prayers, they teach me how to listen" (149). To lessen the grieving, she must let out her secrets "like white doves held captive too long. I am a woman with wings" (273). And, in the penultimate though straightforward statement showing how childhood and adulthood, interest and work, have merged in her life, she says simply that she would like to be a bird (266).

Despite Williams's intimate connections with birds going back to childhood, they provide her no long-lasting refuge, no self-knowledge that will put an end to mourning, until she comes to understand how they "lead secret and anonymous lives" (265). They serve more as escape than the "relational other" until she learns that she must also risk pain, court death, lose herself in wildness. After the death of her mother, when her grieving will not end, Williams slowly comes to recognize the increasing importance of wildness, wilderness, in her life. "Wilderness courts our souls," she writes. Discussing a blank spot on the map, where nothing "human" is filled in, Williams sees such blankness as an opportunity, "an invitation to encounter the natural world, where one's character will be shaped by the landscape. To enter wilderness is to court risk, and risk favors the senses, enabling one to live well" (244). She goes often to the desert, which she believes is holy, "a forgotten place that allows us to remember the sacred. Perhaps that is why every pilgrimage to the desert is a pilgrimage to the self" (148). She desires environments that she hopes will purge her, such as "a holy place in the salt desert, where egrets hover like angels" (237), where she is "saved from the outside world" in a hidden cave, "the secret den of my healing, where I come to whittle down my losses." "Dogma doesn't hold me," she writes, "wildness does."

Wildness can hurt as well as heal, and in some instances the two merge. Williams and her husband, Brooke, go backpacking often in the Utah desert, where one time she becomes scarred and "marked by the desert" when she falls badly and slashes her forehead. A year after her mother's death, Williams goes to Great Salt Lake to help Wildlife Resources count snowy plovers, and like the bird, she goes into the water to cool off. She becomes dehydrated, then nauseous, and is struck with delirium: "The next thing I remember is waking up in a dark motel room in Tremonton, Utah. I call Brooke to see if he can tell me what happened. He is not home. Snowy plovers come to mind. They can teach me how to survive" (260).

As wildness gains importance, Williams's favorite place slowly shifts from the Bear River Migratory Bird Refuge to the Great Salt Lake itself. Compared with the refuge where she went with her grandmother, the lake has few childhood memories attached to it, and her main memory is of sunburn and a reluctance to swim among brine shrimp. The lake is certainly not just a sanctuary. While the refuge has trees, grasses, and marshes, Williams describes Great Salt Lake as "wilderness, raw and self-defined." Wilderness and refuge unite for Williams when Utah resource departments in 1989 nominate the

Great Salt Lake to be part of the Western Hemisphere Shorebird Reserve Network, the wild lake becoming a refuge literally as well as symbolically.

In her narrative's closing scene, which serves as a marker of her recovery, Williams intertwines wildness, the Great Salt Lake, death, and refuge when she describes a canoe trip that she and Brooke take on Great Salt Lake. Shortly before the trip, Williams had gone to Mexico to experience the Day of the Dead, where, weeping silently for all that she had lost, she reentered her "own landscape of grief with perfect recall" and was rewarded: "The voices of my Dead came back to me" (277–78). And as she and Brooke paddle for two hours toward the heart of the lake, which has accepted them "like a lover," Williams tells us that those voices have remained ("Mother and Mimi are present. The relationships continue"), something, she writes, that she did not anticipate. On this excursion Williams wears her shawl from Mexico and carries marigold petals, her mother's favorite flower, emblematic of the Day of the Dead. Floating on the lake, feeling as if "there is no place on earth I would rather be," Williams finally unties her pouch:

Brooke sits up and leans forward. I shake petals into his hands and then into my own. Together we sprinkle marigold petals into Great Salt Lake.
My basin of tears.
My refuge. (280)

And so, except for the epilogue, the book ends. It began with the bird refuge and ends with the Great Salt Lake. It began with a denial of cancer and ends with a burial acknowledging acceptance of death. But if her refuge, here, is the Great Salt Lake, it is more than that. If her refuge exists in her capacity to love—as she has come to understand it—then refuge must entice her outward, toward love. If deep grieving inhibits one's desire to love again, as she had said earlier, then when she is ready to love, she has literally as well as symbolically been renewed, has moved past disabling grief.

It is noteworthy that Williams closes with a burial scene in which she and her husband scatter marigold petals. They paddle together; he pours hot chocolate, she spreads cream cheese on bagels; as she leans into the bow of the canoe, Brooke balances her by leaning into the stern; for hours they float, simply "watching clouds, watching birds, and breathing" (280). At one point during her mother's long illness, Williams had felt overwhelmed with all the sorrow, and she sat home crying, not for her mother but for herself: "I wanted my life back. I wanted my marriage back. I wanted my own time" (164). And in this final scene, she is with her husband, affirming her marriage— a refuge that is the final paradox in a book of surprises.[3]

Williams's changing beliefs about "refuge," the book's title and central metaphor, are at the core of her success in rewriting her past story of grief in such a way that she can imagine a future story of hope. As with Hubbell's *A Country Year,* there is no one epiphany, no one magical moment that turns loss into hope. Commenting on the style and form of *Refuge,* Tallmadge accurately notes that "the story is told as a succession of vivid, epiphanic moments that are strung rather than woven together" (205), though I would add that readers feel these moments as a stringing rather than a weaving because the epiphanies don't last, don't move Williams through her mourning. As Meredith Skura says of a successful analysis, psychoanalytic truth and meaning come from the entire process, which Williams shows in her almost excruciating descriptions of her ups and downs, her continuous turns on the wheel of grieving. But in the end, she has composed a self that in struggling toward acceptance is finally ready to move on. And though likewise exhausted, we as readers are ready to cheer her, deeply moved by our witnessing of her grief.

If refuge and acceptance are at one pole of her response, the metaphor of "unnatural history" and the mode of anger inhabit the other, and together they prompt her social criticism. Williams asserts in her subtitle and in many of her passages that she is writing an unnatural history. *Refuge* is certainly not "natural history" in its style and form: although Williams focuses each chapter on a bird species and announces the exact lake level, she mixes genres and styles in a way that breaks or at least bends our usual expectations of natural-history writing, and she does this within a carefully constructed discourse of gender. But her histories of place and family are also not "natural" because, as she reveals late in the book, she discovers a year after her mother's death that her family had all been exposed repeatedly to above-ground atomic testing, information explaining why seven of nine women in the family had already died prematurely from cancer.

In her epilogue, "The Clan of One-Breasted Women," first published as an essay in *Northern Lights,* Williams tells about her discovery that a recurring dream of a childhood memory, a "flash of light in the night in the desert," was no dream. She learns from her father that the family, driving home from California, had been in the midst of an above-ground atomic-bomb test, and light ash from the fallout rained on their car. Williams is so shocked by the news that she begins investigating what she calls "the years we bombed Utah," when nuclear testing for national security reasons was deemed more important than individual health of citizens. "When the Atomic Energy Commission," she writes, "described the country north of the Nevada Test Site as 'virtually uninhabited desert terrain,' my family and the birds at Great Salt Lake were some of the 'virtual uninhabitants'" (287). Her anger politicizes her: "Tolerating blind obedience in the name of patriotism or religion ultimately takes our lives." The epilogue/essay describes an act of civil disobedience, Williams and nine other women crossing into military lands at the test site, "a gesture on behalf of the Clan of One-Breasted Women" (290). When officers arrest her and find a pen and a pad of paper tucked inside her boot, they ask her what they are. "Weapons," Williams answers.

Atomic testing, cancer, destruction of bird habitat by the rise of the lake, women's roles in Mormonism, the relations between women and nature—Williams connects all these in her social analysis, which has interested critics who have, by and large, used Williams's critiques of technology and the patriarchy to assert, by implication, their assenting opinions. But the contradictions of Williams's ecofeminist and essentialist positions have been danced around. In "Flooding the Boundaries of Form: Terry Tempest Williams's Ecofeminist Unnatural History," Cheryll Glotfelty says that "in a nutshell, the ecofeminist argument is that men dominate and exploit both nature and women" (163). Cassandra Kircher, in an essay that ultimately argues that Williams moves outside of simplistic dichotomies, begins by noting that Williams sets up in *Refuge* an "easy" equation: "Any oppressive forces in the book are male or, more often, are related to patriarchal urban culture" (99). Williams exemplifies such an ecofeminist position in a conversation she has with a friend:

We spoke of rage. Of women and the landscape. How our bodies and the body of the earth have been mined.

"It has everything to do with intimacy," I said. "Men define intimacy through their bodies. It is physical. They define intimacy with the land in the same way."

"Many men have forgotten what they are connected to," my friend added. "Subjugation of women and nature may be a loss of intimacy within themselves." (10)

From such passages and numerous others, Kircher suggests, it could be argued that Williams "relies in part on prefabricated dualisms to structure her book, a decision that reveals an either/or sensibility on her part and a penchant for cliché" (98).[4]

Kircher's essay is certainly insightful about *Refuge*, and her own admitted love for the book makes her want to go beyond her reservations, to turn "problem" into possibility: "Fortunately my criticisms of Williams' dichotomies do not adequately capture the intrinsic complexity of *Refuge*. The ways that Williams problematizes both the female/nature and male/culture alliances and, more important, the way she moves beyond dichotomies to depict a circular notion of family keeps the book from being essentialist" (101). But it is difficult not to see Williams's views as essentialist. "I am desert. I am mountains. I am Great Salt Lake" (29), she writes; "I want to see the Great Salt Lake as woman, as myself, in her refusal to be tamed" (92). Karla Armbruster, in her fine essay on *Refuge*, spends part of the essay explaining the essentialist positions of Williams and part trying to explain away the potential impact of those positions. She says, for example, "From time to time Williams finds it strategic to represent the connection [woman/nature] in a way that could be interpreted as essentialist; if it gives her strength to think that, as a woman, she is in tune with the cycles of nature, she does so—temporarily and consciously" (213). Glotfelty, though praising Williams for her creation of an unusual style and structure, still wishes at the end of her essay that Williams had invoked gender "in the spirit of bridging differences rather than exaggerating them" (166).

Armbruster writes that Williams's book "eloquently illustrates" a genealogy of women and the earth that shows "how human culture has abused the bodies of women and the landscape, thus linking their positions and their fates in this context" (217). But it is difficult to make this ecofeminist argument because one could just as easily change "women" to "men" (if you were willing to include specific men), and say that humans—men and women alike, particularly if they are of a certain race and class—benefit by an exploitation of the landscape, which throughout history has hurt more male bodies than female. New houses in subdivisions are not desired only by men; new clothes in department stores are not bought only by men; and atomic-bomb testing in the Cold War was not done only for men, or only to women. Utah men, not only women, died from cancers. The difficulty for Williams is that she intertwines ideological positions with what she sees in her family and what she feels within herself. Her anguished grieving is enlarged because she projects something particular and personal onto something ideological and general. Nowhere is this seen more clearly than in her inability to separate her mother's cancer from the drowning of the bird refuges.

While Williams structures *Refuge* with the chronology of her mother's illness, death, and her own grieving, she wraps around that chronology a second, contrasting one—the rise and fall of Great Salt Lake. The first chronology comes from what seems unnatural, healthy cells mutating to unhealthy cells for unknown reasons, and the drama of the mother's story is not whether she will live or die but how Williams will cope with her death and move through mourning. The second chronology seems, of course, perfectly natural: heavy snows and rains make a lake rise, and Williams writes at length about the Great Salt Lake, its history, geological makeup, and animal populations, all in relation to this rise. She also details the human drama in response, how politicians worried about reelection try to stop that rise because human businesses are affected. The politicians propose laughably inadequate and expensive projects, such as spending $100 million to pump water into the desert to evaporate. Seemingly no politician or businessperson can just wait until the cycle reverses itself. The fear of high water levels corresponds to the fear of cancerous cells: unnatural disease and private response, natural phenomenon and public response. Williams shows brilliantly humans' inability to stop change.

Over the course of the book Williams lays out specific details of her mother's struggle to fight off the cancer—surgeries, diagnoses, recoveries, and hospital stays—and side by side she relates significant emotional events that bring epiphanies of acceptance or denial. For example, early after the diagnosis she thinks about how cancer's power comes in part from the associated ideas of secret mutation and death that are rarely talked about openly, and she wonders whether our society can rethink cancer. As she ponders how cancer is ironically an individual's own creation that is nevertheless greatly feared, Williams comes to understand its similarities to the creative process: "Ideas emerge slowly, quietly, invisibly at first. They are most often abnormal thoughts, thoughts that disrupt the quotidian, the accustomed. They divide and multiply, become invasive. With time, they congeal, consolidate, and make themselves conscious. An idea surfaces and demands total attention" (44). After watching her mother go through some months of chemotherapy, Williams thinks that "suffering shows us what we are attached to—perhaps the umbilical cord between Mother and me has never been cut" (53). A year later, she has a new metaphor for her experience, imagining herself a piece of clay being repeatedly fired. "My vessel is my body," she writes, "where I hold a space of healing for those I love. Each day becomes a firing" (168). In the last agonizing days of her mother's death, when the family is taking turns changing her morphine drip and nursing her, Williams alternates between two states—between an immense desire to have it all end because it is too painful for everyone and a recognition that in these last days her mother is giving her a reverence for death, and therefore for life, the greatest lesson a mother could teach.

In recent decades, cancer has for many people assumed the level of a cultural referent that functions as a metaphor. A person who has a form of cancer does not just have a specific, usually treatable disease, but "has cancer," which gathers around it disturbing images. A person can even be a "cancer," meaning that in an office, among a group of friends, on a team, that person acts insidiously to harm the group. In her astute book *Illness as Metaphor,* Susan Sontag shows how diseases such as tuberculosis and cancer become "encumbered by the trappings of metaphors" (5). Illness is *not* a metaphor, she insists, and "the most truthful way of regarding illness—and the healthiest way of being ill—is one most purified of, most resistant to, metaphoric thinking" (3), particularly when the disease, like cancer, becomes metaphorically an evil, silent, invincible predator.

Unable to see cancer as a "natural" process of being human, not dissimilar to the flu virus, pneumonia, or AIDS, Williams likewise sees the rise of the Great Salt Lake as devastating to humans at this moment in history. When she praises the Fremont for their ability to adapt to change by simply moving higher in the hills, she does not see that present-day humans acting through government structures to build pumps to control water is just another version—our version— of the Fremonts' moving higher. Both groups are doing what comes "naturally" as a response to their particular needs in time. What would be unnatural today, if we look at human behavior as evidence, is for humans to conserve resources, to avoid building on flood plains, and so forth. Williams criticizes the politicians' ideas about how to lessen the water level, saying that "evidently, to do nothing is not an option" (61). But she certainly wants her mother to "do something" about the cancer, by which she means take any drugs, any version of chemotherapy, that could save her. The technological ability to build sophisticated and large pumps and the desire to use that technology is related to abilities and desires to make and use sophisticated, powerful drugs. So if natural processes are the best solution for one activity (don't pump, do nothing), then perhaps they are for everything (don't medicate).

I am not criticizing Williams here—she is simply being fully human, unable to get her logic and her ideology into line with her personal feelings of despair. Acknowledging the contradictions of her positions does lessen the power of her social criticism, but such acknowledgment does not lessen the humanity coming through her narrative: paradox and contradiction are at the core of us all. Her story of grieving is all the stronger because we see a "self" challenging nearly all social convention under the pressure of grief. But disregarding how these two human responses are related (building pumps to reduce water levels, attacking cancer with drugs) is a simplified reading, a reading that allows one to set "nature" against and above human technology in order to criticize the technology or the ideologies that one wishes to connect to them. Hubbell, in *A Country Year,* serves as a useful contrast, exemplifying one (rather ideal) possibility, in that she seems to have her values and ideology directly in line with her daily life. Hubbell's ability to see herself in multiple webs of textuality in which humans are just another animal helps her to imagine a rich, interconnected life in her future, and coming to this realization marks the end of her grieving. But Williams struggles more than Hubbell, has more difficulties with her grief work, in part, I would speculate, because she is projecting the personal onto these larger ideological issues.

This projection is paradoxical even as the intertwining of personal and political creates much of the text's power. A scene from her chapter "Magpies," recalled from the last year of her mother's life, shows how this projection leads Williams to problematic moments in her grief work. Intense grieving makes all humans flip-flop emotionally, and Williams familiarly describes how one day she hit "rock-bottom," only to "feel stronger" the next. But she generalizes that she feels stronger because she was "learning to live within the natural cycles of a day and to not expect so much from myself. As women, we hold the moon in our bellies. It is too much to ask to operate on full-moon energy three hundred and sixty-five days a year. I am in a crescent phase. And the energy we expend emotionally belongs to the hidden side of the moon" (136). The metaphor is lovely in a way (though many women might recoil at the biological explanation of women's feelings and behaviors), but because the next time Williams feels in despair (perhaps even the very next day) this view will not be able to sustain her, and so she will need an entirely new explanation or metaphor. And she says shortly thereafter that she is not adjusting: "I keep dreaming the Refuge back to what I have known. . . . There is no one to blame, nothing to fight" (140).

Similar attempts to ground her grieving in a mystical ecological view likewise go astray, hindering her grief work. For example, when Williams asserts that a person writing and sending a letter makes a sensual and personal connection to the receiver, she asks how we can connect similarly with the land. She suggests that an ancient pulse still beats in the land and we can be sustained spiritually if we can hear it and find ways to drum back our own heartbeat:

> The heartbeats I felt in the womb—two heartbeats, at once, my mother's and my own—are heartbeats of the land. All of life drums and beats, at once, sustaining a rhythm audible only to the spirit. I can drum my heartbeat back into the Earth, beating, hearts beating, my hands on the Earth—like a ruffed grouse on a log, beating, hearts beating—like a bittern in the marsh, beating, hearts beating. My hands on the Earth beating, hearts beating. I drum back my return. (85)

The passage is finally enigmatic. More is needed to suggest how the land's heartbeats can become audible to the spirit, and what her own drumming back might entail.

Correspondence with the land here concerns knowing and believing, a faith act that comes from a unified vision, but how that translates into behavior is not clear. Language, I would maintain, simply fails Williams at moments like these (and such moments are scattered throughout the text); that is to say, the language does not perform the anticipated act of a healing self-creation. Her descriptions at such moments mirror the writings of people connected to such movements as "deep ecology," an ethical stance toward the environment that Williams in her journey of grieving and recovery embraces.[5] Cultivating a deep ecological consciousness, write Devall and Sessions, "is a process of learning to appreciate silence and solitude and rediscovering how to listen. It is learning how to be more receptive, trusting, holistic in perception, and is grounded in a vision of nonexploitive science and technology" (8). These general ideas certainly find particular correspondences in *Refuge,* as Williams questions, listens, and reshapes her world view in response to her grieving, but they do not appear to help her with that grieving.

Even intertwining the drowning of the bird refuges and her mother's death may hinder acceptance of either loss. For example, throughout the years of and after her mother's dying, Williams mourns the flooding of the Bear River Migratory Bird Refuge, discusses repeatedly how many fewer birds and ducks are there, how many have been killed by rising waters, and so forth. She projects her own loss onto the loss of birds. Mourning her mother's death, Williams finds some consolation when she discovers that many of the Great Salt Lake flocks of birds have relocated to new homes in refuges in Oregon and Nevada. Watching thousands of white-faced ibises, double-crested cormorants, and snowy egrets at the Malheur National Wildlife Refuge in Oregon, Williams feels like she has "come home." All is not lost, she writes: "The birds have simply moved on. They give me the courage to do the same" (253). On one hand, the scene as written works as metaphor, Williams using the birds as lesson, helping her to overcome grief. But on the other hand, this is not good biology: Williams should have known, long before, that the birds had, like the Fremont, moved on, "moved up higher."

Creating an opposition of two worlds, nature and the human-made one, does not serve Williams's grieving well, but in doing this she is closer than Hubbell is to how most readers conceive of themselves. We sympathize with Williams, for example, in her struggles to rethink her understanding of cancer or her role in relation to the Mormon patriarchy; we likewise feel outrage when we read that the government used "national security" to justify above-ground atomic testing. If logically we might believe that humans are a part of biology as everything else is, and therefore everything we do is natural, emotionally we react to Williams's feelings of being betrayed and recognize the rightness of her phrase "unnatural history." We understand her desire to heal herself by setting "bad" human actions against the "natural" world that she loves and that she wants to have serve her as retreat, as refuge.

Recovery comes slowly to her, however, as she realizes months after her mother's death that her grief is much larger than she could ever have imagined. Memories both haunt and heal. Though I have emphasized that Williams's renewal comes primarily from her reconsidering her understanding of "refuge" and is hindered by her need to view her story as "unnatural," these two cannot be totally separated in the book, just as a more "logical" way of seeing ecology cannot necessarily translate into behavior that is totally accepting of what humans do. As Rose says in *Trauma and Mastery in Life and Art,* "logic alone gives a false picture when it comes to the nonrational, imaginative primary process" (191), and in grief work, as in art, one struggles between two mental processes—imaginative, nonlogical thought and cognitive, logical thought. In *Refuge* we behold Williams slowly coming to reconcile these two, making powerful art out of the process of showing grief.

In "The Peace of Wild Things," Wendell Berry, writing not about a specific trauma but a general fear of loss, creates a lovely short poem that resonates with the feelings of Williams in *Refuge.* "When despair for the world grows in me," the speaker says, when fears of the future make uncertain what his life and his children's lives may be, he seeks out a place that calms, a place inhabited by wild animals, who "do not tax their lives with forethought / of grief." The speaker, in this despairing moment, desires to lose one quality that defines us as human, but that can be maddening—the imagining of future grief. For Berry's speaker in this poem, as well as for Williams, these imaginings haunt, and connection with humans only reminds them of old and forthcoming grief. Animals model a totally "present" mode of being that lessens the haunting, and so the speaker goes down to his pond to watch a wood drake swimming and a great heron feeding, as Williams goes to the Great Salt Lake or the Bear River Refuge to learn from "her" birds. For a time, Berry's speaker says, this identification with the animals succeeds: "I rest in the grace of the world, and am free."

Despair . . . forethought of grief . . . coming into the peace of wild things, resting in the grace of the world: Berry takes a moment of immersion into the nonhuman world, where the desire is to get away from human consciousness, and creates a beautiful poem in human language, where the importance of the initial act is then understood or at least refined. With such a performance, we are back to a set of ideas linked by autobiography studies and environmental literature: the individual self may be constructed relationally to nonhuman others; the self makes language and in return the language makes the self. In *Refuge* Williams tells numerous stories that represent her feelings of the moment, and in return those stories construct her: Williams performs grief work not by coming to any one all-encompassing epiphany but by undergoing a long process that leads finally to general insight and a renewal of hope.

In *Nature Writing and America,* Peter Fritzell generalizes that the narrator of the best American nature writing desires to command and master its environment even as it wishes to lose itself in "the unconscious business of identifying its surroundings or in the more mystical experience of being utterly immersed in them" (163). The writers, Fritzell goes on to say, have "argued that the truth of one's relations to nonhuman nature is found . . . not in the opposition of town and country, nor even in the conflict of wilderness and civilization, but in the exploration of . . . the conflict of the civilized and the wild in one's self, in the conflict within one's self between the desire to accept and enhance the orders and distinctions of traditional Western civilization" (167). When *Refuge* is less successful, Williams sets wilderness and civilization, natural processes and unnatural, human-tainted processes, the body and culture, in opposition, in order to accept the death and destruction around her. But *Refuge* is most successful when Williams explores these conflicts within herself and ties the resolutions to her particular family, place, and religion. And when she does this, she writes powerfully, taking her place with those "best American nature writers" that Fritzell names—with Thoreau, Leopold, and Dillard.

4 When All the World Is Cancerous

Bill Barich's *Laughing in the Hills*

The books in this study confound the catalogers at the Library of Congress. *A Country Year* is listed under Natural History, Missouri and the Ozarks; and Country Life, Missouri and the Ozarks. *Refuge* is listed as Williams, Terry Tempest–Health, Breast Cancer Patients Utah Biography; and Natural History, Utah and the Great Salt Lake Region. *Laughing in the Hills,* according to the catalogers, is a book on horseracing and horse-race betting. And indeed, *Laughing in the Hills* is considered one of the finest documentaries of thoroughbred horse racing, but descriptions of thoroughbreds, parimutuel betting, and jockeys all intermingle with reflections on Renaissance philosophy, California geology, and contemporary culture.[1] The reviewer in *Time* magazine compared the book to Robert Pirsig's *Zen and the Art of Motorcycle Maintenance* in its amalgamation of wit, reportage, and philosophy (70). An even more interesting comparison was made by the reviewer for the *Denver Post,* who said that "to believe this is just a book about horse racing is to believe *Moby Dick* is just a book about whales."[2] Barich's strangely juxtaposed discussions are fascinating in their own right, but as with the other writers in this study they are important, too, for their therapeutic effect as he indirectly works through his personal trauma.

Like Williams, Barich is plunged into grieving when his mother dies from cancer. But unlike Williams or Hubbell, he doesn't stay put, writing about the "natural world" while he works through his grief.

In denial of what has happened, and projecting the cancer to all of American society, Barich leaves to spend a season at Golden Gate Fields, a thoroughbred racetrack, a place that "seemed circumscribed and manageable, especially when compared to the complex filigree of nature, hydrogen intertwined with embryos and tumors" (6). Americans, Barich writes, value illusion over substance, which he sees metaphorically as America's cancer. He cites as evidence such disparate modern realities as the damming of rivers to make lakes, the increasing proliferation and importance of television, the closing of museums and libraries, and the lack of interest in history. Deep in depression, Barich goes to the racetrack because horse racing, he believes, stands in opposition to cancerous America. At the track, substance is everything: horses, trainers, and jockeys who do the best job win; quality and effort directly pay off. Such claims, early in the book, appear self-delusory. Is Barich not going to the racetrack simply to escape, to immerse himself in a world where difficult human relationships and social problems can easily be evaded, where the intellectual exercise of handicapping races and the thrill of betting can temporarily lessen his pain? The book's drama becomes Barich's slow and hard-won understanding that his instinct to go to the track is a good one, but for unforeseen reasons.

Barich goes to the "circumscribed and manageable" racetrack in order to assert control and feel a vitality that is becoming increasingly difficult to assert and feel in a world where people get cancer and die, in a world where "progress" seems to be the tearing down of the natural world in order to build a tacky subdivision. The control will come, he believes, if he can find and construct a "prevailing fiction" of the racetrack and master the art of betting. The book, in brief, charts a series of epiphanies that reverses Barich's beliefs about control: he recognizes the necessity of intuition and the impossibility of a coherent fiction; he learns that what he seeks has little to do with betting and everything to do with how humans fit into a universe not divided into self and others. While at first glance, *Laughing in the Hills* seems somewhat unconnected to the other books in this study, in that horse racing has almost nothing to do with environmental literature, Barich's grief work succeeds when he turns his attention away from the racetrack and to the horses themselves. As Barich moves through mourning, *Laughing in the Hills* becomes an "animal book" that segues into autobiography, in its drama of one human's growing relationality to the animal-other.

Cancer, transposed onto all human activities, serves Barich as a public vessel for all his private grief. *Laughing in the Hills* shows him coming to understand that cancer and death are not the same, either literally or figuratively. Barich opens his book in a Hemingwayesque tone with the event that begins his downward slide: "For me it did not begin with the horses. They came later, after a phone call and a simple statement of fact: Your mother has cancer" (1). He flies to New York to see his mother, now "an old woman with bright eyes," ravaged by disease. To escape this image, to return to a time when she was vital, not dying, he wanders his old neighborhood, his boyhood schools, "longing in a not so curious way . . . for innocence, for breath." Emotionally desperate, he begins betting on thoroughbred races, where "anything might happen, could happen, probably would happen." The unpredictability of the horse races becomes a stay against the certainty of death, and soon the entire family begins playing, including the mother, who hears "in the track announcer's call a little pulse of life at the heart of the cancer" (4). The literary act of this opening is marked by the short scenes, the tough-guy pose, the demands placed upon the reader to bring unrelated parts together. Barich's actions are a form of denial—retreating to the past when he and his mother were young, absorbing himself in the horse races as escape; and his narrative voice, like that of the Hemingway narrator, suggests that we as readers are in the know, that we agree with his assessment of society, a voice that invites us to keep listening.

After Barich flies back to California, he falls into deep depression when other relatives get cancer and his wife is operated on for a brain tumor that turns out not to exist. In the fall he quits his job and they move to the country. For a while the isolation in nature helps him, but soon he slides again into depression, arguing with his wife, angry at his inability to write. He makes cancer into the symbolic disease of America, cancer becoming all technological progress, a killer raging rampant without sensitivity or taste. He laments that townhouses and condominiums are devouring orchards and vineyards. He grows angry when he sees a sign for a new subdivision, "Cypress Estates," where no cypresses have ever grown. And he knows his anger is out of control when he flies into a rage upon seeing bulldozers or sewer pipes or even surveyors.

In the spring his mother dies, and Barich, though wanting to forget what has happened, what is happening, wakes at night "to my

mother's face or the memory of my wife lying in her hospital bed."
Longing for "an escape into orderliness," he decides "with the same
hapless logic that governed all my actions then," to leave home and
spend the rest of the spring at Golden Gate Fields, a thoroughbred
track near Oakland, California. He is convinced that there is something special about racing, that he might come away renewed if he
could tap again that pulse of life he'd recognized. Once before he had
escaped in a similar way, leaving his college to spend a semester in
Florence, "wandering instead of studying," reading Italian Renaissance
philosophers. And so, on his way to the track, he throws some of his
old books in his suitcase. Florentines, he says, "had always liked to
gamble" (7).

The summary above covers only the first few pages of the book,
in which Barich details his fragile emotional condition, connects cancer to capitalist America's "progress," and declares emphatically that
horse racing has not fallen victim to this progress. But when he ar-
rives at Golden Gate Fields, Barich is uncertain what specifically will
help him change depression over his mother's death to acceptance. He
does know that cancer and progress represent to him change and
chaos, and so as response he looks to actions that surround handicapping and betting in an attempt to assert control. He begins describing the racetrack by discussing the intricacies of handicapping a
race in order to bet intelligently and win money by gambling. He defines *speed, class,* and *condition.* After compiling a survey of races run
during the preceding racing meeting, showing from which starting-
gate position horses began the race, he explains that at Golden Gate
Fields horses breaking from the middle of the track win most often.
Front-running horses, he adds, win 30 percent of all sprints. Armed
with this information—for its description has been as much for
Barich as for a reader—he goes to the track the first morning both
ready to win money and desiring to fabricate a prevailing fiction
"modeled on notions of symmetry and coherence."

Following Ernest Becker's lead in his monumental work *The Denial of Death,* where Becker articulates "the vital lie" humans tell
themselves in order to deny their own death, William Dowie suggests
that *Laughing in the Hills* illustrates in horse racing the "vital lie" of
sport itself: "The illustration is sharpened by the circumstances of
powerlessness, disarray, and death that led Barich to the track, which
responds, on the initial level of escape, with exactly what he needs:

images of power, order, and life" (27). But the possibility of a fiction of coherence and images of order lasts only while Barich notices how people and the track itself contribute to order and harmony, because once the horses for the first race appear, order gives way to chaos. He bets on a long shot he hadn't even considered when studying the *Daily Racing Form* the night before, and, losing, he overreacts. "All day long," he writes, "I compounded my mistakes, playing the most improbable nags on the card, hoping to get even, to start over, the slate wiped clean" (23). Continuing to lose, he feels defeated, confused, until the following morning when he feels optimistic again because anything seems possible. The next day repeats the pattern, however, as does the next.

If Barich quickly learns that the chaos of the "outside" world is matched by the chaos of the horse races, he still believes that virtue and hard work—not random chance—are rewarded at the track. Shifting his attention from betting, Barich begins exploring the fabric of the racetrack. After watching the horses gallop one morning, he observes the behind-the-scenes business of the "backstretch." Jockey's agents move from barn to barn booking mounts; trainers clock horses and place orders with tack salesmen and feed suppliers; grooms pitch hay. Immersing himself in this world that seems to have a cause-and-effect relationship, Barich finds himself agreeing with Slaughterhouse Red, a gateman, that "anybody who don't like *this* life is daffy!" (30).

Barich identifies with various people on the backstretch, trying to learn from them what will make a coherent life. One "other" is the groom Bob Ferris, whom Barich describes as "the most literate person I encountered" (and who had done most of his reading in prison). Ferris enjoys a freedom that Barich envies. In an old Chevy, Ferris drives wherever he wants, from racetrack to racetrack, encumbered only by his books, not by the past. Barich is also attracted to the trainer Emery Winebrenner, a man who loves his work but isn't happy. Trying to understand why he spends so much time with Winebrenner, Barich decides that "we were both struggling; his confusion resembled my own" (54). He admires the trainer Glen Nolan because Nolan's skill with horses, communicating with a touch or word, gives him pleasure and focuses his life. In a short scene describing his visit to watch John Gibson, the track's announcer, Barich creates an analogy between calling races and his own desire for control—the track announcer's job is difficult, Barich says, because nine times a day you must "lend a sense of order and purpose to animals spilling out of the gate" (93). Though Barich values the way the people on the backstretch care about horses, and though the information he learns is interesting to him, this knowledge does not transfer to the personal narrative, does not help him create a healing story. These people don't serve him relationally.

Visiting the barn of Gary Headley, Barich is attracted to a young filly named Pichi whom Headley is trying to rehabilitate. Pichi had begun racing as a two-year-old at Hollywood Park, a big-time track in Southern California. Nervous and excitable, with an aversion to starting gates, she had performed poorly in the few races she had run. Worse yet, her intractable will had led her trainer to use force, and she had become mean-tempered. By the time her owner gives her over to Headley, Pichi has deteriorated further, physically as well as psychologically. "Another cripple," Headley thinks when he sees her, but liking to work with cripples, to make them fit for racing once again, he patiently brings Pichi round. Barich sympathizes and empathizes with her because she has become a "cripple" in part because of her own nature, in part because of mistreatment and ignorance by humans. For Barich, throughout the book, her progress becomes a measure of his own.

Unable to find meaning in the world of betting and performance, unable to make a signifying story from the fragments of lives he observes at the track, Barich is simply devastated when the races imitate the chaos of the larger world. He had hoped for an experience similar to when he had fled to Florence; after returning to the United States, he writes, he was able to bring the spirit he found in Italy back with him: "My experience in Florence renewed me in many ways and for years after I took sustenance from what had happened to me there. In bad or difficult times I would retreat briefly into memory and think about the Uffizi or evenings spent on the roof of the British Council Library reading Yeats" (127). But at the racetrack, he becomes unsure whether he has any stories that can sustain him and help him move through mourning. Lying in bed one night, remembering back to his boyhood and stickball games under the street lights, Barich realizes that then, as a boy, there were "no races to go to, the racing all inside" (56). And that feeling continued for a time, in Florence, and when he was later in Africa and for short periods after his returns from being abroad. Exhilaration and ecstasy did not have to be sought. "When did the switchback occur?" he asks; he has no answer, but he does know that he is now waiting for the next switchback—an acceptance of death.

As with the other writers in this study, Barich does not dramatize in his text, certainly, the "medical model" of mourning, which sees grief as a disease, a group of symptoms that at some point disappear. Nor does his experience correspond to Elizabeth Kubler-Ross's "stage-model" formulation of how terminally ill people move from denial to acceptance along a path of anger, depression, panic, guilt, and worry. In this model, which proponents articulate rather formulaically and use to describe all mourning, one stage leads, lockstep, to the next and the stages are not recursive, the various feelings of grief not intertwined. A more useful description of the grieving process is John Bowlby's. Applying his attachment theory of mother and child to grief in general, Bowlby argues that grief leads to a disorganization of one's life, and that the grieving process is essential for reorganization, for building up new patterns of behavior. Barich, in a stage of disorganization, cannot (at this point) make relevant to his own life other people's stories or particular information. He cannot, that is, have knowledge function as a metaphor.

For someone who is mourning, the importance of constructing metaphors can hardly be overemphasized. Humans think tropologically, and so metaphor is not simply embellishment, a matter of style.[3] A metaphor "redescribes reality," Paul Ricouer claims; as a comparing of something unknown to something known, or as the intuitive perception of similarity between two things of a different order, a metaphor produces a new order "by creating rifts in an old order" (22–23). What a mourner sees as death-in-life, one way that things are related, must be turned into life-in-life, the opposite relation. Ricouer, reviving Aristotle's use of the verb *metaphorize,* stresses predication over denomination, emphasizing the mental process and making of it an act of the constitutive imagination.

In their persuasive book *Metaphors We Live By,* George Lakoff and Mark Johnson go a step further, arguing not just that human thought processes are largely metaphorical, but that we live our lives within the domains of organizing metaphors. Looking carefully at metaphors that express widely held beliefs in our culture, such as "time is money" or "love is a journey," Lakoff and Johnson demonstrate how such a metaphor structures the behavior of someone who believes in it. For example, if we conceive of time "as the kind of thing that can be spent, wasted, budgeted, invested wisely or poorly, saved, or squandered" (8), then that particular psychology influences how we act in our lives, whether at work or at leisure.

For Barich, the cancer that he sees in everything outside the race-track must be reimagined in terms other than cancerous, and metaphorizing is central to this revision (re-vision). He hinders himself with his reluctance to give up an old version of the past, symbolized by mementos that remind him of a time prior to the cancer of his mother and the metaphorical cancer that is both within himself and without in America. Searching small-town thrift shops for the "history" there, he buys ashtrays shaped like lemons and oranges, souvenirs of the Citrus Fair; he is attracted to "three handtowels from a razed hotel." These items, "precious to me," he writes, are "shards of a human past that was being scraped from the edges of consciousness." The items also become psychological stays against the cancer of technological progress, "another aspect of disease." But the attempt to lose himself in the artifacts of small-town history serves only as a short-term drug. Reconstituting the past with thrift-shop mementos from a time period he idealizes in order to avoid the present becomes merely nostalgia for Barich. He has no lasting engagement with this past, intellectually or emotionally.

What helps him move beyond nostalgia toward the construction of a new understanding is his reading in Renaissance philosophy. His fascination with the Italian Renaissance, he tells us, had begun fifteen years earlier when he spent a college semester abroad in Florence. He had left the United States for Italy after two aimless years in school, years of superficial fraternity pranks and desultory intellectual effort. Disillusioned with college and with the Vietnam War, disillusioned with himself, he found Florence the symbol of something magical. Florence and the Italian Renaissance were to become a useable past.

"Soon after arriving in Florence," Barich writes, "I started wandering instead of studying. The Renaissance became more immanent than historical to me and for six months I lived within its compass." His classrooms were the streets and museums, the alleys and cafes. "The Florence I chose to live in," he recalls, "wasn't an actual city but instead the legendary Florence of Lorenzo the Magnificent. His face was the map of the territory, fleshy, broad, shrewd, a little flushed from drink, and his pursuits, I imagined, were mine: art, women, wine, and poetry" (119). During his present time of trauma, it is not surprising then that Barich attempts to replicate at the racetrack his successful experience in Florence. Nor is it surprising that he turns to Renaissance philosophy for help in understanding and giving shape to his life; Florentines, he says, liked to gamble and knew about death.

Barich is intrigued by Machiavelli, not the writer most of us know, adviser to the powerful, but the man after exile who found comfort in scholarship. Late at night, Machiavelli writes, he went to his study to speak to the dead: "Four hours can pass, and I feel no weariness; my troubles forgotten, I neither fear poverty nor dread death." Barich likewise reads at night, speaking to the ancients of the Renaissance, longing for the same acceptance of death. He is particularly drawn to Pico della Mirandola, who argued that a person's position in the universal scheme is not fixed but fluid, and that one can practice a "natural philosophy" by understanding the ways all things in the world are connected. Barich is interested in Pico's idealism and fascination with magic, "a white and benevolent magic" that works by "sympathy," knowing the "secret charms by which one thing can be drawn to another." Pico's white magic explores affinities and relationships, tries to attract spiritual energy and then to deploy it for the good, in contrast to that other magic "which depends entirely on the work and authority of demons."

The Renaissance becomes Barich's arena within an arena, helping him to understand the racing world. He interprets the track in terms of Florentine life: "I came to think of trainers as Renaissance princes who ruled the backstretch" (57). He observes that the track's backstretch is "as intricately nepotistic as the Medici's Florence." Watching a groom work, he recalls the young apprentices who did "a hundred menial tasks so that Pollaiuolo or Verrocchio or some other master could step up, brush in hand, and apply the final strokes unencumbered" (109). When a horse breaks loose in the shedrow, knocking him down, Barich opens his next section with, "Horses kept breaking loose in Florence, too, all the time, barreling riderless over the cobbles" (151). This kind of transition becomes more insistent as the book proceeds: Barich revolving endlessly in two worlds, trying to understand one from the other through the double vision of metaphor.

This attempt—of seeing American society and his own depression through the lens of horse racing, and seeing horse racing through the lens of the Renaissance—cannot work if Barich idealizes both the Renaissance and horse racing. He escapes to the racetrack because he sees it initially as a world free from death, confusion, randomness. He also goes because the track is a place to construct for himself explanatory stories "modeled on notions of symmetry and coherence"—stories, that is, that give order and purpose to life. His obsession with the art of handicapping becomes, therefore, more than a desire to win money by betting. Handicapping a race accurately is the proof that it is possible, even on the smallest scale, for him to construct such stories. At the track, however, Barich fails to assert the control he desires. At a low point, he realizes that he is getting nowhere: "I sat on the steps and thought about the Unknown and realized that I was pushing at the track, still trying too hard. My disappointment came from expectations, from proposing a shape for the experience I was seeking and then feeling let down when the experience arrived in a shape other than the one I'd proposed" (78). The Unknown, Barich realizes here, can function as a "transformative condition" that grants a new vision, a knowledge of the "mysteries," but only if he is open to considering fresh experiences in a new way.

One morning, deciding that his absorption in winning money has blinded him, he impulsively locks all his money in his glove compartment. The scene echoes a great moment in William Faulkner's *The Bear,* when Ike McCaslin, who without a gun has been tracking Old Ben for nine hours, understands that Old Ben will not allow himself to be seen because Ike is "still tainted" by the watch and compass he carries. Shedding them, losing himself (literally) in the deep wilderness, Ike finally receives his glance, delivering him to the cusp of mysteries that are revealed years later on a December night when he and his cousin go through the ledgers of the McCaslin family. Barich, shedding the material trappings of the bettor, suddenly notices the "awesome randomness" in view, and he understands in a new way the work of thoroughbred trainers: "It was canal work they did, an attempt at channeling energies beyond their control, but they were only intermittently successful. The pulse [of life] kept its own rhythm, somewhere deep inside" (80). Trainers, Barich believes, participate in a Dionysian rite, a celebration of energy and forces beyond anyone's control.

Barich comes to understand that to get past the sadness of death he must tap into this celebration, or something comparable, which

Refiguring the Map of Sorrow

90

leads him to "suspect" that the magical qualities of the track have "more to do with nesting birds than with money, speed, or class" (127–28). But at this point in his narrative he does not know what exactly to do. He does recognize that he is changed as a bettor; he is no longer the hard-nosed gambler, trying to beat the odds with a system or better handicapping. Whereas he once made fun of racegoers who bet because of names or the horse's coat color or the ribbons twisted in its mane, Barich has come to believe that he should follow intuition, that there is something essentially right about betting sentimentally on a horse because the name reminds him of the lake where he and his brother once backpacked. Though Barich wants to measure success by something other than winning or losing at the betting window, he is unable to, in large part because nothing happening at the track gives meaning to life outside the track.

The next day, he reports, he gets news from home about the dam's "progress," where the Corps of Engineers is "plugging up nature with anal fervor." His town is also "progressing" on the speculation of how the new dam and lake will affect business. New tourist-oriented shops are springing up quickly to replace older businesses—the town's hardware store, for example, becoming a theme restaurant. One woman kills herself by jumping off a bridge, free-falling into dust and wildflowers, an act Barich sees "as a wholly appropriate symbol of a more general demise, of the specific sliding into the mass" (145). He still can't shake his metaphorizing of "progress" into disease, can't shake his projecting of cancer onto American society.

Idealization, like projection, inhibits Barich's grief work. If holding on to an idealized version of the past hinders Barich from being able to reimagine life outside the track as something other than cancerous, he likewise hinders himself by idealizing the Italian Renaissance and horse racing itself. Only when he is ready to resee both will he make a turn toward acceptance of death and give up his linkage of America and cancer.

When the Preakness, the middle jewel of horse racing's Triple Crown, is broadcast to Golden Gate Fields, Barich notes how the horses, even on television, look "dense, real, steeped in history." Affirmed and Alydar (the two favorites) "were decidedly not Laverne and Shirley" (160). The race is a beauty, and Barich goes outside afterwards to sit by the bay and savor his racing high, which lasts only until a big rat slinks out from a crevice and drags its tail over moss and potato chip bags. Though at this point in his story the world outside intrudes upon the beauty of the track, Barich begins his next chapter, recounted immediately after, with a reverse image, the story of a horse's death: "Ruling Don was the first horse I ever saw die. He broke down in May, on a beautiful morning with the sun shining" (162). The move from Affirmed and Alydar to Ruling Don, from the glory of the Preakness to a tragic morning gallop, is a crucial marker of Barich's psychological condition. For Ruling Don's death comes to be the event that precipitates his loss of innocence concerning the racing world and allows him to reconsider the world of Renaissance Florence.

Local horsemen attribute Ruling Don's death to two things: the hardness of the track and the drugs that the horse was running on so that he could not feel pain. As Barich begins to explore what the horsemen mean, he descends into a subculture of the racing world he has not yet seen—a "descent" into the white-collar world where the decisions are made. Barich learns that the racetrack has an ugliness similar to the one he has fled. The world of racing, like any business, has financial backers who need a profit and are willing to sacrifice objects to gain that profit, and those backers have employees who will help them.

Barich's research into the history of the racetrack's surface reveals the constant struggle for Golden Gate Fields management to create a surface both soft enough to provide cushion for a thoroughbred's legs and porous enough to drain well after a rain. Because racing on a muddy track leads to slow times, unpredictable races, and scratches by horses that do not like the mud, all of which hurt attendance, management had chosen to make a sandy, hard, well-draining track, a track punishing to the horses. Even more harmful to Ruling Don and to the thoroughbreds in general, Barich comes to believe, is the almost indiscriminate drugging that allows sick or injured horses to run when they should be rested or put out to pasture. When Barich talks to the track's veterinarian, Jay Hoop, he realizes that Hoop sees himself as responsible for keeping a steady procession of "raceably sound" horses moving toward the starting gate, even if the criterion *raceably sound* means they run with painkillers. Hoop, Barich acknowledges, is not a bad man or even negligent; he is simply a loyal employee of a corporation, willing to use language a certain way to mask what is happening. Barich places much of the blame on corporate greed and on persons who seem not to love the horses as grooms or trainers do, but who see the horses as figures on a spreadsheet. Stockholders want profits; employees want rising salaries.

Ruling Don, broken down, is "destroyed" because, alive, after an operation, he is worth less than he is dead with a collected insurance premium. "It seemed to me," Barich writes, "that a subtle balance had gone awry, that the track was grinding up horses for profit, cannibalizing its own best interests" (172). The newly found ugliness of the racing world corresponds to the ugliness Barich discovers about another world he has idealized. He had always imagined Florence's great horse race, the *palio,* "as a majestic event, a ringing forth of bells and horses. . . . But in my reading I'd learned other things about the *palio,* how brutal, ugly, and corrupt it could be" (176–77). Horses, jockeys, and spectators were killed when horses crashed off course; fixers tried to affect the outcome of races with bribes. Barich reads more about the corruption of Florence politics, the martyrdom of Savonarola, and the plagues that struck Florence. While he wants to forget about Ruling Don, Barich says that the breakdown keeps coming back to him, bringing with it feelings of betrayal and helplessness. While there is no single place to fix the blame, he concludes, all of the contributing factors "added up not to an answer but to a familiar syndrome, libraries closing, rivers dammed, condominiums going up, all in the cold blue glow of flickering [television] tubes" (178).

Barich's discovery of the "corruption" at the racetrack or in Florence does not in itself heal, does not move him from "disorganization and despair" to "reorganization." Instead, by losing his idealism Barich gains a distance, which helps him learn what will be therapeutic for him. In their superb book on mourning, *The Meaning of Grief,* Emily Claspell and Larry Cochran extend one strand of Bowlby's work by concentrating on how the grieving person's reorganization flowers into a coherent story of the past and into a dramatic structure of the present that gives meaning to the life. Because the writers in my study are creating stories, making a text, Claspell and Cochran's emphasis on how people's sense of their lives is "dramaturgical" is particularly helpful. A person who is grieving has had his or her life-meaning profoundly altered, perhaps made meaningless. Moving through the mourning process in a healthy way (not making pathology out of the loss) depends on the person's ability, after an extended period of time that varies for each individual, to construct a new drama that contains the story of the "loss" and reinterprets past life-experiences and memories with consideration of that traumatic event. The newly created drama also prompts healthier, less sad ways of responding to present experiences.

Still believing that something special is going on at the track, Barich looks elsewhere and finds a subject—the thoroughbred itself, not horse racing—that eventually helps lead him down that path toward recovery. "All horses are descended from the so-called dawn horse," Barich begins in his fascinating commentary on the evolution of the thoroughbred. Thoroughbred bloodlines have been carefully charted for centuries, and what particularly comes to interest Barich is breeding, the various and nearly innumerable theories about how one attempts to breed horses to run faster and farther. He learns that there are no sure bets; breeders speak of simple, commonsense principles. And yet it is anything but common sense that produces the great champion. One might call it luck or, as Barich comes to see it, something like Pico's "white magic" of benevolent sympathy—another force at work, "something beyond eugenics, the crackling around the bodies of lovers bent on conceiving, heat lightning, what the mystic says in saying nothing: a hole in the smoke" (194). Every now and then a breeder makes contact with this energy, harnessing it briefly, Barich says, but only one person tried to describe it, Federico Tesio, the Wizard of Dormello.

In the early decades of the twentieth century, Tesio ran a carefully managed breeding farm. His genius, like Pico's, "was for registering previously unperceived concordances and applying them to the breeding art" (199). Tesio perceived unities in what might seem dissimilar elements, and he used horses for his speculations about the workings of the cosmos. He insisted on the force of energy, a "Life-force," to move the universe, and in a maxim highly attractive to Barich, he related the perpetuation of this life-force to breeding: horses had to couple fervidly for their favorable genes to be passed on to the offspring. Disregarding genetics, Tesio proclaimed that champion thoroughbreds are not made by breeding two champions, but rather by having the "sexual urge" raised to a "maximum of tension" that endowed "the resulting individual with exceptional energy" (200). He stated his law: All life is based on the consumption of energy to gain supremacy and on rest to restore that energy.

Reading Tesio excites Barich. One afternoon he visits a breeding farm rather than attending the races. Expecting to find a high-tech stud room, sterile and metallic, he is pleased to see simply an old barn, full of baled hay and cobwebs. He likes the stories told by John Ryan, the breeder, about the unpredictability of mares, who rarely conceive when the stud chosen for them is not to their liking. Barich's research into bloodlines and breeding helps him confirm his growing "suspicions" about thoroughbreds: "I thought their attraction was deeply mystical, deriving from some long-standing though lately violated bond between humans and animals, but the traditional view of racing—that it was a gambler's sport dependent on greenbacks for its survival—was at odds with this perception and kept confusing me. . . . Gambling was no doubt central to the racetrack scheme, but the sort of wager being made had a double nature and was of a different order than generally supposed" (203).

As with epiphanies in fiction, Barich leaves sudden insights such as this one unexplained, depending on his readers to use the context (or the entire book) to create meaning. If we compare horse racing to a similar sport, auto racing, we can better understand, perhaps, this crucial passage. A widely held though perhaps cynical view of why people watch Indy cars or stock cars zoom around an oval is the possibility of seeing a spectacular crash. But there is something more at work there. Auto-racing fans like technology and speed. I have known such fans: they are mesmerized by what machines, built by humans and managed by humans, can do, and what they can't do at certain moments. Thoroughbred breeding and racing, we might say, is one sport (or occupation) where science and technology are of little use. A horse is a horse: you can't really build a better horse, even if you can try—within the basic formula, so to speak—to breed the fastest possible horse, and help it to run faster. The cynical view of why people watch horse races is that they like the thrill of gambling and the state lottery isn't as interesting. But Barich here gives a new interpretation of horse racing, perhaps one that any person who feels strongly attracted to a species of animal understands. Barich's "different order" of wager, transcending mere betting for money, is akin to the devotion of mystical faith; the "gambler" bets on renewing a crucial, though perhaps unarticulatable, relationship between human and thoroughbred. The thoroughbred finally serves Barich (and others, presumably, who have devoted their lives to the sport) as a totem.

As totem, the thoroughbred helps show Barich the unity and con-

tinuity he has longed for, not simply the continuity of human generations but the human position in a universe not divided into self and
other. "The human race," writes Freud in *Totem and Taboo*, "have in
the course of ages developed three [unified] systems of thought—
three great pictures of the universe: animistic (or mythological), religious and scientific. Of these, animism, the first to be created, is perhaps the one which is most consistent and exhaustive and which gives
a truly complete explanation of the nature of the universe" (77).
Animism, for "primitive" humans, came unthinkingly; all animals and
plants had souls and a place in the natural order. But Barich, like
many modern persons, is self-conscious, creating thereby both an assertion of separate identity and a desperate loneliness. While reject-
ing science and technology, which he lumps together as societal
"progress" and a cancer, he finds no replacement. And so, while not
turning to myth, he does turn to the idea of a unified universe, of
which the human relationship to the thoroughbred becomes the
symbol.

Disparate elements, Barich says, are beginning to cohere, and this
not only in his understanding of the human relationship to horses but
in his own mourning process. Symbolic of the fragments coming together is that Pichi finally wins her first race. Pichi's running career,
like Barich's recovery, has been slow and painful, full of detours and
false hopes. In her first races at Golden Gate Fields, she finishes far
back. She improves, however, finally capturing a third place, and the
owners and trainer begin believing that she eventually will win a race.
But then on a day when she is even picked by some expert handi-
cappers to finish first, she runs badly, fading to eighth place. Her
trainer is afraid that she is "the sort of horse destined forever to lose
because she burned up if pushed too early and came on too late when
saved for the stretch" (156). Just when everyone's hopes are quashed,
she suddenly wins, running better than anyone thought she could.

Pichi's victory is the last significant event for Barich at the track,
because that night, "sitting in the Home Stretch [the track's bar], high
on Pichi's victory," Barich comes to an acceptance that has previously
eluded him. He had fled to the track because it seemed more causal
and less chaotic than the larger world, but at this stage in his mourning, Barich recognizes a different need, the value of animals for humans. "We [people living in corporate America] were starved," he
writes, "for contact with an animal other and experienced the lack as

a form of sensory deprivation, a diminishment. The corporate fiction into which we'd fallen denied us our passions, and we were hurting because of it" (219). Thoroughbreds, Barich has learned, resist being turned into pets. They keep their wildness, which gives them their dignity. This is the beauty, Barich believes, that humans see in horses: thoroughbreds embody wildness in domesticity.

The animal/human bond may be revitalizing in part because its distinctiveness can lead to unusual self-reflection. Theodora Anastaplo suggests in "Metaxa," a lovely essay about her horse, that the joy she finds in her relationship with Metaxa arises because the horse does not, she believes, remember the past. Unlike humans, who know wrongs and therefore guilt, Metaxa "does not spend her days in the Creek Pasture recounting past and present grievances." And because of this, Anastaplo writes, "this is what happens: I, the human, knowing my own guilt, go to Metaxa, the animal, who does not 'know' what forgiveness is, and Metaxa embraces me with her welcome and says, above all, 'You delight me. Stay awhile.' Love is here in the present. . . . And me, what does that do in me? It strengthens my love for her immeasurably. It makes her big bony bay body beautiful in my eyes, and makes me yearn to visit her when I cannot. This is what true forgiveness is like" (14). For Anastaplo, human love with its wounds and difficulties can restrict her heart and squash her soul, raise her defenses. Animal love can help remind her of how to break down those defenses. As numerous writers are likewise testifying, bonds between species (human and animal) are giving humans new ways of being in a shared world.[4]

Thoroughbred racing in our culture, however, functions primarily as a spectacle for entertainment, and the success of *Laughing in the Hills* depends largely on how convinced we are as readers that Barich is tapping into important relational bonds previously unknown to him. Certainly Barich gets beyond the emphasis on betting to the wildness and unpredictability of the races, to the beauty of the horses, but he has no relationship like the one Anastaplo describes above. The relationality is not between guardian and animal, or even, as with Sue Hubbell, immersion into "texts of suitability" with various animals— the thoroughbred serves Barich as a wild kindred spirit in the animal world. Barich thinks about how watching thoroughbreds run fires every neuron in his body, transforming him "into one long synapse, bits of energy blowing apart" (219). These moments can be subse-

quently renewing for him in memory, like the Wordsworthian spots
of time. If his semester in Florence gave him renewing memories
about living in the moment, his memories from the racetrack teach
him that events and feelings of a life are beyond the control that the
writer brings to his narrative. The flux that brings change and cancer
also brings life. Once Barich feels the truth of that idea, he reorganizes
his vision of the future to match his understanding of the past. "All
connections," he says, are "ever tenuous." But since nothing abides,
there is "no cause for alarm." It is not a revelatory belief, simplified
as it is to a shorthand that stands for all the experiences that gave birth
to it, but when born out of the struggle of mourning, and believed,
it heals. "All connections ever tenuous," he repeats. "I knew what was
happening then. I was letting go of the sadness, letting go of my
mother. Living and dying, winning and losing" (219). Barich had gone
initially to the track because he thought it "circumscribed and manageable"; his subsequent discovery of its unpredictability plunged him
into further despair; now he emphasizes the importance of unpredictability in "a world increasingly controlled and uniform" (219), and
the thoroughbred stands symbolically for that unpredictability.

What carries forward for someone who is moving through the
grieving process is the sure knowledge that what one feels or understands will not continue indefinitely. The psychoanalysts who focus
on narrative—Meredith Skura, Donald Pond Spence, Roy Schafer—
emphasize that a patient's moments of insight and self-consciousness
must be "written into" stories that re-create the past and imagine a
hopeful future. Though he has lost money betting at the track, Barich
writes that the "most important wager I'd made had paid off," which
is that coming to the racetrack would change the direction of his psychological downward spiral.

Barich's act of self-creation in *Laughing in the Hills* is not a "conversion" story, like Augustine's *Confessions,* Malcolm X's *Autobiography,* or many similar autobiographies. Most significant in Barich's
healing process is not any single insight or the recovery of any specific
memory, but rather a gradual working through of his conflicts that
eventually convinces him that there are connections between self and
other. Barich's climactic moment of insight comes when he perceives
that the horse, not horse racing, is crucial to his desires, when the
thoroughbred has become a healing symbol in the way that symbols
have functioned since the romantic movement: fusing subject and ob-

ject, the universal and the particular, order and spontaneity. Not simply the product of a linguistic act, perhaps not even the product of a conscious act, a symbol (the thoroughbred) becomes understandable by intuition and feeling (not rational thinking), and therefore for an individual in a unique way.

In his short epilogue that concludes the book, Barich recounts the end of his depression and how he began feeling restored: "In my mind the dying and the cancer had become separated, almost discrete, the one a natural process of organic decay, the other a cultural hastening of that process" (225). Little is changed in the world around him, or in his personal life, but in one sense everything is changed, because he feels renewed. He sees the world without the cancer that insinuated itself into all his interpretations. "What was any renaissance," he writes, "but a sudden bias in favor of hope?"

In constructing a narrative about his season at the racetrack that folds into it useable elements from his past, Barich comes to understand how to make a continuity from past to present that helps him lessen the anger that causes him to see cancer in everything. *Laughing in the Hills* exemplifies how patients can become, in a figurative sense, their own analysts through the act of writing. Barich's cure reminds us of Schafer's insistence that all a patient and analyst can accomplish is the construction of an explanatory story: a narrative truth that gives new meaning to the disturbing and disturbed present. Rather than continue to lament the building of dams, poorly constructed housing, or the country's valuing of illusion, Barich has come to view his personal history as a narrative fulfilling Schafer's terms of a successful analysis: a comprehensive but modified version of the past, a version "less fragmented, confining, anguished, and self-destructive" (18). His revision of his past experiences and his present situation suggest that he has moved out of depression, if not out of mourning. Barich had originally begun betting the horses in order to get past the sadness of death. And finally, though not by betting, he believes he has.

Laughing in the Hills begins with trauma and loss, ends on a hopeful note, and in between portrays a "documentary" of the animal "other" that makes possible Barich's recovery—a broad outline that all the books in this study share. But Barich's resolution in *Laughing in the Hills* points to the difficulty of this general structure, in that the book ends and we do not see how Barich uses his new knowledge to reconfigure his life outside the track. In a sense, this is the problem of any autobiography whose writer recounts trials and tribulations and then, when they end, closes the book by promising better times to come. The problem becomes more pronounced, however, when the writer tries to understand one world by immersing himself in another, as in Barich's book (or Matthiessen's *The Snow Leopard* and Heat-Moon's *Blue Highways,* in particular among the works in this study).[5] That is, how convinced are we, as readers, that the textual act of self-creation matches the changes that the author announces?

Walden is a classic test case: "I went to the woods," writes Thoreau, "because I wished to live deliberately, to front only the essential facts of life, and see if I could not learn what it had to teach." The life he creates at Walden Pond gives Thoreau a vantage point for his social criticism, and his careful observations of the plants, the animals, the people, and the ponds become inseparable from his worldview. If we think the book succeeds, as most readers do, then when Thoreau leaves Walden Pond we accept that his mind's eye, his mind, and his beliefs have fused into one. We accept his epiphanies in spring as a renewal. Barich went not to the woods but to the track, and likewise, if we believe *Laughing in the Hills* works (as I do), then we are convinced that Barich's immersion into horse racing and the history of the horse, his stories about the track, make a similar fusion and prompt a lasting renewal.

5 Constructing a Self on the Road

William Least Heat-Moon's
Blue Highways

Near the end of his stay at the racetrack, Barich recalls lines from a Grateful Dead song that have taken on symbolic significance: "Lately it occurs to me / What a long strange trip it's been." Though he has left his home and taken up residence at the track, Barich's strange trip has been internal, a matter of emotions and psychology, depression and recovery. In *Blue Highways,* William Least Heat-Moon actually takes to the road, his only plan to circle the country, driving those back roads marked in blue on old maps.

Perhaps because this country's history has been largely a record of people traveling—Indians migrating over the land-bridge connecting Asia and Alaska; peoples of Central America and Mexico moving north; Europeans going west, first to the "new" continent and then across the country—American literature is replete with books about journeys.[1] Groups of people or individuals moving in promise of something better, and moving to regions unlike what they had come from geographically as well as culturally, became and remains a dominant motif of American life. The books that record or create fictions from those moves, from John Steinbeck's *The Grapes of Wrath* to Ralph Ellison's *Invisible Man,* are an impressive body of American literature. But Heat-Moon is not moving to something better or even different. Not moving *on* at all, he simply moves *along* until he comes back to where he had begun. The journey is the point. Jack Kerouac's *On the Road* has given a name to such writing, and like Sal Paradise and Dean Moriarty, Heat-Moon just needs to go.

Not all "on the road" books are the same, of course, because the intentions of the traveler and the structure of the narratives vary. Many resemble the picaresque novel, where the main character (Don Quixote, Tom Jones, Sal Paradise) finds himself in one escapade after another, where scenes pile up like beads on a string, where the hero remains essentially the same from beginning to end.[2] Other road books likewise have an unchanged narrator or main character, but social commentary, not adventure, centers these books. For John Steinbeck in *Travels with Charley* or Peter Jenkins in *A Walk across America*, the intent is to get out and see the United States firsthand in order to report on it. While Heat-Moon structures *Blue Highways* like a picaresque novel and uses his road trip for social commentary, a different purpose motivates him: seeing rural America and writing about it arises from a nearly desperate need to perform an act of self-creation.

On the same day he loses his teaching job, Heat-Moon writes in his opening paragraph, his wife tells him that their marital separation might be permanent. That night, he gets the idea that "a man who couldn't make things go right could at least go" (3). During the next month he outfits a van, orders his affairs, and plans his journey: he will set out on a long trip driving over the back roads of the United States, looking for little towns that show up on a map only because a cartographer has space to fill. Like Barich going to the racetrack because it seemed circumscribed and manageable, unlike human bodies or life, Heat-Moon believes that he can find places with a history and tradition that will be comforting to him, not alienating. The depression he has fallen into and his growing feelings of alienation and futility lead him, he writes, to follow "the open road in search of places where change did not mean ruin and where time and men and deeds connected" (5).

In the book's dust-jacket blurbs, Robert Penn Warren is said to call *Blue Highways* a "masterpiece" and "a book about America," and it certainly is a story-collage of Americans who rarely make the news, who live quietly on country roads. Heat-Moon is accomplished at telling their stories or letting them tell their own, and by book's end Heat-Moon convincingly dramatizes the importance of *place* in human life, the way geography shapes character. But *Blue Highways* is less a book about America than it is about Heat-Moon trying to understand from other people how to live a satisfying life. His act of self-creation is to absorb hundreds of stories from unknown humans, to contextualize those stories into a framework focusing on history and place, and then to see if he can assemble small parts of those stories to serve his own ends therapeutically—a version of "relationality" unrecognizable, I would argue, not only to autobiography critics who focus on the solitary self, but to those critics who emphasize the autobiographer's critical relation to one other person, usually a relative.

Halfway through the journey, talking to a young Hopi Indian, Kendrick Fritz, Heat-Moon is startled when Fritz shows him the emergence symbol of the Hopi:

The lines of this symbol, Heat-Moon writes, "represent the course a person follows on his 'road of life' as he passes through birth, death, rebirth . . . a kind of map of the wandering soul." Struck by the similarity to his own journey, Heat-Moon uses a replica of the symbol before each of the ten sections of his book. The book's drama centers on Heat-Moon's attempts to have such wandering perform grief work. What will Heat-Moon know and feel as he emerges from his journey and returns home to write? How does he turn life lived on the road into a shapely and healing story?

One of Heat-Moon's first encounters on his trip occurs in Shelbyville, Kentucky, and the way he structures it shows the tension between his writing a documentary of rural America and his use of unknown people's stories in an act of self-creation. Walking the main street of Shelbyville, Heat-Moon stops to watch a man strip asphalt siding from a small house that is turning back into a log cabin. He helps the man jack the doorway straight and then gets a tour of the old cabin that was built 150 years earlier with ax, adz, froe, and wedge. Bob Andriot, the new owner, tells Heat-Moon about his research that led him to think the house was a cabin underneath the siding and sheetrock. Heat-Moon is delighted when Andriot pulls out a wooden peg, hand-whittled from an oak that was probably alive in 1776. "Gives you a real sense of history. Take it with you," says Andriot, and he and his workmen drink Cokes with Heat-Moon and tell him of the town's and the log cabin's history. Explaining why he wanted to restore the cabin, Andriot says, "This old place makes a difference here. To us, of course, but to the town too before long. I feel it more than I can explain it. I don't know, I guess rescuing this building makes me feel I've done something to last" (14). After taking a picture of the crew standing in front of the cabin, Heat-Moon drives on east, reflecting on what he had heard, and he closes the chapter with what the encounter means to him: "I thought how Bob Andriot was rebuilding a past he could see and smell, one he could shape with his hands. He was using it to build something new. I envied him that" (14).

The subjects of all travel books or documentaries, certainly, are viewed through a particular person's eyes, though in most instances how the person shapes the viewing is not made part of the text. In a fine article on George Orwell's encounters with and observations of the working class in *The Road to Wigan Pier,* Philip Dodd argues that Orwell, unlike many travel writers of his time, is aware that "What he can see and know . . . is determined by the place from which he sees. . . . Epistemological questions are not sociologically inert" (134–36). Nationality, race, class, gender, sexual orientation—the list is long about what influences not only a person's interpretation but what even gets noticed.

In *Blue Highways,* Heat-Moon makes certain that personal psychology tops the list. On the second page of the book, he writes: "A Pledge: I give this chapter to myself. When done with it, I will shut up about *that* topic." In this short chapter he tells us that he is mixed-blood Sioux with Anglo features; that his wife is mixed-blood Cherokee; that he named his van Ghost Dancing, "a heavy-handed symbol alluding to ceremonies of the 1890s in which the Plains Indians . . . danced for the return of warriors, bison, and the fervor of the old life that would sweep away the new" (5). After he hits the road, he doesn't shut up about his life, of course. He doesn't tell us directly about his distant past (childhood, parents, hometown) but does keep at the forefront of the text his own responses to the present. Heat-Moon is thirty-eight years old, a time in life when American culture sends strong messages that men should be leading satisfying lives of family and career, and his losses of job and marriage lead directly to his strong feelings of personal alienation and futility. His estrangement dictates an "organizing" metaphor for the road trip, a desire to find places where time and men and deeds still connect. This metaphor, like Barich's of an American culture consumed by cancer, dominates not only what and how he understands, but also how he shapes narrative. As we see with the encounter in Shelbyville, a man tearing down "new" asphalt siding to reveal a log cabin catches Heat-Moon's attention, and Andriot's own gloss on his work (to be part of history, to be part of community by restoring the old) becomes the compelling interpretation.

In a later section of this chapter, I will discuss the evolution of Heat-Moon's journey, suggest the arc of the trip, and to do so will bring up many examples of his experiences with other people. But this episode with Andriot has a shape that occurs countless times. Heat-Moon actually knows little about Bob Andriot (though he does not highlight it in his text, for obvious reasons). Heat-Moon doesn't talk long because he needs to be back on the road. He assumes much about the man from Andriot's explanations for why he chose to restore a log cabin for his picture-framing and interior-design shop. What Heat-Moon foregrounds is the way some people have managed to put together lives that do not follow the compartmentalized "modern" life that separates a person's work, home, entertainment, personal past, the history of their town and region, and so forth. Andriot's story, in brief, fits nicely into Heat-Moon's quest to find where "time and men and deeds connected."

In an essay on Jonathan Raban's *Old Glory,* Roger George compares a "critical" reading (a second or even third reading) of a travel book with writing an account of a journey: "Experience is linear, as is a 'naive' first reading. But critical reading is recursive, as is the writing about an experience. On his boat, Raban drifts downstream with the current, in one direction, and so does the reader who reads only for pleasure. But a critical reader repeatedly heads upstream, revisiting literary 'landmarks,' creating an entirely new 'map' by combining elements in thematic patterns and overriding the sequence of events, discovering meaning *in retrospect* in the same way that the traveler discovers meaning and significance in the act of writing about the journey, after the experience is finished" (257). What George refers to as critical reading is what I will do in this chapter, teasing out the symbolism, noting the epiphanies, making my own map of the text by constructing a psychoanalytic framework. But George's remarks are equally useful to consider the *writing*, not just the reading, of *Blue Highways*.

Heat-Moon, trying to have his narrative faithful to the journey, seems to have simply written down what he was thinking and learning, what other people have done and said. But any "true" account of a journey is problematical, because the subsequent thinking about, sorting through, and composing a narrative for changes the experience of the journey to something more like the illusion of the experience of the journey. The only way around this is to publish, without editing, one's notes taken on the trip, but unedited notes or journal entries usually are mundane or even boring. For this reason, most travel narratives are shaped carefully and read as much like a novel as a journal. The writer constructs a story of the journey, a story that takes form in large part according to how the experiences can fit into and with the accounts of other experiences that the writer has stored away.

Heat-Moon sets out on his journey hoping that life on the road meeting unknown Americans might give him understanding and wisdom, might help him therapeutically; the danger of such purposes is that they shape the journey and the narrative so much that distortion is inevitable. The desires of the self rule supreme. But Heat-Moon writes that he returned to Columbia, Missouri, a changed man because he had traveled the country listening to and absorbing the stories of those who had stumbled—stories that gave him a new angle of vision, a way out of the excessive turning inward that leads to ego's impossible desires. The book ends with the journey's end, but there is tension here between living the life (taking the journey) and writing the life (writing the journey). Because *Blue Highways* ends before the difficult task of Heat-Moon translating new knowledge and feelings into living a better, everyday life, readers have no textual "evidence" to help them decide whether the optimism of the ending is justified, whether the new angle of vision that Heat-Moon says he has gained on the journey enables him to make that better life.

The self-creation that readers encounter in *Blue Highways* and the other books in my study is a textual construct, of course. Unless we turn to biography for verification (of a kind), we do not really know how this self-creation continues past the events of the narrative. What we have with these books is autobiography, a "life" not as it relates precisely to the life lived—which we can't know—but a life as it is constructed in the text. Paul de Man, in a controversial article "Auto-biography as de-Facement," suggests that the relation between the life of an autobiographer and the autobiography is multidirectional: "We assume the life produces autobiography as an act produces its consequences, but can we not suggest, with equal justice, that the autobiographical project may itself produce and determine the life" (920). De Man's position seems counterintuitive, in that most autobiographers, writing about the past, did not live that past believing that they would one day be writing about it. (Though the next step, that the writing of an autobiography influences the future life, seems incontrovertible.) But De Man's conception here has particular relevance to Heat-Moon. In a symbolic move, and typical of most road books, early in *Blue Highways* Heat-Moon inventories the items he stocks in his small van, a vehicle he has converted into a six-by-ten bedroom, kitchen, bathroom, and parlor. He takes necessities to live self-sufficiently, and other items that few people would deem "necessary": two books (John Neihardt's *Black Elk Speaks* and Walt Whitman's *Leaves of Grass*), notebooks, two cameras, and a cassette recorder. Thus Heat-Moon sets out on his journey because of depression but takes the requisite equipment to record that journey, as if he already knows the subsequent literary act will be essential.[3]

Textual self-creation is doubly complicated with *Blue Highways,* suggesting yet again the shrewdness of de Man's remark that the autobiographical project may determine the life. After Heat-Moon returned home he wrote the book and began sending the manuscript to agents and publishers. After three years, numerous rejections, and six revisions, Heat-Moon, who went then by his Anglo name Bill Trogdon, recognized one night while working on the docks that he had been ignoring his Native American heritage.[4] That night, he returned to the manuscript, put "William Least Heat Moon" on the title page, and began a revision that emphasized his "Indian" way of seeing. The result—publication of a book that stayed thirty-four weeks on the *New York Times* bestseller list. A second result—Bill Trogdon becomes the famous author Heat-Moon, an act in which a literary pseudonym is not an identity disguise but a persona inevitably wedded to the "self" in a transformation that leaves both radically changed. Few examples so vividly demonstrate the self-write-life connections of autobiography; just as the self constitutes language, so language constitutes the self.

The inventory of "tools" that Heat-Moon takes on his trip indicates that he knows beforehand that he will photograph subjects, tape conversations, and record observations, all to the purpose of writing a book about his journey. The metaphor of "time-men-deeds-connect" suggests that Heat-Moon frames his quest from the beginning in such a way that it influences his "life" on the trip and his subsequent retelling of that trip (and life) in a book. This is not to say that Heat-Moon goes looking for something he already knows about and then "finds" it. Such an act has probably been passed off as a kind of quest many times, with only the writer knowing how the journey has been manipulated to produce certain results. Heat-Moon doesn't know what he wants, but he does know what he doesn't want: life as he finds it in the news, in cities or suburbs, in chain stores, shopping malls, or interstate highways. "Life doesn't happen along interstates. It's against the law," he writes, implying that a life without difference, uniqueness, is no life at all. And journeys don't take place on interstates—unless you want only to be Anne Tyler's "accidental tourist"—because journeying is, almost by its definition in travel literature, something that tests the traveler because everyday experiences are not habitual. At one point, late in his trip, Heat-Moon comes upon a circular privet-hedge labyrinth, planted to be symbolic of the "Harmonist concept of the devious and difficult approach to a state of true harmony." He walks the rungs and curves of the maze without a single wrong turn, because the right way "was worn so deeply in the earth as to be unmistakable. But without the errors, wrong turns, and blind alleys, without the doubling back and misdirection and fumbling and chance discoveries, there was not one bit of joy in walking the labyrinth. And worse: knowing the way made traveling it perfectly meaningless" (411). Heat-Moon does not want his journey to resemble such a maze, which is why he sets out without an itinerary but with a purpose.

In *Blue Highways* Heat-Moon submerges to some degree his own role in the "facts" that he is reporting, whether the presentation of people's stories or information about history and geography. As he tells the people he encounters why he is traveling, and then asks them questions and responds to them, he is, as social scientists have explained so convincingly, presenting a "public" self that becomes inextricable from any "private" self. George J. McCall argues that humans' ability to have self-awareness results from seeing themselves through the reactions of others, thus learning how to appraise themselves as an object. Erving Goffman suggests that the self is finally the character performed. Just as the performance cannot be separated from the performer, what is and is not a "mask" becomes difficult to know. Acting out particular scenes in a social situation, then reflecting upon those actions, and finally writing about them becomes a change in self.

Coleridge's Ancient Mariner felt compelled to expiate his crime of killing the albatross—compelled to exorcise his guilt—by telling his story over and over. Heat-Moon is a kind of reverse, latter-day Mariner who doesn't know his crime, knows only his own inner doubts and confusions, and attempts to exorcise them by listening to other people's stories over and over, stories that he guides by his actions and questions about change and history. Such a structure can become repetitive for a reader, though Heat-Moon avoids this in large part because the people and geography are so different as he travels around the country. But its strength for Heat-Moon psychologically is in its very repetition: any one of the tellings subtly influences the quest, and his own response to the stories gives them personal significance and shapes what is still to come. In this way, his travels and conversations with the disparate people he meets function much like the *process* of psychoanalysis.

There is little, particularly on the text's surface, that invites a psychoanalytic reading; Heat-Moon does not structure his narrative the way that obviously symbolic fiction is structured. And there is little exploration on his part of what is much of the usual psychoanalytic material: one's past, relations to parents, relations to siblings. Not much can be used as psychoanalytic explanation that exists for the most part at the level of abstraction or generalization—"explanations" of behavior, for example. But the structure of *Blue Highways* can be considered, figuratively, as a series of sessions in which other people do the talking and Heat-Moon does the thinking, constantly revising in his mind what his old stories have been and how he might rethink those stories in order to put together a satisfying life. "New ways of seeing," he writes, "can disclose new things: the radio telescope revealed quasars and pulsars. . . . But turn the question around: Do new *things* make for new ways of seeing?" (17). He sets out on his quest only because he already believes he knows this answer, and that it is *yes,* and that a journey will be, for him, a new thing.

If a writer suspects at the beginning that a literary act might serve acute psychological needs, then that act needs to be prepared for. As the preparation shapes the journey, the journey in turn shapes the literary act. The writing, however, subsequently shapes the story of the journey in *memory*. Because *Blue Highways* is both a book of travel about "others" and a response to a personal crisis, it highlights this recursive process, critiquing our notions of "self-creation" at the same time that it insists there are "real" and "textual" subjects. I have been emphasizing the complicated relations between author, purpose, subjects, and text both to complicate Heat-Moon's intentions and to honor the complexity of his task. *Blue Highways,* even more than the books discussed earlier, unsettles readers' desires to have literary nonfiction seemingly work as a straightforward representation of experience.

Heat-Moon's is not the "night journey," the short odyssey of a hero or heroine who finds in the landscape a mirror for the psyche or soul, Young Goodman Brown discovering evil and his own capacity for sin and then returning to his wife and village a different person. Nor is it a journey *to* somewhere, where an event or encounter will change the hero—Ahab finding the white whale. The structure of Heat-Moon's journey (and his book) is a wandering and then a return to the place he began, Columbia, Missouri. "Following a circle," he writes, "would give a purpose [to the trip]—to come around again—where taking a straight line would not" (3). And if his quest is fulfilled, he will return knowing something to help him change, to help him create "home."

Heat-Moon begins the journey by looking for the life that happens in towns and among people who are distinctly part of a region, having been shaped specifically by geography and history. Though he thinks that his own past is a predator capable of eating him, he believes that for some people the past must center life. His journey first takes him east-southeast, through Kentucky, Tennessee, and North Carolina, where he finds people who have lived long enough in one place to know its old stories. Eating buttermilk pie with the Wattses, who tell him how their town long ago came to be called Nameless, Tennessee, Heat-Moon thinks, "It is for this I have come" (33). When he looks for a two-hundred-year-old grave of a Piedmont Lancashireman, William Trogdon—the patriarch of Heat-Moon's (that is, Bill Trogdon's) white-blood clan—he is helped by Noel Jones, who has lived on the land for perhaps seventy years and knows both its history and its swamps and trees. Heat-Moon drives to old fishing villages that have not marketed themselves for tourists, and he visits Fort Raleigh, the first English settlement in America, whose settlers vanished and left behind only a single word, carved in a tree, *Croatoan*. But the history that can become meaningful is not only old history, as Heat-Moon discovers one evening when he sits down to watch some tennis players and has a conversation that "changes the direction of the journey" (91). He is urged to go to Selma, where Martin Luther King Jr. had organized the march to Montgomery, to see if change has happened there. In Selma, Heat-Moon talks to a white man in a bar who spouts race hatred; he talks to black men who tell him, "Things slippin'. Black man's losin' ground again," and he is harassed by the police. As he drives through the South and into the Southwest, his night in Selma helps attune him to similar dark history—government policy and individual acts that exploited black people or Native Americans. He becomes interested in how people respond to their victimization. He meets a machinist who cannot get work after leaving the army and has come to realize that his uncle, who had difficulty finding work and then was shot dead in Dallas, was not the bum he once thought. Heat-Moon meets Barbara Pierre, a single mother who is putting herself through school and is insistent enough about changing things that she is often ostracized by the whites in her town. Heat-Moon finds their stories powerful, in part because for them change does not mean ruin: they want the change that he fears.

I have characterized the books in this study as blends of autobiography, environmental literature, and literary nonfiction, and in these snapshots of life in rural America, related in part through the people's own words, Heat-Moon works squarely within the contemporary tradition of literary nonfiction and travel writing. But in this genre *Blue Highways* is unusual because of Heat-Moon's frequent reminders of his psychological state: he talks to people in part simply to escape from troubling or even debilitating memory. In Louisiana, one-quarter of the way through his planned trip, Heat-Moon takes stock of what he has learned: "Reading my notes of the trip—images, bits of conversation, ideas—I hunted a structure in the events, but randomness was the rule" (115). He considers ending his journey, returning to comfort and friends, thinking that his wish for the road was a craziness, but he heads on, soon to have one of his epiphanic experiences. In eastern Texas, sitting and eating his lunch on the burial mound of a thousand-year-old Caddoan Indian village now overgrown with wild blackberry bushes, Heat-Moon recognizes suddenly that time, change, and process are resistant to certain kinds of understanding: "My rambling metaphysics was getting caught in the trap of reducing experience to coherence and meaning, letting the perplexity of things disrupt the joy in their mystery. To insist that diligent thought would bring an understanding of change was to limit life to the comprehensible" (133).

As he drives the lonely roads that carve the plains of Texas, the deserts of New Mexico, Arizona, and Nevada, Heat-Moon finds people who live lives that they believe are satisfying, even though an outsider to the town and that life might see it as impoverished: Claud Tyler, in Dime Box, Texas, who began cutting hair, giving shaves, and pressing clothes in 1925; Virginia Been, proprietor of "a genuine Western saloon," one of two businesses in Hachita, New Mexico; Margaret Chealander, who runs a cafe in Frenchman, Nevada—population, four. When Heat-Moon asks about the loneliness in a town of four people, Chealander says, "You get to know yourself out here—you have to. . . . I think it's the distance between us that keeps us close. Everything here is important because there isn't much of it—except weather and dust. Once you see that, you're not lonely" (202). When Heat-Moon stops for breakfast at Southern Utah State College in Cedar City, he meets Kendrick Fritz, a Native American student who is studying to become a physician so that he can return to his Hopi community and practice medicine. Fritz gives Heat-Moon a taste of piki, shows him the Hopi emergence symbol, and explains the Hopi Way.

Heat-Moon likes these people, who seem content with where they are, who tell him stories and give him information. He is far less kind to others, particularly anyone he sees at a distance (travelers driving an interstate in their station wagon), or anyone as uncentered as he is. One night, for example, he meets in the Chiricahua Mountains a man he calls "The Boss of the Plains," whose age, marriage, and job problems make him an ironic mirror image of Heat-Moon. Heat-Moon reacts strongly to the Boss's self-pity, saying that he "wanted to slap him around, wake him up. He had the capacity to see but not the guts; he mucked in the drivel of his life" (165). Readers might think that the words could apply, at this point, to Heat-Moon himself.

In a review of *Blue Highways,* John Updike criticizes the book because the encounters and information do not add up to enough. "One doubts," Updike writes, "if William Least Heat-Moon learned much about himself or about America that he could not have discovered in Columbia, Missouri" (126). On one hand, Updike's statement is ridiculous exaggeration, in that Heat-Moon knows much about geography, history, and many particular lives that he didn't know before—and that is learning something about America. Readers learn that, too. But Updike's charge has merit, I would suggest, for those readers who want the events to work more as fiction does. The avoidance of epiphany, avoidance of turning all experience into meaning, can be a problem for a *writer,* whose very goal is to show—subtly or more obviously—what significances lie in the words. But nonfiction, even when it is written stylishly with literary (fictional) constructions, has a different set of constraints on it. While novelists stand poised to make up a world, construct a world that slides and forms and moves under their control, writers of nonfiction must follow events and character already there, though they may shape a story.

Just as there is tension in books like *Blue Highways* about the relation between describing life on the road and preparing for a journey in a way that creates a particular life, so there is tension between making an artful narrative and making things up. Because Heat-Moon generally avoids epiphany and symbol, the shaping that most fiction has, the book in its descriptions and events seems closer to life, we might say, as it is lived day to day. Or, as Heat-Moon puts it: "Other than to amuse himself, why should a man pretend to know where he's going or to understand what he sees? Hoping to catch onto things, at least for a moment, I was only following down the highways a succession of images that flashed like blue sparks. Nothing more" (192). Kendrick Fritz's reminders that people who feel a part of all living things can take that spirit wherever they go, or Chealander's idea about loneliness and living, useful as they are for Heat-Moon, cannot be absorbed and made significant immediately. He has come to understand that he can't model his life after someone else's—you can't change yourself as you can change a hat, he says—as he is past trying to turn experience into coherence. The lives of the people he is meeting work in a particular place, and only for them. At this point, Heat-Moon is committed only to driving, listening and talking, and feeling.

In northern California, after driving thousands of miles, he realizes that while he "had failed to put any fragments of the journey into a whole," he "did have a vague sense of mentally moving away from some things and toward others" (206). One subject he has been wrestling with, and it comes up often when he meets someone, is "work." Alfred Kazin has said that the question, "What do you do, bud?" is "the poignant beginning of American conversation," and that question has tormented Heat-Moon throughout his journey, both because he never knows how to describe the purpose of his trip (that it is not a vacation), and because by not working at all, in the sense of how people mean it when they ask the question, he loses his sense of what he is. Early in the trip, Heat-Moon meets a metallurgical engineer who works for General Electric in Louisville, and the man insists that there is a difference between work and a job. "A job," he says, "is what you force yourself to pay attention to for money. With work, you don't have to force yourself." The reason he only has a job, he adds, is that "what I do begins and stops each day. There's no convergence between what I know and what I do. And even less with what I *want* to know" (11). Heat-Moon keeps running into people who have versions of these ideas. Madison Wheeler farms poor land because factory work, while easier, isn't good for the soul and "a man becomes what he does" (31). Brother Patrick, a former Brooklyn policeman now a Trappist monk, has become the monastery's forest ranger because working in the natural world puts him closer to God and to making himself whole. When Heat-Moon meets a Mr. Watkins in northern California, he is ready to receive Watkins's simple wisdom that good work always comes from a good man, because work is what we do all the time, it's all of our actions. Separating out what we get paid for from what we do the rest of the time doesn't make sense. "A man's work is doing what he's supposed to do," Watkins tells Heat-Moon, and so driving around the country is not only nothing to be ashamed of but something to be proud of—it's good work (212).

The next day, thinking back to his meeting with Watkins, Heat-Moon reflects on the contemporary sense of the word *error*, which has come to mean "a mistake," though in its originations it meant to wander about, as in *knight-errant*: "If a man can keep alert and imaginative, an error is a possibility, a chance at something new; to him, wandering and wondering are part of the same process, and he is most mistaken, most in error, whenever he quits exploring" (215–16). If his journey is to be good work, then, the issue for Heat-Moon is to do it in the right spirit, as a wanderer and wonderer. At this stage of his trip, however, he is still subject to his life outside the journey, and so when he calls his wife and she doesn't want to talk to him, he begins "fighting the fear" that he "was about to lose heart utterly and head back" (221). But his depression lasts only overnight, and the next morning, recalling his experiences, realizing that he has to keep going on because only in going does he keep thinking, he resumes his journey with feelings that he has hurdled a tall barrier.

In an essay about his second book, *PrairyErth,* Heat-Moon says that James Agee's *Let Us Now Praise Famous Men* is "the greatest book of twentieth-century American travel" because it solves so "originally and richly the centrifugal-centripetal problem of one writer's explorations" (23)—that is, having the self prominent enough to make literature (and not just journalism) but not having it so prominent that the writer falls into a solipsistic hole. Heat-Moon's acclaim of Agee's book as travel literature is somewhat surprising, but *Blue Highways* is related closely to *Let Us Now Praise Famous Men.* Agee's writing about Alabama sharecroppers whom he lived with for three weeks during the Great Depression alternates between careful description of the family members and attentive reporting of Agee's feelings, and his insistence on details reflecting his own desires and imaginings admits to a subjectivity that writers of nonfiction often attempt to conceal. Agee explicitly portrays the enormous impact of these people on him—his effort in the book, he says, will be "to recognize the stature of a portion of unimagined existence." Though at times insistently entering the narrative, Agee as often writes himself completely out of the text, striving for "objectivity," striving to make an inevitably inaccurate medium more accurate. The book's form shifts back and forth between these poles.

Heat-Moon has followed this example in one major way, in that he generally allows the people he meets to tell their own stories, to use their own words, and only afterwards does he follow up with his own thoughts. His quest, however, as he knows well, has been self-obsessed, perhaps to the detriment of these people he meets. But halfway along now, he experiences some things that change him, change the quest, and perhaps lead him to his reverence for what Agee accomplishes in *Let Us Now Praise Famous Men.*

In Oregon, during his lowest time of depression, Heat-Moon begins a book he had bought in Phoenix: *The Sacred Pipe,* Black Elk's account of the ancient rites of the Oglala Sioux. When Black Elk contrasts "the good and straight red road of life" with the blue road, "the route of 'one who is distracted, who is ruled by his senses, and who lives for himself rather than for his people'" (219), Heat-Moon is stunned. Was it racial memory, he asks himself, "that had urged me to drive seven thousand miles of blue highway, a term I thought I had coined?" He suddenly understands his trip in a new way, that his "skewed vision was that of a man looking at himself by looking at what he looks at" (219). He chides himself for making a "traveling companion of the great poet of ego, the one who sings of himself."

Of the two writers whose books accompany Heat-Moon on the journey, Walt Whitman dominates the first half of the book. When Heat-Moon is hitting the open road, wanting to feel free, the American poet of the adventurous life seems a suitable companion, singing his "Song of the Open Road," the praises of traveling, not being contained by walls, expectations, habits:

> Aloof and light-hearted I take to the open road,
> Healthy, free, the world before me
> The long brown path before me leading wherever I choose. (1–3)

With a "modern" transcendentalist view—against consumerism, business, the "developing" of the natural world, and conformity—Heat-Moon attempts to construct a satisfying, coherent, transcendent self.[5] But the freedom of the open road does not translate for him into this self.

The change of reading from Whitman to Black Elk, which gives Heat-Moon a new paradigm for his journey, takes place in southern Washington on a high hill overlooking the Columbia River. In this place where coastal rains meet desert sun, a turn-of-the-century "visionary," Sam Hill, believed he could create an agricultural Eden: in addition to laying out a town he named Maryhill, Hill constructed a museum of fine arts and a rendition of Stonehenge. This setting sparks Heat-Moon's most philosophical reflections of the trip. Looking up at the stars, looking out to the lights of cars traveling an interstate that buried the old Oregon Trail, looking across the flat plain at stones that in the faint light looked considerably like Stonehenge but was a memorial to the dead of World War I, Heat-Moon thinks that "the journey had led here" (240).

When Heat-Moon departed Missouri, feeling as if he lived in an alien land, fearing his past and yet fearing more the uncertain future, he hoped to find where "time and men and deeds connected," where change did not mean ruin. Ironically, he understands best how these come about when he is alone on this hill, where there are no deeds being performed and no other people. When he gazes at the stars, he thinks about time and how, with powerful enough telescopes, we could, astrophysicists say, look back into the past. When he gazes at the mighty Columbia River, he understands the equally mighty succession of geology leading to fish leading to Indians leading to all the new people who swarmed into the Northwest after promises. When he gazes in the direction of the towering peak of Mount Hood, fifty miles into the distance, he realizes that its volcanic eruptions have buried life many times. He thinks of Whitman's line that "a vast similitude interlocks all." The nature of things, Heat-Moon reflects, "is resistance to change, while the nature of process is resistance to stasis, yet things and process are one, and the line from inorganic to organic and back again is uninterrupted and unbroken." The Ghost Dancers, he continues, "showed both man's natural opposition to change he doesn't understand and his natural failure in such opposition. But it is man's potential . . . to see that changelessness would be meaninglessness, to know that the only way the universe can show and prove itself is through change" (241).[6] The changes of the universe dwarf humankind, Heat-Moon thinks, but if knowing that "dims egocentrism, that illusion of what man is," it need not dim the self, which he has come to understand in a different way: "Ego, craving distinction, belongs to the narrowness of now; but self, looking for union, belongs to the past and future, to the continuum, to the outside. Of all the visions of the Grandfathers [his Native American forebears] the greatest is this: *To seek the high concord, a man looks not deeper within—he reaches farther out*" (241). Whitman, we might say, teaches similar lessons, but Heat-Moon gives the last word here to his Native American ancestors, and it is this idea that he refers to repeatedly as he completes his journey. While he had earlier explained his ideas and feelings (or even felt them) with references to Whitman's poetry, that role is taken over by Black Elk, whose visions of a people united and connected to the earth, living a life of simplicity and harmony, have great currency for Heat-Moon.

In his wide-ranging book about postmodernism, *The Saturated Self: Dilemmas of Identity in Contemporary Life*, Kenneth Gergen argues that the modern advancements in communications technology result in people becoming immersed in a myriad of social connections that are constantly forming, adjusting, breaking. Compared with life just decades ago, when a person's relationships were usually direct and limited to people seen, contemporary technologies make possible the sustaining of relationships with an ever-expanding range of other persons. "We are reaching," writes Gergen, "what may be viewed as a state of social saturation," which he equates with the condition of postmodernism.

This saturation of self in contemporary life has placed in jeopardy "all previous beliefs about the self . . . and with them the patterns of action they sustain" (7), particularly the beliefs about the self that Gergen calls the romanticist and the modernist. The romanticist view of the self emphasizes characteristics of personal depth, passion, soul, creativity, and moral fiber, a "vocabulary essential to the formation of deeply committed relations, dedicated friendships, and life purposes"; the modernist view of the self emphasizes humans' ability to reason, to think through beliefs, opinions, and conscious intentions, which leads modernists "to believe in educational systems, a stable family life, moral training, and rational choice of marriage partners" (6). People today, believing in either of these views of the self but "thrust into an ever-widening array of relationships," often feel caught, Gergen suggests, in contradictory or incoherent activities, which they then anguish over because of the violation of their sense of identity. But as social saturation continues, "this initial stage is superseded by one in which one senses the raptures of multiplicitous being . . . one opens an enormous world of potential." The final, future stage in the transition to the postmodern, Gergen says, will be "reached when the self vanishes fully into a stage of relatedness. One ceases to believe in a self independent of the relations in which he or she is embedded" (17).

Gergen's provocative views are useful to frame Heat-Moon's evolving quest because it is precisely this attempt to hold back the postmodern self—to return to a place and time where personal integrity is prized and deeply committed relationships might flourish, where one's sense of identity can remain constant—that motivates Heat-Moon at the beginning. And it is a version of the postmodern self (to reach further out, not look deeper within) that he adopts as part of his personal philosophy, though the version is given to him by his

Native American ancestors who decidedly did not have postmodernism in mind. Ironically, once Heat-Moon believes in reaching further out, not looking deeper within, the need to be on the road becomes less important.

Even with his new insights, Heat-Moon remains emotionally fragile, unable yet to transfer rational understandings into stable feelings. He repeats a pattern that, when life on the road is good, his hopes rise and a fantasy denying his loss percolates to the surface—he thinks he can return to Columbia, put his marriage back together, and make a success of his life. But life on the road is not always good; driving across the great northern Plains of Montana and North Dakota, the immensity of the landscape slowly eases him down the spiral to another low point. For a person driving the Plains, he says, the "isolating immensity reveals what lies covered in places noisier, busier, more filled up. For me, what I saw revealed was this (only this): a man nearly desperate because his significance had come to lie within his own narrow ambit" (274). While Gretel Ehrlich expresses similar ideas but has the opposite reaction in her acclamation of "the solace of open spaces," Heat-Moon, in a foul mood, pushes himself relentlessly, wanting to simply leave the plains and put miles behind him. In Wisconsin, when he can't find a good place to spend the night and mosquitoes begin biting him, he realizes that though he had come on the trip to change routine and be inconvenienced, the inconvenience is now just making him irritable, unhappy. He crosses Michigan, seeing many people, "but not often learning where our lives crossed common ground" (290). The fault is his, certainly.

When Heat-Moon comes to upstate New York, his mood changes. He stays three nights at a friend's house, helping him build a rock wall, taking walks, writing letters, eating and drinking well. He visits families who own neighboring vineyards. His spirits restored, he drives across the Adirondacks, up Lake George and Lake Champlain, crosses Champlain on the ferry, drives south and spends the night in a tourist home in the beautiful village of Woodstock, Vermont. Hope rising within, having a dream one night that his wife offered a "new marriage," he tries to reach outward, not look inward, as Black Elk had said. "Certain things among the shadows of a man's life do not have to be remembered—they remember themselves," he writes (327), and so he calls his wife. But they talk at cross-purposes; she gives him no hope. When he resumes driving the next morning, he admits the futility of his attempt to mend a broken marriage by taking it on the road for eleven thousand miles, to poke into things in order to hold back the feelings of failure.

Blue Highways fits in with the other books of this study in that trauma and loss motivate Heat-Moon to embark on his trip, and in that his subsequent literary act of writing the self through writing others accomplishes his grief work; if, however, we take *A Country Year* as the norm—Hubbell elegantly weaving her daily life into her farm's ecology as a way to move through mourning—then *Blue Highways,* in its move toward telling the stories of human others and neglecting the nonhuman world, pushes the parameters of this subgenre.[7] Travel books can be nature writing—one recalls Edwin Way Teale's *The American Seasons*—but Heat-Moon in his travels is oriented toward the human world and not the animal and plant world. Ecocritics have claimed Heat-Moon as one of theirs, nevertheless; he is in the canon of contemporary American nature writers.[8] The reputation is earned, I would agree, with *PrairyErth,* a nearly exhaustive "thick description," to use Gilbert Ryle's term that Clifford Geertz made famous. In that book, a cultural geography of one county in Kansas, Heat-Moon constructs what he calls "verticalities" or "excavations" to go deep into the history of a place, history that encompasses the nonhuman as well as the human.[9] In an otherwise insightful essay on Heat-Moon, David Teague claims that these verticalities work likewise in *Blue Highways,* but such a view is simply a stretch. "Excavation" (digging deep) and traveling thousands of miles of blue highways simply do not go hand in hand.

There are moments in *Blue Highways* when Heat-Moon does what naturalists are likely to do. Stopping in the Texas desert, he sits and makes a list of thirty items he sees, as a counter to the typical belief that there's nothing "there" in a desert (149). Or, when memory becomes too strong, he turns to the eye to watch "particularities," and then makes the following observations:

Item: a green and grainy and corrupted ice over the ponds.
Item: blackbirds, passing like storm-borne leaves, sweeping just above the treetops, moving as if invisibly tethered to one will. . . .
Item: uprooted fencerows of Osage orange (so-called hedge apples although they are in the mulberry family). The Osage made bows and war clubs from the limbs. (5–6)

Perhaps because he is on the road looking out at the world through his windshield, or that he simply can't take the time in one place to observe particulars, most of his natural history comes from books, from his reading when he is later back in Columbia. Gathered together, his "items," his frequent observations of details in the scenery, and his pronouncements about landscape lend the air of natural-history writing, of environmental literature, but in *Blue Highways* the "nature writing" primarily serves as texture, not substance.

Near the end of his journey, however, after he has accepted the end of his marriage, accepted that there will be no quick gain to compensate for his losses, Heat-Moon does write scenes with a different emphasis than earlier material: he seems more interested in placing people he meets into a longer and fuller history that, if not approaching a verticality, might be the step between what has happened earlier in *Blue Highways* and what he does with *PrairyErth*. When, for example, Heat-Moon meets Marion Horner Robie in Melvin Village, New Hampshire, he is finally ready to rethink his earlier preconceptions about change and ruin, which helps him "hear" and understand in a way he had not previously. At age eighty, living in the house she was born in, Robie has become her town's historian, and she tells Heat-Moon that what looks like change has gone on in Melvin Village for centuries. What he sees as a preserving of the "old" (and desirable) is no such thing, she says. Change has been a constant. But change does not mean loss. "And that's what I mean by abiding. Things remain," she says, "even when we think they don't" (335). She sends him to her second cousin, Tom Hunter, the fifth generation of his family to tap maple trees for syrup. Hunter tells Heat-Moon that "outlanders" get upset when they see his family cutting down trees for firewood, but they "don't see that those trees are growin' in an old field" (340). In his sketches of Robie and Hunter, Heat-Moon has them lead to their own revelations without his own preconceived ideas to shape the context, and he does not feel obliged to give a final commentary on their stories.

On this last leg of the trip, Heat-Moon gives up his mandate to drive blue highways, looking for oddly named towns to discover the "history" there. Instead, as with Robie or Hunter, he simply follows up leads on interesting people. He is invited by Tom West, the skipper of a fishing boat from Cape Porpoise, Maine, to learn for himself how "a flounder gets from twenty leagues down to the A and P" (346).

In a slow-paced sketch, Heat-Moon describes a day in the life of some ocean fishermen, and one thing he discovers is that despite all of the new high-tech equipment, in many respects these fishermen are doing what they have done there for several hundred years. Change does not mean ruin; some things abide.

Heat-Moon's most important connection occurs at the Eastern Shore of Chesapeake Bay, when he departs for an overnight stay on Smith Island. The octogenarian Alice Venable Middleton teaches him about the island's ecology and how humans have interwoven themselves into that ecology in such a way as to preserve, not destroy, what they found. David Teague has suggested that Middleton is the only person in all Heat-Moon's travels that the author of *Blue Highways* identifies with (518), and certainly she gives him several useful metaphors for reconceiving his life. She compares the network of waterways on the islands to crabs, noting that both of them go forward by going sideways: "That's how they get the feeling of the territory. Narrow at the head, wider at the shore. A picture of a life lived well, I deem" (393). Middleton speaks of history and connections, and tells him that the hardest thing about living on a small, marshy island is "having the gumption to live different and the sense to let everybody else live different" (397). Implicitly, Heat-Moon suggests that they are words for him also to live by, and the world need not be remade if he can remake himself.

When Heat-Moon leaves Smith Island he is soon in the midst of a thunderstorm, and so he stops. Lying on the bunk in his van, he thinks over his journey and, instead of the usual fragments, indecisions, and reproaches, he puts together a new understanding. "In his time on the blue road," he writes, "the immaterialist Black Elk often heard voices from the clouds; in my season on the blue highways, the voices I heard were those of men—men [and women] who knew about stumbling not from observation as gods know it, but rather from having stumbled. For that reason, their words carried a force cloud voices could not match." These human voices, he says, "showed the power not of visions but of revision, the power to see again and revise." Ego, "that excessive looking inward," had run amuck "like a crazed enemy." His life with his wife was over, but, he realizes, what was not over was a chance to begin again, to find "an angle of vision" that could adjust to circumstances, could accommodate change: "By seeing both the futility in trying to relive the old life and the danger in trying to obliterate it, man can gain the capacity to make anew. His very form depends not on repetition but upon variation from old patterns. . . . And what of history? . . . Etymology: *educate,* from the Latin *educare,* 'lead out' (399–400). Change is constant; educate yourself to know what can abide.

In "Journeys into Kansas," a talk delivered for a Modern Language Association session on contemporary American travel writing, Heat-Moon says that for *PrairyErth* he wanted at all costs to avoid a kind of writing that he sees "as the major threat to good travel reporting today: the journey that exists primarily to explore the soul of the traveler" (21). He confesses that he used this "descent into self" himself in *Blue Highways,* plunging into the topography of self for half the journey before he realized "the futility of that course." Though perhaps Heat-Moon lets himself off too easily by saying that a descent into self structures only the first half of the book, the remarks, years after *Blue Highways,* reveal his beliefs about the limitations of travel literature.

Late in his trip, Heat-Moon begins one morning to muse, to fall inward and take his "darker self . . . seriously," but, as a measure of his personal change, he resists brooding and gets in the van simply to resume driving. He thinks of Henry Miller's line that our destination "is never a place but rather a new way of looking at things" (359). As he turns west for the homestretch of his journey, he is not motivated to investigate history, nor to talk much. He has given up the metaphor that once shaped his journey's purpose, to find where men, time, and deeds connect. He has given up criticizing American culture in order to proclaim his own values. He's ready for the road trip to end.

If Heat-Moon begins his quest by seeking out places in rural America where little change has occurred, he ends his quest by coming to understand that change itself is not the problem, and moreover that he himself must give up his previous version of "self" for a more fluid, adaptable one. No single specific moment, no one or two people, teach him this. But the months of driving, talking, reading, and observing lives anchored to a specific place do help him end seeing the world only through the prism of his grieving. The arc of his journey is a slow move toward involving himself with others in an open, curious way, which lessens preoccupation with self and loss. The driving trip functions, that is, much like the process of psychoanalysis, as Heat-Moon uses new information and insights to rethink and eventually rewrite the "meaning" of his story, even if the facts of loss will not alter.

Contradiction is at the heart of *Blue Highways*. The text tries to fuse "good travel reporting" and an exploration of the soul. Heat-Moon sets himself up as a critical commentator on American life by returning to its "true and best source," rural people who have been less affected by cultural changes than most Americans, but paradoxically he then implicitly shows in his book that his preconceptions about such people's lives are mostly wrong. He sets out on his driving trip in order to affirm his sense of self by contrasting what he believes with what our culture seems to value, but he then discovers that self-consciousness does not lead to self-knowledge or self-creation. Late in his trip, Heat-Moon acknowledges that you don't solve your marriage problems by going on an eleven-thousand-mile trip; we might add that you don't set out to raise yourself from depression by poking into other peoples' lives and having them tell their stories. And yet the text suggests that in fact this might work. Heat-Moon does say that he returns to Columbia a changed man. How much we, as readers, are convinced by this depends largely on whether we believe the lessons of the road can be transferred to off-road, at-home life.

If we take *Blue Highways* as evidence, it is unclear whether his journey, resembling the Hopi symbol, leads him to an emergence that he understood upon his return. But if the "story of the book" can only remain somewhat ambiguous about whether Heat-Moon has finished his grief work, we can still say that the autobiographical act is, eventually, an unqualified success. In the writing and rewriting of his manuscript, he half-discovers, half-creates (to echo James Olney about the autobiographical act) a persona that is able to compensate for his loss. Driving rural roads to hear stories in which time and men and deeds connected has not worked as anticipated, but his telling of these stories, set in the context of a quest, necessitates that he must attempt to make his own time and deeds and character connect. And they do. In the move from Bill Trogdon to a new self, the writer William Least Heat-Moon emerges, finally formed in relation not only to all the people he has met, but in relation to those Native American ancestors who had shaped his way of comprehending the world and his own desires.

6 A Pilgrimage to Fashion a Zen Self

Peter Matthiessen's *The Snow Leopard*

Like Heat-Moon, Matthiessen begins a journey in grief, leaving for a two-month trek through the Himalayas not long after his wife dies of cancer. But unlike Heat-Moon, who sets out with no plan other than to drive the blue highways of America in a loop, Matthiessen intends to make a religious pilgrimage to the Crystal Mountain in Inner Dolpo, Nepal. A student of Zen Buddhism, he hopes to visit the Lama of Shey, the most revered of all the *rinpoches,* the "precious ones" of Tibetan Buddhism. To go step by step across the greatest mountain range in the world, Matthiessen believes, will be "a true pilgrimage, a journey of the heart."

In *The Snow Leopard,* his award-winning account of his journey, Matthiessen embeds a text of grieving and recovery within a journalistic account of his Zen pilgrimage. The book blends description of a Tibetan world that few Westerners have ever entered and research about Zen into an adventure narrative filled with physical hardships, brushes with death, difficulties with weather, and "treacherous natives"—adventures enough to make a Hollywood movie. But the main action, less suitable for a movie, unfolds in Matthiessen's heart and mind as he travels, seeking acceptance of death and a meaning for his future life. For the epigraph to book 1, "Westward," Matthiessen uses a passage about pilgrims from the Lama Govinda's book *The Way of the White Clouds:* "Just as a white summer cloud, in harmony with heaven and earth freely floats in the blue sky from horizon to horizon following the breath of the atmosphere—in the same way the pilgrim abandons himself to the breath of the greater life that . . . leads him beyond the farthest horizons to an aim which is already present within him, though yet hidden from his sight" (9). By immersing himself in a Zen culture and then undertaking a pilgrimage in Tibet, Matthiessen hopes to go beyond horizons that he knows; by giving up control, by attempting to feel free and ready to pursue whatever lies ahead, Matthiessen hopes to discover the aim present but hidden within him, a life purpose to help him move through mourning.

Like Barich and Heat-Moon, Matthiessen at the time of departure wishes to convert pain, anger, and depression into a new story. His journey seems less escapist than Barich going to the racetrack or Heat-Moon driving the blue highways, in that Matthiessen chooses a quest linked to his spirituality. Trekking through the Himalayas— talking, reading, thinking, writing—Matthiessen confronts directly the relations between human culture, the self, and nature. He recognizes the difficulties he has in shedding psychological defenses and entering the world "wholly present" because he is an American, and a man. At the end of his pilgrimage he perceives that, like a snake shedding its skin, he is "no longer that old person and not yet the new" (300). The literary act that describes his journey and his grief work will become ultimately that new skin, elegantly showing what the journey teaches, also demonstrating what it costs. Questions emerge with this journey and its construction into narrative: Can a Westerner truly absorb Eastern precepts, gain enlightenment, and convert Zen principles into a lived Zen life? Does the journalistic and autobiographical act conflict with the lived life? If the geographic setting is crucial for Matthiessen's self-creation, can he return successfully to life in the United States? And, as with Heat-Moon, do the lessons of the road transfer?

The spiritual forces surrounding the word *pilgrimage* have never had potency in American culture. Even the most noted religious pilgrims in American history, those early settlers at Plymouth Rock, did not follow the normative pattern of leaving, journeying to a sacred place, and returning home. In Protestant Christianity and American Catholicism, pilgrimage is largely absent compared with Hinduism, Buddhism, or Islam, whose followers are urged to visit holy places; Muslims are in fact obligated, if physically and financially able, to make at least one visit to Mecca. In this country, people routinely use *pilgrimage* in a secular, usually diminished way, as when a group goes on a "pilgrimage" to Hollywood's Avenue of the Stars or to all of major-league baseball's stadiums, or when Elvis devotees visit Graceland. The pilgrim, in America, has become a tourist with an interest and a credit card.

Matthiessen is no tourist and his pilgrimage is an incredibly difficult physical and mental endeavor. As a journey, it is not, however, new to him. Daniel G. Payne has observed that Matthiessen's trek through the Himalayas "is similar in pattern and approach to his earlier travel books: he journeys through a remote region of the globe studying the wildlife and ecology of the area and observing and learning from indigenous cultures" (609).[1] But noteworthy to this expedition is that Matthiessen undertakes it because the journey's goals—to visit the Lama of Shey, to see and experience the daily life of primitive peoples practicing Buddhism, to see the snow leopard—are connected to his deep feelings of loss over the death of his wife, Deborah Love, who was a convert to Zen and introduced Matthiessen to Zen practice. Through attempts to model Zen practice and behold Buddhist models in the Tibetan people, Matthiessen can demonstrate in *The Snow Leopard* how journey becomes religious pilgrimage. Unlike Heat-Moon, Matthiessen knows where he is going and for what set of reasons. Descriptions of wildlife and ecology, sketches of Tibetan people and life, revelations of his own spiritual quest—these can all be joined, resulting in an unusual relational autobiography.

Though Matthiessen undertakes a spiritual journey with a specific destination, the ultimate pilgrimage in Zen Buddhism is to discover the Buddha within oneself—to become enlightened. The ten phases of enlightenment are described, in one formulation, by the oxherding pictures, which evolved in twelfth-century China to depict the spiritual quest as the search for an elusive ox that roams wild in the rain forest (Hixon, *Coming Home,* 60). In the first picture, "Seeking the Ox," the quester's focus on the "true nature of consciousness" creates an illusory duality between the one who seeks and the object that is sought. During this phase, the seeker comes to understand that the ox will never be found on one of the nearly infinite paths, but that the ox is the rain forest, the paths, and the seeker. In the second picture, "Finding the Tracks," the quester learns that the teachings of the masters are the tracks that can draw him into deeper meditation. In the third phase of enlightenment, "The First Glimpse of the Ox," the seeker understands that the ox cannot be searched for, that it does not even exist in abstract contemplation, but it might reveal itself momentarily in direct experience, in the natural world. The fourth picture, "Catching the Ox," shows the seeker as having found and embraced the ox, though the sustaining of his perception of True Nature is not easy. Only with total discipline, compassion, and truthfulness can the seeker hold the ox; at this stage, the seeker has become a practitioner whose "system of values and even his physical nervous system must be reconstituted as to harmonize the energy of Enlightenment with personal and cultural being" (Hixon, 60–64).[2]

He once had, Matthiessen recalls, an experience of True Nature, of the One, early in his days as a Zen student. After spending a Saturday intensely meditating, he returned to his room, was greeted by his wife, Deborah, and suddenly intuited that she was dying. The next day, when the two sat across from one another during the morning prayer service, Matthiessen chanted the Kannon Sutra with such fury that he lost his "self" and had an extraordinary moment:

In my journal for that day, seeking in vain to find words for what had happened, I called it the "Smile." The Smile seemed to grow out of me, filling all space above and behind like a huge shadow of my own Buddha form. . . . it was I who smiled; the Smile was Me. I did not breathe, I did not need to look; for It was Everywhere. Nor was there terror in my awe: I felt "good," like a "good child," entirely safe. Wounds, ragged edges, hollow places were all gone, all had been healed; my heart lay at the heart of all Creation. . . . For the first time since unremembered childhood, I was not alone; there was no separate "I." (106)

Matthiessen feels, because of the Smile, acceptance of what he perceives to be his wife's fate, and when she is soon diagnosed with cancer, the "state of grace" that began that morning prevails throughout her dying, giving him "an inner calm in which I knew just how and where to act." His Zen teacher tells him that he has transcended, and Matthiessen feels forgiven, not just by Deborah but by himself, a forgiveness that "strikes me still as the greatest blessing of my life" (107). But after her death, he discovers that he cannot sustain the inner calm, that a power is seeping away from him, and he comes to believe that his enlightenment had occurred only because of his wife's crisis. In this period of his mourning, the zoologist George Schaller invites him on a journey through the Himalayas to the Crystal Mountain, and Matthiessen accepts.

Matthiessen's initial transcendence and subsequent inner calm correspond to the fourth phase of enlightenment, "Catching the Ox." But when he begins his Himalayan trek, he has realized, as the Zen masters said, how hard it is to continue his progress to the next stage, "Taming the Ox," when an "effortless intimacy or friendship with the Ox" is established, when the practitioner learns that discipline and purity are no longer necessary and are even harmful to further progress. Matthiessen even suspects that he has regressed, has slid back down the path of enlightenment, and that perhaps he will not be able to continue.

The problem for Matthiessen (like so many humans) is that he cannot internalize into a way of being what he knows and desires intellectually or rationally. His interest in Zen, he recounts early in the book, has culminated a thirty-year exploration of how to get rid of his pain and anger. With no insight as to what was causing the dread in his life, he "only knew that at the bottom of each breath there was a hollow place that needed to be filled" (43). He studied the writings of the mystic-philosopher George Gurdjieff and experimented with hallucinogens used by shamans in the jungles of Peru to induce supernatural states. "I never saw drugs as a path, far less as a way of life," he writes, but for ten years he used them regularly, searching for a vision that would give him, or teach him, peace. Though his drug journeys sometimes lightened his rage and pain, he could not transfer the feelings into daily life. "Old mists may be banished," he says, "but the alien chemical agent forms another mist, maintaining the separation of the 'I' from true experience of the One" (47).

What unites Matthiessen's various searches is his attraction to things mystical. He believes that he can learn peace and a kind of wisdom from mysticism, by which he means not what we call the occult but what "is only another aspect of reality" (55) for prehistorical people, or Easterners with little contact with Europeans, or Native Americans. A difference, Matthiessen writes, between the mystic and the scientist, between Eastern and Western modes of thought, is that the Westerner attempts to understand reality and the Easterner desires to experience it directly, with no need to articulate or even consciously understand what has been experienced. Matthiessen's companion, George Schaller, is the scientist who "refuses to believe that the Western mind can truly absorb nonlinear Eastern perceptions" (61). Matthiessen hopes that Schaller is wrong.

Though Matthiessen agrees that everything about him and his culture makes it difficult to be a mystic, he wants to explore, like all introvertive mystics, the inner layers of feeling and experience that lie beneath our customary responses and thoughts. To help him explore these inner layers and not be preoccupied with the outer ones, Matthiessen, early in his journey, begins shedding: he cuts his hair, throws away his wristband and watch. Such shedding, however, is only symbolic, Matthiessen knows, because American culture and books, his entire life experiences, have made it difficult for him to live in the moment, to live without the extreme self-consciousness characteristic of Westerners. But how does an American change an emphasis on things to an emphasis on the spirit?

Matthiessen's "way," his spiritual path, is Zen Buddhism, but the ideas and feelings of American transcendentalism are congenial to him, in part because Ralph Waldo Emerson and Henry David Thoreau read widely in Eastern religious philosophy. Matthiessen particularly connects to the transcendental belief that nature is God's scripture to be read by everyone, which corresponds closely to Zen's precept that the universe itself is the sacred scripture and that religion, in Matthiessen's words, "is no more and no less than the apprehension of the infinite in every moment" (35). At one time in American culture, Matthiessen says in *The Snow Leopard,* writers such as William James, Emerson, Herman Melville, and Walt Whitman had articulated ideas of "a clear and subtle illumination that lent magnificence to life and peace to death." Those ideas, which Matthiessen calls mystical, were then "overwhelmed in the hard glare of technology" that has dominated American life since. The light was put out, and "now we are full of dread" (63).

In modern techno-land, in capitalistic America, Christianity has adapted itself to the temptations of the immense quantities of available goods: there is little emphasis on Jesus' teaching that a rich man has a better chance of getting through the eye of a needle than going to heaven. Religion seems something for Sunday, with little connection to the paradoxes of the life led the other six days. The Zen mystics, on the other hand, begin with the belief that everything one does is religious—that everyday life, conducted with the proper attitude, is a form of prayer, which Matthiessen finds particularly attractive. For Zen Buddhists, as for Native Americans, Matthiessen says, "the religious ceremony is life itself" (56).

Matthiessen's interest in the unification of religion and daily living is acute because of his overwhelming feelings of being alienated from all things, not only the nonhuman world but other humans and, more often than he desires, himself. He comments repeatedly about feeling split into different selves, as, for example, the night early in his journey when he notes "how strange everything is," because "one 'I' feels like an observer of this man who lies here in this sleeping bag in Asian mountains; another 'I' is thinking about Alex [his son]; a third is the tired man who tries to sleep" (41). We know that there is no "inner self," that the self cannot be divided up into parts or into layers. But the metaphor can be useful for someone like Matthiessen who is not trying to explain away the difference between what he feels and what he does (a common reason in pop psychology for talking about the inner self) but is trying, metaphorically, to understand why the source of his peace or joy can rarely be gotten at.

Children, Matthiessen believes, see and live freely, without the self-consciousness that separates adult humans from each other and the world. He tells how his son, when he was young, would stand rapt in his sandbox, surrounded by birds, the leaves dancing, the clouds flying: "The child was not observing; he was at rest in the very center of the universe, a part of things, unaware of endings and beginnings, still in unison with the primordial nature of creation, letting all light and phenomena pour through. Ecstasy is identity with all existence" (41). The delight of children with their world, the mystery and promise of life, is slowly lost as they grow up, and Matthiessen neither sees in others nor himself feels any recompense.

A goal of the journey becomes, then, the desire to unite different "selves" through the literary act. If one self observes Tibetan culture, another self merges into a "oneness" with plant and animal life in this ecosystem that few Westerners have visited, and a third self reflects back on the past to understand how past is connected to present and future, then the resultant writing as a blend of genres can aid the pilgrimage. In other words, the roles of the nature writer, the writer of literary nonfiction, and the autobiographer are three kinds of "seeing" that can lead to three kinds of "being," which Matthiessen wishes to combine into a new way of seeing/being that will help him in his grief work.

For the epigraph to *The Snow Leopard*, Matthiessen quotes Rainer Maria Rilke: "The experiences that are called 'visions,' the whole so-called 'spirit-world,' death, all those things that are so closely akin to us, have by daily parrying been so crowded out of life that the senses with which we could have grasped them are atrophied. To say nothing of God." By journeying to a remote place where few reminders of Western life can reach him, by removing himself from the daily parrying of his life, by observing adults who feel the world as a unified whole, Matthiessen hopes to bring back senses to grasp the spirit-world, or God. He might perceive as he did in childhood, he writes, "the wildness of the world," where he was not separate from flower or bird, or himself—the wildness present before the "armor of the 'I' begins to form" (42) and creates separation and loneliness.

Matthiessen uses the metaphor of "screens" to describe those things that we carry with us and that shape how we respond to everyday events, and he means something more than Freud's defense mechanisms. Defense mechanisms are certainly a kind of screen, but Matthiessen's screens are those things that separate us from feeling. Using anger to control, holding back tears, or not acknowledging tenderness can slowly harden us, when done countless times, into something impenetrable. Like looking through a window with layers of dirt, we can hardly see out, and what we see is not clear but is our way of seeing "screenlike," which we might believe is normal. Matthiessen likes to quote William Blake, perhaps the quintessential poet who recognized the various ways humans enslave themselves: "Man has closed himself up, till he sees all things through the narrow chinks of his cavern" (42).

As he walks up mountain passes and down through narrow valleys, surrounded by mountain peaks soaring twenty-six thousand feet into the sky, as he writes about this landscape and his past, Matthiessen emerges a version of the Romantic Hero, the Solitary, the Wanderer. His predecessors are not only Zen pilgrims and religious seekers, but Shelley's Alastor, Byron's Manfred, Yeats's Oisin, and other characters of the romantic quest-romance. And yet, Matthiessen knows, the romantic tendency to exalt the artist's powers of imagination and to proclaim the urgency of the spiritual quest often leads, as it does with these characters, into a quicksand of self-consciousness and ego because the imagination so overwhelms the natural world. The mystical search is dangerous, he says, because it can lead down a path to isolation and madness. He seeks to bypass this morass in two ways. One, by looking carefully at other humans—Schaller, the porters and sherpas who aid the expedition, the Lama of Shey—he can learn how people live fiercely in the moment, without dread of the future or sorrow about the past. And, two, by connecting physically, not just imaginatively, with the natural world, he might come to empty his mind in such a way as to have the universe come "to attention, a Universe of which one is the center, a Universe that is not the same and yet not different from oneself" (210).

The drive to gain the knowledge that comes from pursuing the quest-romance has been seen as particularly reflective of men's interests and desires, but Matthiessen exemplifies a latter-day version in that he wants his exploration of the mystical to lead back eventually to domesticity and fatherhood. He does not want to be the isolated mystic or a monk but a spiritually communal man. Matthiessen treks in Tibet because he desires to see the Lama of Shey, but it also makes symbolic sense that he leave the United States. Much in American culture reinforces the masculine codes that Matthiessen believes have hobbled him, codes that explicitly and implicitly tell men to pay attention to work or entertainment but not to matters of the spirit, to be unfeeling, not to confess weakness. For Matthiessen to see fully and clearly without screens, to emerge from the closed cavern, or to shed the armor of the I is to admit to emotions that American masculinity has defined itself against. The path home, he says metaphorically, is overgrown with thorns and thickets of ideas, fears, and defenses. In one sense, donning armor is a useful act to proceed through thickets, but knight's armor is hot and cumbersome, good for displays of power but bad for freedom of movement, litheness, the feeling of soaring.

Matthiessen wants to make himself receptive to the most mundane parts of human existence in order to help him lose self-consciousness, and so he is critical of his inability to be direct or open to emotions, his propensity for falling into a kind of intellectually cold thinking and responding. He admires the Tibetan people, who lead their lives so differently. The sherpa assistants, for example, accomplish their work cheerfully, their dignity unassailable. "The service," Matthiessen writes, "is rendered for its own sake—it is the task, not the employer, that is served. As Buddhists, they know that the doing matters more than the attainment or reward, that to serve in this self-less way is to be free. Because of their belief in karma . . . they are

tolerant and unjudgmental. . . . These simple and uneducated men
comport themselves with the wise calm of monks, and their well-
being is in no way separable from their religion" (33–34). When one
sherpa drops the head sherpa's sleeping bag in a river—making necessary the difficult task of building a fire, drying it, and then catching
up with the other walkers—all the sherpas laugh, amazing Matthiessen with their easy acceptance and lack of anger.

An important lesson about acceptance comes from the Lama of
Shey. En route to the Crystal Mountain, Matthiessen had "entertained
visions of myself in monkish garb attending the Lama in his ancient
mysteries, and getting to light the butter lamps into the bargain; I
suppose I had hoped he would be my teacher" (191). Eventually they
do meet, though it is hardly Matthiessen's fantasy, and the lama
teaches Matthiessen something important simply with an answer to
one question. The lama is crippled from severe arthritis and so cannot walk the steep trails or ever leave the high mountains; when
Matthiessen asks him about his unchangeable isolation, the holy man
laughs and cries out, "Of course I am happy here! It's wonderful! *Especially* when I have no choice!" (246). Matthiessen feels deeply
moved by the lama's wholehearted acceptance of what is, and hiking
down the mountain from the monastery, he thinks, "Have you seen
the snow leopard? No! Isn't that wonderful?" (246). In following days,
Matthiessen recalls frequently the lama's response, which gives him
courage to accept his own losses.

Matthiessen is not an ardent propagandist for Tibet or the primitive peoples he meets: he decries waste or environmental degradation
when he sees it, notes with sadness the numerous people who barely
survive their difficult life, and judges harshly those who in a dumb
fury of response mistreat children, women, or animals. Matthiessen
does not romanticize the difficulties of people's lives—he is not looking to escape the United States, escape his community or history—
but he does seek a resilience that he believes the Tibetan people have
gained from their high-mountain lives and from Buddhism. Inherit-
ing a Western belief system that has shaped his character greatly, but
trying to change that character, Matthiessen is metaphorically neither
of the West or East. On his trek, he uses two men to think through
how he might create an East-West blend to serve him therapeutically:
George Schaller, a zoologist studying the bharal sheep in their native
habitat, is the "Western scientist"; Tukten, a "disreputable" porter who

carries gear for the expedition, is the Eastern mystic. In *The Snow Leopard*, Matthiessen shapes these two figures to stand in symbolically for each culture, to oppose one another and to represent admirable traits of East and West.

Matthiessen calls Schaller the "finest field biologist working today" and admires his strong work ethic and fundamental human decency, the "fine, old-fashioned qualities" that he has in abundance. Schaller's "mix of brains, strength, and integrity is not so common," Matthiessen writes, "and counts for a lot on an expedition such as ours: how many of one's friends, these days, could be entrusted with one's life?" (36). But Schaller is intensely private, uncomfortable with emotions and other people, and so independent that he is happy on the trek only when they are far away from other people, or when he is alone, pushing himself against the elements, collecting data on the blue sheep. Matthiessen sees exemplified in Schaller many of his own traits that he wants to change. While Schaller believes "that Eastern thought evades 'reality' and therefore lacks the courage of existence" (61), that Eastern people are passive, too accepting of their lives, Matthiessen struggles with the difficulties that trauma and loss bring to an ambitious, high-achieving Westerner like himself, unable to accept death or one's present circumstances. In his unspoken argument with Schaller, Matthiessen replies that "the courage-to-be, right here and now and nowhere else, is precisely what Zen, at least, demands: eat when you eat, sleep when you sleep!"

Matthiessen has near at hand a model of someone who accepts life's hardships with a Zen grace. Tukten, Matthiessen says, "radiates that inner quiet which is often associated with spiritual attainment" (52). But the other sherpas don't trust Tukten, telling Schaller and Matthiessen that he has a reputation for swearing, drunkenness, and causing trouble. Matthiessen, however, notices something different, that "all animals and wayfarers are Tukten's friends, and listen to him carefully, yet he rarely speaks except when spoken to, and never seems to speak too much; without obtruding, he becomes the center of each situation, so naturally does he belong where the moment finds him" (303). Matthiessen believes that Tukten is somehow known to him, like a dim figure from another life:

> Tukten himself seems aware that we are in some sort of relation, which he accepts in a way that I cannot; that he is not here by accident is, for me, a restless instinct, whereas he takes our peculiar bond for granted.

More often than I like, I feel that gaze of his, as if he were here to watch over me . . . the gaze is open, calm, benign, without judgment of any kind, and yet, confronted with it, as with a mirror, I am aware of all that is hollow in myself, all that is greedy, angry, and unwise. (53)

Tukten is never downhearted or tired and does not respond with sullenness or rudeness to Matthiessen's fits of temper, which amazes Matthiessen, given his own mood swings, his doubts and insecurities.

If Matthiessen's spiritual quest for thirty years has been to discover how he might lose self-consciousness and re-create frequently in daily life those rare moments when he has felt at one with everything, including his own past and present, then Tukten shows him the way. With his intellect and his energy, Matthiessen can learn about what he desires, but the next step is to not allow intellect to hold back the direct feeling of emotions, to hold back the world. At Kathmandu, finished with the journey, Matthiessen says goodbye to Tukten, only then realizing that although he had gone to the Crystal Mountain hoping that the Lama of Shey would be his teacher, his teacher had accompanied him on the entire journey, showing him how to live a Zen life: "Without ever attempting to speak about it . . . in his life in the moment, in his freedom from attachments, in the simplicity of his everyday example, Tukten has taught me over and over. . . . 'When you are ready,' Buddhists say, 'the teacher will appear.' In the way he watched me, in the way he smiled, he was awaiting me; had I been ready, he might have led me far enough along the path 'to see the snow leopard'" (316–17).

Because feelings of alienation and loneliness come from Matthiessen's following Western and masculine codes, human relationality to men leading lives far different than his own is one thread of Matthiessen's drama of self-creation. Equally important, he explores how he might move closer to the nonhuman world, a separation that likewise contributes to self-consciousness and its subsequent loneliness. I quote the following passage at length because it is a paradigmatic moment in *The Snow Leopard*, where Matthiessen's attention to the natural world makes for beautiful writing but does not bring him what he desires:

Wind brings swift, soft clouds from the south that cast shadows on the snow. Close at hand, a redstart comes to forage in the lichens, followed soon by a flock of fat rose finches. I do not stir, yet suddenly all whir away in a gray gust, and minutely I turn to see what might have scared them.

On a rock not thirty feet away, an accipitrine hawk sits in silhouette against the mountains, and here it hunches while the sun goes down, nape feathers lifting in the wind, before diving after unseen prey over the rim of the ravine. Then the great lammergeier comes, gold-headed and black-collared, a nine-foot blade sweeping down out of the north; it passes into the shadows between cliffs. Where the river turns, in a corner of the walls, the late sun shines on a green meadow, as if a lost world lay in that impenetrable ravine, so far below. The great bird arcs round the wall, light glancing from its mantle. Then it is gone, and the sun goes, the meadow vanishes, and the cold falls with the night shadow.

Still I sit a little while, watching the light rise to the peaks. In the boulder at my back, there is a shudder, so slight that at another time it might have gone unnoticed. The tremor comes again; the earth is nudging me. And still I do not see. (109)

Matthiessen, perhaps, seems too humble here; certainly this description is possible only because he pays close attention to what is visible and, furthermore, has considerable knowledge of the natural world. But his view is diminished, he suggests in that final paragraph, because it is a Western, naturalist's view. He cannot see as he wants to, see what he knows is just beyond him—cannot, that is, connect seeing to being.

In his long essay *Nature,* Ralph Waldo Emerson created a metaphor that has come to symbolize a transcendental moment when seeing merges into being:

Crossing a bare common, in snow puddles, at twilight, under a clouded sky, without having in my thoughts any occurrence of special good fortune, I have enjoyed a perfect exhilaration. . . . . There I feel that nothing can befall me in life,—no disgrace, no calamity, (leaving me my eyes,) which nature cannot repair. Standing on the bare ground,—my head bathed by the blithe air, and uplifted into infinite space,—all mean egotism vanishes. I become a transparent eye-ball. I am nothing. I see all. The currents of the Universal Being circulate through me; I am part or particle of God.[3]

There is, perhaps, no passage more useful for understanding Matthiessen's desires while he sits on the mountain, watching the lammergeier. Like Emerson, Matthiessen wishes to see everything and become nothing; if he can lose self-consciousness, he might become interwoven into the currents of the universal being. But this is exactly what he feels unable to do, even there.

On a religious pilgrimage, the physical journey takes on increasing significance when it becomes infused with the archetypal emotions and ideas of the spiritual quest; conversely, the ineffable spiritual path becomes partly expressible when language and images emerge from the activities of the earthly pilgrim. For instance, when Matthiessen successfully traverses a steep and narrow mountain path and is elated by the view of tremendous mountain peaks that greets him at the end, he notices, upon the path, "in the glint of mica and odd shining stones" a yellow and gray-blue feather of an unknown bird. This discovery leads suddenly to a revelation: "And there comes a piercing intuition, by no means understood, that in this feather on the silver path, this rhythm of wood and leather sounds, breath, sun and wind, and rush of river, in a landscape without past or future time—in this instant, in all instants, transience and eternity, death and life are one" (131–32). The moment is, for Matthiessen, a fine Zen moment, a fusion of the physical world, intellect, and emotion that can help him heal, can move him through his depression about his wife's death and his own emptiness at the core of his soul. And these moments are repeated during his journey: when he sees himself simultaneously as himself, the child he was, and the old man he will be (171); when he learns the "secret of the mountains" (212); when he thinks that he has grown into the mountains like moss, has become bewitched, and wishes never to leave the Crystal Mountain (232).

The arduousness of the journey, the immersion into Tibetan culture, the etched brilliance of the mountain peaks surrounding him— all of these begin to punch through Matthiessen's screens, to help him shed the armor of the I. He feels "open, clear, and childlike" in the snow mountains, "bathed by feelings" and near tears (169). Gazing at the Crystal Mountain and meditating one day, Matthiessen experiences his body dissolving into the sunlight, tears falling "that have nothing to do with 'I.' What it is that brings them on, I do not know" (248). He comes to "love the common miracles . . . the hardship and simplicity, the contentment of doing one thing at a time: when I take my blue tin cup into my hand, that is all I do" (232). Wind and sun, he says, pour through his head as through a bell; though he talks little, he is never lonely: "I am returned into myself" (232). In the United States, his days would be considered "empty," but he sees them as full—full of thinking, observing, meditating, walking.

At Crystal Mountain, Matthiessen comes to realize that his reasons for undertaking the quest have changed, and one measure of this transformation is his relinquishing the desire to see a snow leopard. Before he began the pilgrimage, Schaller had told him that only two Westerners (and he was one of them) in twenty-five years had ever laid eyes on the Himalayan snow leopard in the wild. In part because of the challenge, Matthiessen writes, "the hope of glimpsing this near-mythic beast in the snow mountains was reason enough for the entire journey" (3). By journey's middle, however, Matthiessen realizes that it would not be enough to see the snow leopard, because he wants most of all "to penetrate the secret of the mountains in search of something still unknown that . . . might well be missed for the very act of searching" (126). At Crystal Mountain, Matthiessen says, he is happy to know simply that the leopard exists and that it is around somewhere (242). Like the ox in the oxherding pictures' third phase of enlightenment, the snow leopard might one day reveal itself briefly, unexpectedly.

In his last days at Crystal Mountain, Matthiessen realizes that he will not, on this journey, gain a quiet, enduring acceptance of his life. But he has begun going down the right path: "[In] some way, on this journey, I have started home. Homegoing is the purpose of my practice, of my mountain meditation and my daybreak chanting, of my *koan:* All the peaks are covered with snow—why is this one bare? To resolve that illogical question would mean to burst apart, let fall all preconceptions and supports. But I am not ready to let go, and so I shall not resolve my *koan,* or see the snow leopard, that is to say, *perceive* it. I shall not see it because I am not ready" (256). Matthiessen links seeing to being, and though his weeks in the rarified air of the Crystal Mountain are marked by a level of openness and feeling that he had not achieved before, he is unable to sustain these feelings as he begins his trek back to civilization, back down the trails he had climbed, months before.

On this return trip, Matthiessen occasionally has moments of great joy, moments connected with the immediate present and memories of his past and present life. But more often, he is filled with dread, wanting simply to cover ground, put miles behind him. He notices little of the physical beauty about him, and reacts critically to the Tibetans who accompany him. He asks himself why he hurries so and wonders if he has learned nothing. Though he recognizes that after such an experience "it is crucial to emerge gradually from such a chrysalis, dry-

ing new wings in the sun's quiet, like a butterfly, to avoid a sudden tearing of the spirit" (297), he plunges anyway into savage self-scrutiny
where he decides that nothing has changed, that he is "still beset by the
same old lusts and ego and emotions, the endless nagging details and
irritations—that aching gap between what I know and what I am"
(298). The next day, Matthiessen feels less gloomy, recognizing that
"a change is taking place, some painful growth, as in a snake during
the shedding of its skin. . . . It is difficult to adjust because I do not
know who is adjusting; I am no longer that old person and not yet the
new" (300). This realization lightens his spirits, helps him leave "the
tragic sense of things behind." His mood rising, Matthiessen has an
epiphany that is, perhaps, the most important realization dramatized
in the text: "the journey to Dolpo, step by step and day by day, is the
Jewel in the Heart of the Lotus, the Tao, the Way, the Path, but no
more so than small events of days at home" (300). Knowing that his
transcendence will be fleeting, he is happy, anyway, "so light do I feel
that I might be back in the celestial snows" (301).

As a Westerner attempting to become an adept in an Eastern religion, Matthiessen believed that in order to move along the path toward enlightenment, extraordinary measures were necessary: an ar-
duous, dangerous trek, a religious pilgrimage to see the Lama of Shey.
His journey was to be an attempt to give him the power to proceed
with his ultimate pilgrimage, the discovering of the Buddha within
himself. Ironically, the journey is in large part paradoxical to the prin-
ciple in Zen that enlightenment is attained through staying put, living life simply, and sitting zazen (the Zen form of what Westerners
call meditation). A question remains: Is Matthiessen undertaking a
religious pilgrimage to gain a mode of being that is not fully possible
for him? Or does the pilgrimage help him construct a self that, while
not totally "Zen-like," is altered enough to help him move out of depression and through mourning? Upon his return, he looks into a
mirror for the first time in months and sees "the face of a man I do
not know" (317). He does know that the journey has transformed him,
but he is uncertain in what directions the transformation will lead.
Most crucial for him, however, is his newly won ability to simply accept, not fear, change itself.

Near the town of Gaya, in the fifth century, Sakyamuni—later to be
known as Sakyamuni Buddha, or "the awakened one"—sat beneath

a pipal tree, vowing that he would meditate and not move until he had attained supreme enlightenment. A Buddhist temple now stands beside an ancient descendant of that *bodhi* tree, or enlightenment tree, and one night before beginning his journey, Matthiessen sat underneath that tree with three Tibetan monks to watch the rising of the morning star. He came away, however, "no wiser than before" (19).

The Snow Leopard dramatizes many such moments, where Matthiessen places or finds himself in situations where he attempts to replicate the experiences of a Buddhist. If he is unsuccessful at the time, unable to get outside his ordinary consciousness, he does have, in effect, a chance for a different kind of success at the time of writing, when he can recount the event and surround it with a context that provides compensatory gain. In one sense, this is what Hubbell, Williams, Barich, and Heat-Moon do also—they seek experience that will divert them, or teach them, and then in the autobiographical act they discover and create a construction of that experience that is ultimately therapeutic. This certainly does not mean that they falsify experiences. Matthiessen, like the others, seems almost painfully scrupulous to record every up and down of his travels and his pysche. And he knows that any falsifying would hinder his quest and be alien to his pilgrimage. But for Matthiessen, the undertaking of a mystic quest in the heart of a Buddhist culture becomes therapeutic (if not enlightening) in part because of the immense knowledge he acquires by doing so.

Compared with *A Country Year, Refuge, Laughing in the Hills,* or *Blue Highways,* Matthiessen's book is learned, even scholarly. *The Snow Leopard* has footnotes. Matthiessen immersed himself in scholarly works about Zen Buddhism and in the travel narratives of everyone who ever journeyed in Tibet, and he weaves into his story extensive information about the history of Zen Buddhism and the history and culture of the Tibetan peoples he encounters. For example, when he passes a lone hut displaying a brightly colored fresco of seven Buddha figures symbolizing Sakyamuni's life, Matthiessen discusses how Buddhists adapted and adopted local deities rather than eradicate the old religions:

In the first centuries after Sakyamuni's death, certain yoga teachings of Vedic origin became systematized in esoteric treatises, called Tantras (it is sometimes claimed that they are the fifth Veda) and the Tantric influences of these yoga cults brought about the creation of female wisdom principles. . . . By the sixth century A.D., Tantric worship of female energies was dominant in both Hinduism and Mahayana Buddhism, and it was this Tantric form of Buddhism that was carried north into Tibet. (116–17)

Matthiessen continues with a three-page history of the interminglings of Eastern religions in that specific area of Tibet. At such times, Matthiessen presents this information as if it is important for its own sake, as if his audience were readers who would have prior interest in the subject. At other times, he weaves the information into his personal quest. For example, before he writes about sitting under the enlightenment tree in imitation of the Buddha, he summarizes Sakyamuni's Four Noble Truths, which have a resonance because of their relation to Matthiessen's needs: "that man's existence is inseparable from sorrow; that the cause of suffering is craving; that peace is attained by extinguishing craving; that this liberation may be brought about by following the Eight-fold Path: right attention to one's understanding, intentions, speech, and actions; right livelihood, effort, mindfulness; right concentration, by which is meant the unification of the self through sitting yoga" (17).

As I have discussed in earlier chapters, all autobiographers dramatize, implicitly if not explicitly, that their books are fusions of two stories, past and present, the events as they were lived through and the autobiographical act that constructs those events into story. What Matthiessen shows in *The Snow Leopard* is an unusual, self-conscious purpose for the past and present stories. His pilgrimage is a deliberate setting forth to live a kind of life and to have experiences that will teach him about his life's purposes, that will show him what his past might mean. In the book, Matthiessen structures this story by creating a present sequence of events, writing the narrative in present tense, and referring back to the rest of his life to show what is at stake for him emotionally and spiritually. The autobiographical act has then a twofold purpose: Matthiessen dramatizes the hard-won emotional gains of the pilgrimage and simultaneously grounds himself intellectually in Buddhism, both of which are useful for his grief work. In this respect, he comes close to exemplifying what Paul de Man suggests in "Autobiography as de-Facement," that the autobiographical project produces and determines the life as much as the life produces the autobiography.[4]

The Snow Leopard, although in journal form, is not unedited notes from Matthiessen's journey. The two years after his return to the United States were for Matthiessen a time of intense Zen practice, during which he sat zazen daily and participated in frequent sesshin (three- to seven-day retreats), putting in long hours crosslegged in the lotus position. When this infatuation with Zen practice subsided, when "the flowers were just flowers once again" (*Nine-Headed Dragon River,* 64), Matthiessen turned to writing *The Snow Leopard.*[5] In addition to shaping and polishing his journals from the Himalayan trek, he read deeply about Zen Buddhism, gaining from his study immense knowledge that he then wove into his narrative. This intertwining of event and learning is one of the distinctive features of Matthiessen's autobiographical act.

Though Matthiessen begins his pilgrimage with some knowledge and experience of the cultures he will encounter, he becomes more of an insider as he travels and again as he studies and contemplates the culture from afar. Matthiessen has written numerous books of nonfiction about the natural world and primitive peoples. His writing is marked by his careful attention to detail, to getting the "facts" right, and so he routinely submits his manuscripts to expert naturalists, anthropologists, zoologists, or ornithologists (depending on what disciplines bear on his work).[6] Because Matthiessen tries to understand his experiences with Tibetan culture and Zen Buddhism in this same way, one of the basic issues he explores is how he can trust his interpretation of what he sees, which leads him to his experiential insights about the differences between Western and Eastern ways of seeing. Because he desires to "transcend" his ego and lessen his grief, he pursues the study and practice of Zen Buddhism; because he knows that Western modes of perception can hinder understanding of Eastern experience, he studies Zen Buddhism to help him shape his observations of and reflections about Tibetan life. That is, Matthiessen's own personal needs and his religious interests spiral together, the dramatization of which becomes a spiritual autobiography, like Augustine's *Confessions* or Kathleen Norris's recent *Dakota.*

Ironically, the act of writing an autobiography and the text itself—a journal with daily dated entries, scholarly footnotes to identify sources, and maps to orient those who desire to follow the journey—perhaps measure best how impossible it is for him to get outside Western consciousness. By its very nature, autobiography demands and promotes self-consciousness, self-scrutiny. A narrative that creates simple cause and effect, that implies a logic, seems at odds with a meditation that is supposed to empty the mind, "to return it to the clear, pure stillness of a seashell or a flower petal" (91). Autobiography, as text, is in an altogether different dimension than a *koan*, "a Zen paradox, not to be solved by intellect, that may bring about a sudden dissolution of logical thought and clear the way for direct *seeing* into the heart of existence" (130). Before Matthiessen had left on his journey, his Zen master, Eido Roshi, had given him a *koan* to contemplate: "All the peaks are covered with snow—why is this one bare?" If Zen sitting is intended to make concepts such as death, life, time, space, past, and future disappear in order to lay one open to the fullness of the moment, then the writing of *The Snow Leopard* seems to the layman to be antithetical to such enterprise.

I bring up these points only to suggest that a "Zen autobiography" is probably an impossibility for Matthiessen. But if he is unable to get into the enlightened mindset, unable to transcend ego so that, for him, all existence would collapse into the One, he has accomplished much for himself, in a Western way, by creating an explanatory narrative. The trek through the Himalayas, he said, pointed the way home, even though he is not ready at the end of the journey to live in the moment, away from the past and the grieving that is there for Deborah's death. At least, in writing *The Snow Leopard* Matthiessen fashions a text of consolation and compensation to fill the hollow in his heart.

7 Making a Home on the Range

Gretel Ehrlich's *The Solace of Open Spaces* and Western Myths

We all know now how the founding of the American West was made legendary, was and is romanticized. We know that there were and are many Wests, and that this "founding" of a land that had been found centuries before uprooted long-established cultures of Native Americans and Mexicans. We know that the history of the European-settled West is most notable for its boom-and-bust cycles, for how states took government handouts while proclaiming independence. But years after the correctives, we also realize how enduring are the heroic images of Western frontier life.[1]

James Olney has written, in words numerous critics have echoed, that autobiography is "the most elusive of literary documents" ("Cultural Moment," 3–4), and perhaps even more than the books by Barich, Williams, Heat-Moon, Matthiessen, and Hubbell, Gretel Ehrlich's collection of essays about Wyoming, *The Solace of Open Spaces,* appears elusive and resists definition. The other writers, even if their subject matters and book structures are not the usual fare for autobiographies, do describe events in a span of time; Ehrlich, however, makes no chronological beginning, middle, and end, and instead the book's structure dramatizes Ehrlich's slowly understood realization that Wyoming is indeed where she belongs, where she has made "home." Perhaps, one might argue, Ehrlich's book is not an autobiography and she is simply writing a series of personal essays about Wyoming, particularly given that several chapters of the book were first published individually. But the new essays, the way Ehrlich arranges the sequence of chapters, and the material she includes about her fiancé David's death suggest that she is doing grief work by constructing a life-story that will give meaning to her past as it is lived from the present into the future.

In the preface to *The Solace of Open Spaces,* Ehrlich says it is "impossible to speak of writing this book without mentioning the circumstances and transitions taking place in my life at the time" (ix), though interestingly she alludes only to a "tragedy" that disoriented her, that made it difficult for her to know exactly where she was. She explains that what she did know was that she had no desire to resume her life in New York City, with old friends and familiar comforts. Though friends asked her when she was going to stop "hiding out" in Wyoming, she recognized that "for the first time [she] was able to take up residence on earth with no alibis, no self-promoting schemes" (ix).

Ehrlich wrote her book in "fits and starts"; it began in the form of raw journal entries sent to a friend in Hawaii. Explaining the choice of this friend to read her journal, Ehrlich writes: "I chose her because she had been raised in a trailerhouse behind a bar in Wyoming; she then made the outlandish leap to a tropical climate and a life in academia. I was jumping in the opposite direction and suspected we might have crossed paths midair somewhere" (x). The move to Wyoming, Ehrlich says, was a long, arbitrary detour, until she recognized that the detour had become the actual path; likewise, in her writing, the "digressions" about Wyoming become her story.

Similar to Hubbell in *A Country Year* questioning remaining on her Ozark farm, Ehrlich is wondering whether to stay in Wyoming. In an autobiography, the writer's "story" is, as Olney says, half-discovered in memory and half-created by writing, and likewise Ehrlich is half-discovering and half-creating what in Wyoming might make it "home." Ehrlich takes up familiar subjects that have been essential to the mythmaking of the West: cowboys, rodeos, ranch life, sheepherding, the Indian Sun Dance, Wyoming weather and landscape. The book records Ehrlich's intellectual and emotional sorting through of her responses to these Western images, to Western life and landscape. Reacting strongly to animals, to cowboys, to ranching women, and to the forbidding, harsh landscape, she discovers useful relations among human and nonhuman others previously unknown to her, all of whom aid her act of self-creation by teaching her about what she is coming to love.

In unfamiliar territory, literally and figuratively, Ehrlich performs a literary act of grief work by pursuing what Wyoming might mean to her linguistically and psychologically. She weaves sketches of Wyoming life and people, near-ecstatic celebrations of landscape, and descriptions of her own recovery from loss. Collectively, the essays in *The Solace of Open Spaces* become an autobiography of a grieving woman who finds in her construction of "Wyoming" the rhythms of and pattern for a satisfying and purposeful life.

Nonfiction is often read naively: as if it isn't shaped, as if the text's structure does not influence a reader's understanding, and as if the content, the "information," is all that matters. Fiction, of course, invites interpretation at all times: reading parts in terms of the whole, which is understood because of the parts, and so on in that delightful process often called the hermeneutic circle. Though Ehrlich cannot create a structure or invent stories in the way fiction writers can (if she does so, she cheats the writer-reader "pact" of autobiography),[2] she does interpret life symbolically in her present attempts to endow it with meaning.

With her first chapter, "The Solace of Open Spaces," Ehrlich intertwines information and art to enact implicitly a process of self-creation. She begins with a sentence that works rhetorically on several levels: "It's May and I've just awakened from a nap, curled against sagebrush the way my dog taught me to sleep—sheltered from wind" (1). There's a double awakening here, for the natural world and Ehrlich, and though only the first is explicit (by human knowledge of spring's rebirth), Ehrlich's awakening works symbolically. At a different rhetorical level, the first sentence plunges most readers into an unusual world, where humans nap (outdoors, no less) during the day, where they look to their dogs for instruction, where they are sheltered from the natural world, the wind, by only one of the flimsier plants, sagebrush. In following sentences, Ehrlich quickly sketches her situation: she is herding sheep in bad weather, high in the mountain plateaus of Wyoming. Though herding the sheep is difficult, it seems far preferable to what she has come through. Ehrlich opens her next paragraph by saying "winter lasts six months here," and in winter "the landscape hardens into a dungeon" where your mind and body do not work (1). Whether her mind and body function or not, a rancher does work, often outside, and during one of those dungeon days, riding to find a new calf, finding her jeans frozen to the saddle, Ehrlich says that "in the silence that such cold creates I felt like the first person on earth, or the last" (2).

That such moments give her life meaning, Ehrlich says, is unfathomable to most people who have either driven through Wyoming as if there's nothing to stop for or who have skied in Jackson Hole. For the epigraph to her book, Ehrlich uses several lines from Joseph Brodsky's poem "Strophes," including the following: "And geography blended / with time equals destiny." The geography that Ehrlich begins with, Wyoming's vast landscape, is crucial for many reasons, but none more so as this chapter unfolds than how it affects Ehrlich's perceptions of everything around her. "To live and work in this kind of open country," she writes, "with its hundred-mile views, is to lose the distinction between background and foreground" (2). Having lost that orienting view, she is unsure of what she sees or feels, is unsure as to what Wyoming is to her. And other people, she quickly realizes, can't help her know. Even for people who have lived in Wyoming all their lives, the high plains and higher mountains mean different things. Ehrlich quotes two old-timers whose beliefs are contradictory and therefore of little help: to one, Wyoming is "all a bunch of nothing—wind and rattlesnakes—and so much of it you can't tell where you're going or where you've been"; to the other, "Open space hasn't affected me at all. It's all the people moving in on it" (2). Ehrlich will need to find her own description, which is what the rest of the essay (and on a grander scale, the book) tries to do.

Ehrlich begins her second section of the essay by implying why orientation—seeing and feeling—has been so important to her: "I came here four years ago. I had not planned to stay, but I couldn't make myself leave" (3). The second sentence is interesting grammatically because, though it suggests that she has no volition, it is in active voice. Things have worked on her, kept her in Wyoming, though she is unsure what they are, having lost the ability in this strange land to understand background and foreground, what is important and what is less important. Her life in Wyoming, so different from what she came from, has separated her from the habits of seeing and feeling built up over a lifetime. Her unsureness leads to paradox or to contradiction, which is another way of saying that she has lost the ability to judge. These early pages of the essay, much of the "introduction" readers get to Wyoming and to Ehrlich's mind, work by contrasts. As with her effective turn of phrase, "first person on earth, or the last," she writes: "Instead of producing the numbness I thought I wanted, life on the sheep ranch woke me up" (3–4); "The arid country was a clean slate. Its absolute indifference steadied me" (4); "Despite the desolate look, there's a coziness to living in this state" (4); "Longing for human company, I felt a foolish grin take over my face; yet I had to resist an urgent temptation to run and hide" (5); "good-naturedness is concomitant with severity" (5). Often, the contrasts mirror what is, for Ehrlich, the state's chief characteristic, that "Things happen suddenly in Wyoming, the change of seasons and weather; for people, the violent swings in and out of isolation" (5).

Recognizing early the attraction this life has for her, Ehrlich makes herself anew on the surface. She cuts her hair, throws away her city clothes. The changes, one imagines, allow her to do ranching work better. But cutting hair and getting new clothes is also a way for her to announce a fresh start, to begin the process that will result in her becoming, as she says, a "culture straddler," one who is both insider and outsider. Becoming an insider takes much more, of course, than these kinds of changes. She learns that ranch work "is a matter of vigor, self-reliance, and common sense" (5), and that she can slowly acquire those attributes. She learns that ranch work is lonely, with periods of solitude broken only occasionally by human contact, though the infrequent community and the absolute need to rely on one's neighbors makes human relations seem more important than in other places. What ranch life adds up to is a model of living far different than the one she had before. On the range, she says to conclude this second section of the essay, "a person's life is not a series of dramatic events for which he or she is applauded or exiled but a slow accumulation of days, seasons, years, fleshed out by the generational weight of one's family and anchored by a land-bound sense of place" (5). In this striking statement, Ehrlich demonstrates that she has come to understand what might give her a satisfying life, though she also suggests, ironically, that she will always in a sense remain the outsider (therefore a culture straddler) because she does not have that "generational weight" of family on her side.

In an astute piece of social psychology, *Mindfulness,* Ellen Langer shows how people usually go through their daily lives on a kind of mental cruise control, what she calls mindlessness. Mindless people, she asserts, are often trapped by categories, or behave automatically as if there is one set of rules, or act only from a single perspective. To help increase mind*ful*ness, a person must become more aware of process, of context, and of having more than one view. In one sense, getting past grief is learning, again, to be mindful. The mourning makes the griever see in only one way and one context: through the framework of grieving, through the frame of loss and diminishment.

One way to describe Ehrlich's sense of audience (and therefore what she chooses to write about and how) is to say that she writes as an outsider now turned culture straddler to the outsiders who are curious. That is, she seems at times to be explaining herself to people on the East or West Coast, explaining why someone like her would choose to live in Wyoming. Equally important, however, she seems to be making herself mindful once again by marshaling reasons for herself, marshaling ways of constructing a life and thinking about Wyoming that serve her. As she describes Wyoming, what she tackles indirectly in the next sections of the essay are issues or problems that she must face if she is to live there. By finding deeply felt resolutions to those issues, Ehrlich can, in essence, answer those friends who think Wyoming is "a landscape of lunar desolation and intellectual backwardness."

One such issue concerns the paucity of talking. "The solitude in which Westerners live makes them quiet," Ehrlich writes. "They telegraph thoughts and feelings by the way they tilt their heads and listen" (6). She describes meals eaten without any words being said except a "thank you" at the end; she describes driving with company in a pickup and spending hours in total silence. Imagining Ehrlich's previous life in California and New York City, a life of intellectual and emotional talk, one could well believe Ehrlich's surprise at this. And yet she finds compensatory rewards: "Instead of talking, we share one eye. Keenly observed, the world is transformed. The landscape is engorged with detail . . . the air between people is charged" (7). Silence, she says, becomes profound. For the Westerners she is coming to know, there is "no vocabulary for the subject of feelings." Conversation that she does have often goes on in what seems a private code, in which "a few phrases imply a complex of meanings" (6). Sentence structure "is shortened to the skin and bones of a thought," with adjectives, adverbs, and sometimes even verbs dropped out. But what emerges is something she values, because "language, so compressed, becomes metaphorical" (6). She cites as an example a rancher who ended a relationship with one remark—"You're a bad check."

When Ehrlich takes up spring weather, she indirectly writes again about what is not there, what she can't expect. The weather is not temperate and beneficial, but a weather of extremes. It is "capricious and mean," she says, snowing one day and then being extremely hot the next. It is weather that breeds tornadoes. The aridity means that she cannot take water for granted (water, she writes, "is like blood"), and the one constant in the weather is the wind, "the meticulous gardener" shaping the landscape. Wyoming is one of the windiest places in the country and she has a "romance with this wind-swept state" (8). Romance for one is nightmare to another, however, and in the next section of her essay, about wilderness and settlement, Ehrlich contrasts the ways Native Americans roamed the land, at home in large spaces, with the sodbusters who arrived on the high plains encumbered with ways that could not be transplanted. "The emptiness of the West" was simply hardship for them. But for others who arrived, without family perhaps, with no intention of farming, Wyoming was "a geography of possibility." Territorial Wyoming "was a boy's world," with "room enough, food enough, for everyone," at first. But boys grow up, and "history" gets complicated, as Ehrlich shows by telling brief stories of Wyoming's cowboy past, the range wars between the wealthy and the poor, the fencing of the vast land that made it seem lesser.

The legacy of the frontier past is continued when Ehrlich takes up values and morality. She believes that in Wyoming honesty and rock-bottom truths are more important than conventional morality. People are blunt with one another, strong on scruples, but also tenderhearted about quirky behavior. The Western Code, "a list of practical do's and don'ts," arises from the contradictions of Western life, from a blending of "formality that goes hand in hand with the rowdiness" (11). Knowing the history of one's region is important to feel connected to place, but it is difficult to tell whether Ehrlich is glorifying Wyoming's frontier past or criticizing it. On one hand, she laments the lawlessness, the murders over land, the way fencing abrogated space and caused the loss of the land's integrity as a geographical body, and yet she also believes that such living generated individualism and optimism that have endured. These qualities, prominent in Western myths, she finds life-enhancing—not surprisingly, we might say, for someone who is moving through stages of grieving.

In general, Ehrlich views optimistically the possibilities of present-day life in Wyoming, but she is equally aware of how such life can go wrong. "The dark side to the grandeur of these spaces," she writes, "is the small-mindedness that seals people in. Men become hermits; women go mad. Cabin fever explodes into suicides, or into grudges and lifelong family feuds" (13). The trick, Ehrlich implies in the passage, is to be large-minded, not small-minded; when she begins a new section immediately, without commentary, about a pack trip she took into the mountains, she suggests that one can open oneself to ranching life and the natural world in such a way that the gains outnumber the losses.

Ehrlich structures her essay as a series of short vignettes—a collage of facts, impressions, history, anecdotes, description—whose connections must be made by the reader. But in the final section of the essay, she speaks her message directly. "Space represents sanity, not a life purified, dull, or 'spaced out' but one that might accommodate intelligently any idea or situation" (15). "Americans are great on fillers," writes Ehrlich, using the mineral bentonite (a filler in candy, gum, and lipstick) as a metaphor: "[it is] as if what we have, what we are, is not enough." We build our houses against space, we fill up space when we can, which only "further obstructs our ability to see what is already there" (15). Past uncertainty, Ehrlich has moved away from paradox, contradiction, multiple possibilities. She defends what her city friends would misunderstand or despise. The solace of open spaces has led to a gradually growing love for Wyoming, a love revealed in this sweeping description of landscape, history, and people.

Because *The Solace of Open Spaces* is a book about psychological rebirth, Ehrlich must give us the "death." The second essay in the book, "Obituary," tells the demise of a once-thriving, eighty-seven-year-old sheep ranch, a "miniature society" that only eight years previously employed a hundred hands. In particular, Ehrlich is interested in the sheepherders who live a nomadic, isolated life tending the sheep. The herders still live alone in wagons, moving the animals during the summer from one pasture to another. "In the hierarchy of a ranch," Ehrlich writes, "herders are second-class citizens," because "to have chosen a life of solitude is seen as a sign of failure" (20–21). The similarities to Ehrlich herself, a different kind of outsider who has recently left a city life to live in Wyoming, are obvious, and she writes affectionately about these people, suggesting that in their isolation "they may learn what makes the natural world tick and how to stay sane" (21). But she recognizes the cost paid for abandoning the world, as in essence these sheepherders have done, not for reasons of spiritual transformation but for social defects: "women troubles, alcohol, low self-esteem" (21). A suicide, a jailing, an accidental death, their binge drinking—these seem an inevitable part of the sheepherding life.

In the book's third chapter, "Other Lives," Ehrlich turns directly to her past, writing about the trauma that precipitated her depression, showing us implicitly why she identifies with the sheepherders. Without this story, *The Solace of Open Spaces* would be a different book, a rich but rather straightforward description of people, places, events. When Ehrlich, then a New York filmmaker, went to Wyoming to film a PBS documentary on sheepherders, her fiancé and partner in the project, David, had to stay in New York because he had developed cancer. In "Other Lives" she describes him, their love, the initial hope that his cancer would go into remission and they could have a life together, and the subsequent realization that there would be no remission. He eventually joined her in Wyoming, but stayed only briefly because the majestic landscape reminded him of possibility, of the life they couldn't have. After he left, Ehrlich says, the film "became an absurd chore," and every few days she would drive down the mountain to call him, to listen to his increasingly thinner voice. On the day she was packed and ready to fly east to see him, she received the phone call telling of his death.

After David's death, Ehrlich writes, "a wheel of emptiness turned inside me and churned there for a long time" (39). She writes of traveling for two years trying to escape the grief, but it is only after returning to Wyoming, taking up a life of ranching mixed with intervals of solitude, and writing about her new life, that the past becomes less debilitating. In *A Grief Observed*, C. S. Lewis notes that mourning is not a state but a process, needing not a map but a history (47), and in the essay "Other Lives" Ehrlich gives a concise history of her sorrow and how she gradually begins to feel it less intensely when she works as a ranch hand, learning endurance and toughness, when women befriend her, when she spends a winter alone, hoping "that solitude might work as an antidote to solitude" (42). And it does, partially. Ehrlich discovers in Wyoming's open spaces and extremes of weather a hard life that scrubs her from the inside out. "True solace is finding none, which is to say, it is everywhere," she writes. She comes to like the openness of the Western landscape and links the spaces with her emotional recovery: "Space has a spiritual equivalent and can heal what is divided and burdensome in us." The following spring, she moves to Shell, a town of fifty people, where she meets several women who ranch alone or with their husbands, and they mentor her and model for her the life she could lead there. She meets a man who is attracted to her, and she surprises herself when she responds to him. "For the first time," she writes, "the concussive pain I had been living with began to ebb. One never gets over a death, but the pain was mixed now with tonic undulations" (48).

"Other Lives," the most revealing essay in the book about Ehrlich's past, shows that the creation of "Wyoming" has significant personal meanings for Ehrlich because of David's death. From the time she moves to Wyoming, feeling depressed and wondering what life is good for, until she begins to consider staying there, and on until she and her new husband buy a ranch high in the Big Horn Mountains, Ehrlich is involved in a drama, a life-story full of turns and twists and reevaluations, that she constructs and reconstructs in memory and then in writing. Like many who went to the unsettled or frontier West, Ehrlich confronts the landscape and myths that both attract and threaten her. She enacts in her writing how her need to find language to describe this new place is essential to her evolving selfhood. These first three essays of the book function as a unit, in that they introduce "Wyoming" and show Ehrlich's recent past, which includes trauma and loss. In the essays following "Other Lives," we begin to glimpse how Ehrlich constructs Wyoming to serve her. From here on, the essays as a whole will focus on subjects that Ehrlich uses to demonstrate her recovery from that loss, subjects that she uses to write a relational autobiography.

In *The Children at Santa Clara*, a book that likewise blends documentary and autobiography, Elizabeth Marek describes a year she worked in New Mexico at a center for emotionally disturbed children who had been through horrific family experiences. Marek fled there from Harvard University when she was twenty years old, unable to continue her studies:

> I had lost my self, submerged it in a sea of demands and expectations.
> I had made myself up according to too many scripts. I was the under-

standing girlfriend . . . the cheerful friend . . . the sane, successful daughter. If I stopped playing any of those roles, there, at Harvard, at home, I risked losing the love I knew in my heart was based on their convincing enactment. But if I could get away, go somewhere that no one knew me, I would be free to invent myself for myself, to make myself over, at last, in my own image.

Marek's words give a personal spin, her feeling of being submerged by too many different demands, on an experience remarkably American, lighting out for the territories, inventing oneself anew. In one sense, Ehrlich does likewise, though her efforts differ from Marek's in two ways. Ehrlich fashions this new self by taking on the traditionally "male" versions of laborer and provider; and unlike Marek, who after a year returns to Cambridge and her family, Ehrlich stays in her chosen place, weaving herself into the web of life there.

Ehrlich composes the story of this life to make a "truth" *for herself* that will serve as grief work, doing consciously and carefully in an extended way what all humans do in their minds—using language to express what is remembered and observed, structuring memories and observations into story. Memory, we might say, is simply our latest "version" of an event or scene, our most recent storytelling. But writing can alter that memory, can turn disabling loss into manageable sorrow. Ehrlich's construction of a text that we might call "Wyoming," her observations and feelings articulated into stories, give her reasons to live there. Wendell Berry is fond of saying that if you don't know *where* you are, you don't know *who* you are, and Ehrlich's writing suggests that she would like that formulation.

Like the other writers in this study—Barich, Heat-Moon, Matthiessen, Hubbell, and Williams—Ehrlich exemplifies that people's sense of their lives is "dramaturgical," to use Claspell's and Cochran's phrase, and that someone who is grieving has had their life-meaning shattered. Moving through the mourning process depends, then, on the person's ability to construct a new drama to give meaning to past, present, and future experiences. Ehrlich's chapters function as pieces of a puzzle that, once put together, display a newly written dramatic story, one that heals and shows healing.

Annie Dillard, on the paperback cover of *The Solace of Open Spaces,* is quoted saying that "Wyoming has found its Whitman," and indeed the book was widely reviewed and widely acclaimed, particularly by the Eastern establishment where Ehrlich is well connected. She won an award from the American Academy of Arts and Letters. The book's individual chapters immediately became popular pieces for composition anthologies and collections of "nature writing." But literary criticism didn't follow.

In her recent book, *Landscapes of the New West: Gender and Geography in Contemporary Women's Writing* (1999), Krista Comer, noting the abundance of criticism on writers such as Leslie Marmon Silko, Maxine Hong Kingston, Louise Erdrich, and Sandra Cisneros, asks this provocative question: "As of mid-1998, hardly a single critical piece has been published about the most popular of white women writers: Barbara Kingsolver, Terry Tempest Williams, Mary Clearman Blew, Kim Barnes, Gretel Ehrlich, or Pam Houston. Why?" (8).[3] The answer is complex and individual, certainly, but at a meeting of the Western Literature Association in the early 1990s, at which I delivered a paper on Ehrlich, I discovered that not all avid readers of Western literature like Wyoming's new Whitman. When a large group talked informally about Ehrlich's book, only myself and one other person expressed admiration; the other person was an Easterner, coincidentally. The rest of the group revealed ambivalence or even hostility to the book. Since then I have spoken to other Western academics with a similar perspective. Criticisms range widely. Some say the book is overwritten, overly dramatic. A woman raised on a ranch was furious with Ehrlich for even presuming to write about rodeos, horses, or ranching—a view suggesting to me the classic mistrust of established generations for the newly arrived. Other less personal objections raised intriguing intellectual issues, and I began to understand how this text becomes, in an academic context, entwined in the recent scholarly arguments about the history and literature of the American West.

In her essay "What on Earth Is the New Western History?" Patricia Limerick summarizes the work of the "New Western" historians by emphasizing their rejection of three things: one, "the old model" of progress and improvement; two, Frederick Jackson Turner's frontier thesis; and three, an exclusively white-male viewpoint. These revisionist historians, among them Donald Worster, Elliott West, and Peggy Pascoe, as well as Limerick, stress continuities in Western history—the repeated boom-and-bust cycles, the central role of the government, the importance of ethnic and racial groups to this history, the eternal attempts to find a "solution" to the aridity of the region.

Revisionist historians are as likely to focus on Western urban centers as on the rural West, as likely to develop insights from Western banking as from ranching. Literary criticism of Western literature has gone down the same trail, for the most part. Whereas writers who wrote about life in cities or suburbs once were not seen as "Western," a less narrow geography and a rejection of the frontier myth means that these are also important writers for understanding Western experience, as are the many superb Native American, Chicano/Chicana, and Asian American writers who address the impact of their peoples on Western life, whether the past or the present.

The West, once a relatively unexamined historical site for environmental, gender, and racial issues, now seems a battleground. Not only does Ehrlich's book lie outside these newer concerns, these attempts by many Westerners to establish a less mythic, less narrow, more inclusive history and literature, but her support of ranch life has put her in opposition to those who view cowboy mythology as a danger to important things such as conservation of the land and issues of justice.[4] And for those still compelled by the traditional myths, *The Solace of Open Spaces* can be disliked anyway. It doesn't celebrate the cowboy myth in the kind of provocative way that Pam Houston, for example, has done with her collection of short stories *Cowboys Are My Weakness,* in which Houston's women narrators like men distilled to pure, tough, "cowboy" essence. The responses to *The Solace of Open Spaces* suggest that books about the West are being increasingly reacted to in rather narrow "political" ways.

Battlefields demand participants to be on one side or the other, but Ehrlich frustrates such a wish. In a Bakhtinian interpretation of the book, "Desire of the Middle Ground: Opposition, Dialectics, and Dialogic Context in Gretel Ehrlich's *The Solace of Open Spaces,*" Bonney MacDonald focuses on Ehrlich's trope of the "culture straddler," saying that an "open exchange is generated at the interface between Ehrlich, the observer and interested visitor on the one hand, and the Western community and culture on the other. . . . She does not completely impose an eastern literary training in order to reshape or overtake her surroundings, nor does she attempt to discard her background to become indistinguishable from the Wyoming setting. She stands in both places at once and enacts, in so doing, what Bakhtin takes to be central to dialogic encounters with another person or culture" (144). Ehrlich stands alternately on both sides, insider and outsider at one and the same time. Or, to be more precise, Ehrlich wishes to describe and then inhabit common ground that has led her to a new understanding of herself, her grief, and her future life.[5]

Much of that common ground centers on one important reality in every rancher's life: physical labor, done outdoors, that involves birth and death. From her immersion in ranching labor comes Ehrlich's new and healing understandings of her life and desires. She does not get them from the usual autobiographical source, the memory. Her important relations are fresh things she is encountering—cowboys, animals, and the landscape—which help shape her self-creation. Ehrlich first went to Wyoming to make a documentary on sheepherders; when she returns, depressed and aimless, she herself hires out on a sheep ranch. Hard physical work mixed with solitude combine to begin her regeneration. In the chapter "From a Sheepherder's Notebook: Three Days," Ehrlich equates what she learns about herding sheep with what she is learning about herself. She finds the unpredictability disconcerting and attractive at the same time. She has to move sheep who follow their own unfathomable desires, who can scatter because of a rainstorm or for reasons known only to sheep. Her attention to the sheep makes her intensely aware of her surroundings: she likes morning when "blue air comes ringed with coyotes" (56); she is ecstatic when she reaches a mountain ridge that gives her a hundred-mile view. "To herd sheep," Ehrlich writes, "is to discover a new human gear somewhere between second and reverse—a slow, steady trot of keenness with no speed." Despite all of this, she recognizes, however, that something is missing: "The constant movement of sheep from water hole to water hole, from camp to camp, becomes a form of longing. But for what?" (59).

The answer to her question starts to come clear for Ehrlich when she moves across the state to the small town of Shell and begins cowboying. When she takes up, in her essays, the subject of cowboys, we, too, begin to see the answer. In several ways, a cowboy's life is similar to that of a sheepherder's: the work takes patience; they both toil outdoors with animals; they often drift from job to job, ranch to ranch. And yet cowboying is fundamentally different, Ehrlich suggests, in that the sheepherders pay a high price for their apartness, for their inability or lack of desire to be with others. Ehrlich's longing is for community, and cowboys are part of various communities.

Ehrlich admires cowboys, and many of her observations seem aimed to overturn the stereotypes usually associated with them, to overturn the myth of the quintessential Western man. When Philip Morris, in 1954 the country's smallest cigarette maker, decided to change the image of its Marlboro brand cigarette, it went to a Chicago ad agency to design a campaign. The agency decided that the cowboy was the most masculine American image, and so the Marlboro Man—strong, silent, tough—"became" the cowboy. The figures on those Marlboro ads, Ehrlich says in her essay "About Men," reminded her of no one she knew in Wyoming: "In our hellbent earnestness to romanticize the cowboy we've ironically disesteemed his true character" (49). What Ehrlich sees and esteems is an "odd mixture of physical vigor and maternalism." Toughness masks tenderness: "Ranchers are midwives, hunters, nurturers, providers, and conservationists all at once" (51). Though they don't "know how to bring tenderness into the house" and "they lack the vocabulary to express the complexity of what they feel," it is not because cowboys make themselves invulnerable, hard: "Because these men work with animals, not machines or numbers, because they live outside in landscapes of torrential beauty, because they are confined to a place and routine embellished with awesome variables, because calves die in the arms that pulled others into life, because they go to the mountains as if on a pilgrimage to find out what makes a herd of elk tick, their strength is also a softness, their toughness, a rare delicacy" (52–53).

Another Westerner might disagree with Ehrlich's interpretation of cowboy character, or might argue that she, though in a different way than Philip Morris did, simply romanticizes cowboys, but what we see in these ideas is Ehrlich creating a "story" of cowboying that is useful to her. For example, Ehrlich wants to turn upside down the notion of what toughness is, which, she says, is not "a martyred doggedness, a dumb heroism," but "the art of accommodation." "To be tough," she writes, "is to be fragile; to be tender is to be truly fierce" (44). What she is learning from her own ranch work is toughness and independence. She learns the joy of participating in the cycles of life and death that are ever-present on a ranch. She projects, we might say, the balance of hard and soft within her on cowboys in general, believing that they come from the opposite end, from a patriarchal, "hard" model that becomes softened by working on a ranch.

As Ehrlich works and lives in Wyoming, she comes to understand that what gives her strength, what makes the place renewing, is the kind of community that arises from ranch life. Many of Ehrlich's cowboy or ranch stories are about people working together. She loves the camaraderie that comes when she rides as a team with two other women and one man for branding, spring roundup, and fall gathering, or when she helps to calve late at night during a storm. She tells of cowboys moving stock together, or rescuing a partner's horse. Ehrlich greatly admires the many women ranchers that she meets, seeking them out as mentors and being rewarded by their willingness to help her.

Usually the frontier West has been seen as the place where self-fashioning takes place outside of community. For an archetypal example, Boone Caudill, in A. B. Guthrie's *The Big Sky,* leaves the East and goes West (like Ehrlich), but he is looking for the West to be an unspoiled paradise, a natural world where a person can be a "natural man." Loving the West is, for Boone, loving his freedom from responsibility. He avoids community and makes of Teal Eye, his Native American wife, an exalted domestic slave. (The irony and necessity of the novel is that Boone has to leave the life and land he loves after murdering his best friend.) Ehrlich, however, moves toward the kind of community that she finds in the West. Solace and open spaces are important to her, but as the book progresses, we see that equally necessary is the particular community created because of the open spaces. She means to stay in Wyoming. Looking for ways of being in the world that can give her emotional strength, Ehrlich finds it to a large extent in this community that builds from shared work done under physical conditions that often try human capabilities to the extreme.

In a moving and elegantly written essay on digging clams, but also about the experience of being human in community, Robert Finch affirms the importance of such connections in words that apply well to Ehrlich's changing life:

I think of cities I have known, and of the profound loneliness of urban crowds that is the loneliness of a thing unto itself, however large or extensive. True belonging is born of relationships not only to one another but to a place of shared responsibilities and benefits. We love not so much what we have acquired as what we have made and whom we have made it with. There is, at least, the figure for such a love here. And paradoxically, it is in such broad, spacious settings as this—raking the flats, handlining on the banks, working by himself in some common field of endeavor—that a man may feel least alone. The more he allies himself to some varied and interdependent whole, the less he is subject to sudden and wholesale bereavement by chance. His heart rests at the bottom of things; anchored there, he may cast about and never be at sea. ("Scratching," 196)

Ehrlich, coming to find herself "allied to some varied and interdependent whole," is less subject to disabling bereavement. Though often alone, she perceives herself as part of working communities—comes, perhaps, to appreciate the figure for a love such as Finch describes.

In her narrative about these Wyoming "others," Ehrlich underscores that community also comes when emphasis is placed on what you can do and not what you have. For Ehrlich, moving to Wyoming created an opportunity that allowed for the blossoming of a rich inner life because the outer life was simple. Ranch life, which she describes as a version of the "simple life," has traditionally gone against materialism by subordinating the material to the spiritual and ethical, substituting in place of consumerism and a status-orientation "the small achievements of the human conjoined with the animal, and the smaller pleasures—like listening to the radio at night or picking out constellations" (43–44).

As her increasingly important connections to ranch work and cowboys help Ehrlich move through grieving, her relations with animals become surprisingly important to her. Frequently Ehrlich writes about the joy that comes from working with animals or learning how to rope and then using that skill when working with stock. In her celebratory essay about domestic and wild animals, "Friends, Foes, and Working Animals," she says that she likes working with horses and dogs because animals sense "what's bedrock and current in us: aggression, fear, insecurity, happiness, or equanimity. Because they have the ability to read our involuntary tics and scents, we're transparent to them and thus exposed—we're finally ourselves" (64). Animals hold us to "who we are at the time, not who we've been or how our bank accounts describe us" (63–64).

Because our land is being "developed" at an exponential rate and because the loss of countryside means that fewer people have connections to animals other than as pets, many humans in recent years have been proclaiming the value of human-animal relationships. As Renee Askins says:

Something mysterious happens to us when we hear the howl of a wolf, or look into the eyes of a wolf. Something familiar is calling back to us, or looking back at us. Ourselves? Yes, but we also see an other. We see something that is in us, and yet outside us, something we know, but perhaps lost, something we fear, but are drawn toward. We recognize wildness . . . our own and an other's. The "other" is very important because it is through the presence and respect for the "other" that we recognize and heal ourselves. ("Shades of Gray," 377)

Deena Metzger, "working against the assumption of human preeminence and entitlement," tries to see herself and the world "through the animal's eyes while respecting the animal's subjectivity" ("Coming Home," 362). Her desire for an intimate connection, she writes, comes from "an increasing and powerful longing to live in . . . sacred relationship, in what Buddhists might call right relationship to all beings" (363).[6] All the writers in this study (except for Heat-Moon) testify to their growing realizations that relationships with animals are crucial to their move through depression. Wild animals come in for their due when Ehrlich writes that "what we may miss in human interaction here we make up for by rubbing elbows with wild animals" (68). She and her husband even go to the National Finals Rodeo for their honeymoon, which she says is better than going to Paris because at a rodeo you can learn important lessons for marriage: that "the point of the match is not conquest but communion: the rhythm of two beings becoming one"; or that "in this match of equal talents, it is only acceptance, surrender, respect, and spiritedness that make for the midair union of cowboy and horse" (101). Certainly Ehrlich proceeds from her own psychological needs, but her praise of animals—working with them, observing them—also demonstrates her position as a culture straddler. She uses her new sense of being in partnership with animals in order to praise Wyoming life.

Living in California and New York, Ehrlich had no opportunity (or desire) to do hard ranch work, mix with cowboys, or depend on a horse or dog; equally important to her new self-creation is how Wyoming landscape and weather shapes her character. In her essay "The Smooth Skull of Winter," Ehrlich writes about the emotional feelings that result from weather-caused isolation (for one of her first winters in Wyoming, Ehrlich stayed alone in a cabin). Winter's storms, she says, give her "peripheral vision," a snow-covered view that widens what she can see of the world and her life. The deep ache of the cold is "the ache in our lives made physical." Ehrlich values this weather because by stripping "what is ornamental in us" (72), it aids her in stripping herself emotionally, trying to get at the core of her being. While winter isolates humans, it also strengthens the desires for companionship: "Part of the ache we feel is also a softness growing. Our connections with neighbors—whether strong or tenuous, as lovers or friends—become too urgent to disregard" (72). People help each other constantly because of hardship; the difficulty seems less important than the need for intimacy. Winter has a dark side, Ehrlich acknowledges. People can become crazy or mean. The turning inward of the mind can lead toward explosive, pent-up wildness. Ehrlich's views about what winter weather does to people's psyches are paradoxical, if not contradictory, but she wants to stress that Wyoming—its weather and people, the open spaces—wakes her up, helps her brain work at its sharpest, neither of which was true before she came to stay.

"There is nothing in nature that can't be taken as a sign of both mortality and invigoration" (83), Ehrlich writes in "On Water," and if her views about landscape are paradoxical, it is because of this quality in nature. She relishes such paradox, however, in part because nature serves as a barometer of her own emotional state and a force to influence her character. "Everything in nature," she says, "invites us constantly to be what we are" (84). One of the most interesting stories she tells is about a rancher who likes to irrigate more than he likes to ride a horse. Because Wyoming is arid, ranchers are dependent on capturing the run-off when the snowpack on the mountains melts. Frank Hinckley, waiting on a warm May day with his tarp dams set so that he can divert the run-off over his alfalfa fields, is a model, Ehrlich writes, of someone whose long-term enthusiasm has turned "a discipline—a daily chore . . . into a fidelity" ("On Water," 75). The words echo what Ehrlich has understood is central to herself: if she can live her life in tune to the landscape and weather, if she can work for the satisfaction of a job done outdoors and well, if she can make her emotional life respond to nature's dictum to "be what you are" and not the social need to create roles, then she can put an end to mourning.

Unlike the other books in this study, which end with the writer finally coming to accept their trauma, feeling as if they have moved beyond painful grieving, and promising a better future, Ehrlich in

The Solace of Open Spaces shows herself arriving in that future.[7] With the chapter "Just Married," the book takes a decided turn, as the title suggests. In one of those unusual ironies that one finds mostly in fiction (because who could invent a better story?) Ehrlich meets her husband-to-be at a John Wayne film festival in Cody, Wyoming. He, like Ehrlich, is a culture straddler, able to "talk books as well as ranching, medieval history and the mountains, ideas and mules" (86). "Here's to the end of loneliness," Ehrlich toasts after the wedding ceremony, and though she didn't believe such a thing could come true, it does when "love gone deep into a friendship" gives her a sense of peace greater than she ever anticipated. The marriage gives Ehrlich not only a partner, but a place. After "spasms of soul-searching" about where to live—fundamentally a decision about whether to end their "bachelor lives," their chronic vagrancy that leaves them with a certain kind of freedom—they decide to buy an isolated ranch high in the mountains, not to own it, but "to rescue the ranch from the recent neglect it had seen" (89). But rescuing turns into something more, into ownership of a different kind. "The land was ours before we were the land's," wrote Robert Frost, and in the penultimate passage in the essay (and one of the penultimate passages in the book), Ehrlich shows how she has understood her outright gift:

> If I was leery about being an owner, a possessor of land, now I have to understand the ways in which the place possesses me. Mowing hayfields feels like mowing myself. I wake up mornings expecting to find my hair shorn. The pastures bend into me; the water I ushered over hard ground becomes one drink of grass. Later in the year, feeding the bales of hay we've put up is a regurgitative act: thrown down from a high stack on chill days they break open in front of the horses like loaves of hot bread. (90)

Stephanie Kaza has suggested that Ehrlich is one of only a few women nature writers whose work embodies physically the "power and attraction of the land" (257), and Ehrlich's lovely fusion here of land, work, and self becomes emblematic of the rebirth into the erotic that living in Wyoming has brought her.

Whereas the chapters from the first two-thirds of the book show Ehrlich confronting her traumatic past, writing about her attraction to Wyoming, and sorting out her responses to Western life, "Just Married" and the final three chapters (about the National Finals Rodeo, a Crow Fair and a Sun Dance, and the passing of autumn) convey the repose of someone who knows she is staying. In these essays, Ehrlich's tone is softer, muted. There is more straightforward description, less urgency in the assertions, fewer attempts to dispel myths, and so less of the back-and-forth argumentation that comes from dealing with paradox.

The subjects in these three essays (rodeos, festivals, autumn) all concern, in one sense, things passing that become reborn, either because of the rhythms of nature or because they are important enough that some people will not let them go entirely. Ehrlich particularly likes the elaborate rituals surrounding these events and the community that is fostered. She sees rodeos as a symbol of the Western way of life and the Western spirit, in which "two great partnerships are celebrated"—one between human and animal, and one between human and human, cowboy against cowboy. When she describes the Sun Dance and Crow Fair, Ehrlich emphasizes how Native Americans live "in two worlds." They are culture straddlers, she says, of a different kind, finding renewal from one for the difficulties of the other. The dancers sacrifice for the tribe in "an old ritual: separation, initiation, return." Ehrlich's observations of rodeos or the Sun Dance, at this point in her book, apply implicitly to herself, and when she concludes with an essay on autumn, we have come half circle seasonally but a full circle symbolically from the opening lines of the book when she was awakened from a nap on a spring morning. Autumn, as Ehrlich describes it, is nature's ripened sexuality, a ritual of death that will go into rebirth. "There's a ceremonial feel to life on a ranch," she writes. "It's raw and impulsive but the narrative thread of birth, death, chores and seasons keeps tugging at us until we find ourselves braided inextricably into the strand" ("To Live in Two Worlds," 103). Ehrlich herself has gone through a cycle—from initial trauma and loss, through and out of the process of grieving—to be reborn in deep joy, in connectedness, as one braid in a strand.

In the tradition of any writer of regional literature, Ehrlich grounds her observations and subsequent beliefs in the land and life around her. But like Sue Hubbell, she is certainly not that "regional nature-describer" that Carol Bly has described, even if Ehrlich doesn't write directly about politics or ethics. She dispels myths and argues for her positions not for political reasons but out of deep psychological needs to help her through mourning. Embedded in the people and landscape around her, Ehrlich shapes her text to create her own linguistic and psychological state of "Wyoming," an act inseparable from her own reinvention of self. She models how being anchored to place paradoxically sets one free.

Ehrlich's self-creation emerges in the language she finds to convey her new and important relationships with cowboys, animals, and the Wyoming landscape. I have described how Ehrlich's writing has the texture of fiction—her transitions are almost always associative rather than logical, and usually she desires metaphor to carry her argument rather than discursive prose. I have conveyed what is characteristic of her mind-at-work, noting that she begins her book with back-and-forth argumentation that relies on paradox and contradiction, but after she has decided to make Wyoming her home, she turns more directly to straightforward description. I wish to close this chapter by looking at Ehrlich's style more closely, in part as a way to return to the metaphor of the "culture straddler."

Ehrlich invents, as with the other writers in this study, a style that enables her to perform grief work through the literary act. Style, that is, becomes inseparable from the insights and emotions found and felt. A belief that self and language are dependent suggests a connection to therapy. Freud's belief that patients must recover and then work through their pasts has been modified, as I discussed in chapter 2, by psychoanalysts such as Roy Schaefer, Meredith Skura, or Donald Pond Spence who emphasize the importance of patients creating their own life-stories to give narrative truth to their experiences. These stories all contain in them "versions of the self" (to use words from John N. Morris's title), in which the self has various degrees of self-agency, self-knowledge, self-consciousness, and so on. There are certainly differences between writing one's autobiography and undergoing therapy. The relationship between patient and analyst, and the process of transference, does not exist when a person writes the story of her life, and writing makes demands that speech does not. And yet for Ehrlich, constructing the text of "Wyoming" is done only *in* a style, and therefore that style is what we can know of her grief work and her self-creation.

Honest enough to acknowledge that she is not the total "insider," and not just because she wasn't born in Wyoming but because her sensibilities, her way of seeing and being, have been shaped by different and strong influences, Ehrlich emphasizes her role as a culture straddler. The unusual insights that come from such a stance has gained increasing attention in recent years (though most often the "straddle" concerns race). In her book *Borderlands/La Frontera: The New Mestiza,* Gloria Anzaldua says that borderlands are physically present "wherever two or more cultures edge each other, where people of different races occupy the same territory, where under, lower, middle and upper classes touch" ("Preface"). Living on borders and in margins, whether physical, psychological, sexual, or spiritual, Anzaldua says, is exhilarating and joyful. But it's also a "place of contradictions." Many Chicano and Chicana writers have their characters perform extensive language switching from English to Spanish; they speak "Spanglish" to reflect more honestly how the characters living in these borderlands really talk and think. And in a sense, this is what Ehrlich does with her style—it switches repeatedly from being spare to being lush. This switching most marks the style of the book and, I believe, measures how well Ehrlich has carved out as a culture straddler a place that gives her wholeness and comfort.

Consider the following passage:

Conversation goes on in what sounds like a private code; a few phrases imply a complex of meanings. Asking directions, you get a curious list of details . . .

Sentence structure is shortened to the skin and bones of a thought. Descriptive words are dropped, even verbs; a cowboy looking over a corral full of horses will say to a wrangler, "Which one needs rode?" People hold back their thoughts in what seems to be a dumbfounded silence, then erupt with an excoriating perceptive remark. Language, so compressed, becomes metaphorical. (6)

The clipped, skin and bones voice here, and Ehrlich sounds often like this, is that of the cowboy. But then we hear another voice, when she writes about the land:

To offset Wyoming's Arctic seascape, a nightly flush of Northern Lights dances above the Big Horns, irradiating winter's pallor and reminding us that even though at this time of year we veer toward our various nests and seclusions, nature expresses itself as a bright fuse, irrepressible and orgasmic. Winter is smooth-skulled, and all our skids on black ice are cerebral. (74)

In an essay "The Pleasures of Voice in the Literary Essay," Peter Elbow uses Ehrlich (among others) to talk about what readers hear when they encounter particular styles. He identifies in *The Solace of*

Open Spaces four distinct voices in a polyphonic self: "a laconic tough guy who refuses to name feelings. sudden infusions of a deft lyrical voice. Notes of a metaphysical, playfully intellectual voice . . . Occasional soundings of long periodic poetic voice" (220). Elbow's four voices might be five or more to someone else, but in order to continue Ehrlich's own binary, I group them into two: a spare voice that sounds like Westerners talking; a lush voice that comes from books, intellectual conversations, or nature poetry. This switching of voices demonstrates Ehrlich's culture straddling as crucially as any hard physical labor she does or belief system she espouses. Moreover, her ability to combine these voices is the demonstration of the self that she has constructed in moving through grief, the self that gives coherence to her life.

In "Landscape," an essay she wrote for a photo-journalism book, *The Legacy of Light,* Ehrlich says that "scape" is simply the "projection of human consciousness" onto the land: "It is a frame we put around a single view and the ways in which we see and describe this spectacle represent our 'frame of mind,' what we know and what we seek to know" (17). The passage speaks loudly not just about humans viewing the land, but also about Ehrlich's task in *The Solace of Open Spaces.* Style is the frame by which she, and then we, see Wyoming, its land and people and animals. And style is the standard by which we understand her grief work.

Epilogue

"We Tell Ourselves Stories in Order to Live"

Joan Didion, in a masterful essay about California culture, "The White Album," juxtaposes fifteen vignettes to capture the bizarre qualities of the sixties, from the politics of the Black Panther Party to the nihilism of The Doors' Jim Morrison. Her collage of snapshots attempts to make sense of a time that has become so senseless to her that she winds up in a psychiatric hospital, unable to cope with the effort to comprehend and then mediate reality. She is supposed to have a script, she says, a plot, but she has mislaid it. Life is not meant to be all improvisation, a succession of images with no meaning, a cast-off film on a cutting-room floor, mixed up and cut up. "I wanted still to believe in the narrative," she writes, "and in the narrative's intelligibility, but to know that one could change the sense with every cut was to begin to perceive the experience as rather more electrical than ethical" (13). Her own condition mirrors society's, she continually suggests. Neither one has a coherent script. And yet we go on, she concludes, because "we tell ourselves stories in order to live."

Hubbell, Williams, Barich, Heat-Moon, Matthiessen, and Ehrlich—all have come to feel, likewise, that because of trauma and loss they have incoherent scripts for the world as they have known it. Like Didion, they tell stories in order to live, stories of human and nonhuman others that might teach them how their script coheres.

Peter Fritzell, in *Nature Writing and America,* calls such attempts to locate oneself "settling stories," suggesting that the earliest stories

of people writing about place were literal attempts to map the territory and name its inhabitants, human and nonhuman. The best
American nature writers, Fritzell proposes, have continued in this
vein, and the drama of their writings "has thus mirrored one of the
essential forms of American experience, both actual and mythic: the
experience of a self-conscious human individual attempting to come
to terms with what we far too innocently and unconsciously call 'the
land'" (8). The result, for writers such as Thoreau, Leopold, Dillard,
and Abbey, has been a combination of natural-history writing and
spiritual autobiography, and a tension that comes from two extreme
positions, egoistic self-celebration and self-deprecation.

In considering Hubbell, Williams, Barich, Heat-Moon, Matthiessen, and Ehrlich as nature writers, we may refine Fritzell's thesis. The
stories they tell are a version of settling the country, but they write
about the land and its inhabitants for a different purpose: their settling stories are attempts to locate themselves first within and then
outside a story of trauma and loss. While they write directly about nature (including humans), their self-creation becomes spiritual autobiography because only in that form are they able to transcend their
loss. The tension of their narratives—and the alternation of voice—
concerns the psychological swings between grieving and a hope that
grieving is coming to an end. These books are a psychological version
of settling the country.

In the introduction I suggested that the books I take up intersect
at the edges of autobiography studies, environmental literature, and
literary nonfiction. *A Country Year, Refuge, Laughing in the Hills, Blue
Highways, The Snow Leopard,* and *The Solace of Open Spaces* all occupy that small area where those three genres overlap. On one hand,
genre seems analogous to *species* in biology, a grouping for closely related objects with similar identifying characteristics. But for these
writers, the term *genre* has more to do with three frameworks for "seeing"—into the self, into humans and culture, and into nature.

Collectively the books address a large number of related topics:
sustainability, animal species, Western myths, women's work, travel,
Zen Buddhism, ecosystems, atomic testing, cancer, rural life, and
friendship, to name just a few. But what unites the explorations of
these subjects are the writers' desires to explore the world and tell its
stories as an attempt to make sense of their own lives. Hubbell talks
about living the questions, Heat-Moon finding the places where men

and time and deeds connect; Ehrlich quotes Brodsky to maintain that "geography blended / with time equals destiny," and Matthiessen cites Lama Govinda, who believes that the pilgrim must "abandon himself to the breath of the greater life that . . . is already present within him." For all, the searching meshed with writing ultimately completes the act of self-creation.

In these books, as we have seen, the "self-life-write" of autobiography takes place not in the usual ways—neither through an examination of the writer's past life nor in relation to a family figure such as a parent. That is, these writers neither devise the typical self-at-center autobiography nor the typical relational autobiography. Instead, relationality is spread out to numerous human and nonhuman others that are rarely the subjects of "classic" autobiographies. Hubbell constructs herself as a text of suitability woven into numerous ecological webs of life on her farm; Barich comes to understand his strong attachment to a totemic animal, the thoroughbred; Williams finds herself absorbed into all things wild, from the Great Salt Lake to deserts, which helps her challenge accepted beliefs of her culture. And so on for the other writers, whose connections are to mountains or animals or rural people.

Mary Oliver's poem "Wild Geese" echoes themes encountered in all of these books. The speaker says,

> Tell me about despair, yours, and I will tell you mine.
> Meanwhile the world goes on.
> . . . .
> Meanwhile the wild geese, high in the clean blue air,
> are heading home again.
> Whoever you are, no matter how lonely,
> the world offers itself to your imagination,
> calls to you like the wild geese, harsh and exciting—
> over and over announcing your place
> in the family of things.
>
> (from "Wild Geese," in *Dream Work*)

Variations of Oliver's constellation—human despair, storytelling, wild geese, the imagination, and our place in the family of things—appear in all the books in this study. Oliver sees the essential role of language as a pathway to community, in her emphasis on the absolute necessity of using and listening to the voices of both humans ("Tell me about despair, yours") as well as nature ("the world . . . calls to you /

over and over announcing your place"). Similarly, these books, each in their own ways, develop the notion of language as a kind of refuge, a literary act as a kind of grief work. They demonstrate a self-creation that interlocks humans, the land, and all its inhabitants.

Notes

Introduction

1. Much of the interest in relational autobiography has been ideologically driven, with feminist and multicultural critics rightly showing that emphasis on the solitary self has implications for gender and race and has often excluded certain kinds of writing by women or people of color.

2. As quoted in the epigraph to Kathleen Norris's *Dakota*.

3. On the title page of *Blue Highways,* the author is presented as William Least Heat Moon. The subsequent difficulty of knowing what were the middle and last names spawned, I believe, the official change to Heat-Moon (i.e., with a hyphen) as his last name—a practice I have followed even when referring to the author of *Blue Highways*.

4. The label *spiritual geography* comes from Kathleen Norris's powerful meditation on rural life, *Dakota*. Popular beyond anyone's expectations, filling a spiritual need for many readers, Norris's book shows how spiritual geography transcends the maps and statistics of high-school geography to become a knowledge of the land that attaches itself to her personal history and common humanity.

1 Writing the Self through Others

1. Concomitant with the defining of the genre as a whole, critics began creating an early canon for American autobiography; see, in particular, Mutlu Blasing's *The Art of Life: Studies in American Autobiographical Literature;* Thomas Couser's *American Autobiography: The Prophetic Mode;* James Cox's "Autobiography and America"; Daniel Shea's *Spiritual Autobiography in Early America;* and Albert Stone's *Autobiographical Occasions and Original Acts:*

Versions of American Identity from Henry Adams to Nate Shaw—all dating from the late 1960s to the early 1980s.

2. For a fine overview of this history of American literature criticism, see Richard Brodhead's essay "After the Opening: Problems and Prospects for a Reformed American Literature." Brodhead also looks to the future, remarking on what the next stage of literary studies might look like.

3. For more on how women's autobiographies challenge the norm of self-hood creation, begin with the collections of essays by Benstock; Brodzki and Schenck; Smith and Watson; and Ashley, Gilmore, and Peters; and articles by Hooten, Mason, and Smith.

4. For one example, Chodorow begins with the assumption that children are parented by their mothers. Although it is true that more mothers than fathers stay home with their children, and true that more mothers than fathers are the primary caretaker of children, most children in two-parent families are parented by both women and men, and, moreover, the effectiveness or influence of parenting is not always directly connected to the amount of time spent. Obviously, not all women are good at intimacy and relationships, and not all men are bad at them.

5. A revised and extended version of this address is chapter 2, "Relational Selves, Relational Lives: Autobiography and the Myth of Autonomy," in Eakin's recent *How Our Lives Become Stories*.

6. I am thinking here in particular, among numerous others, of arguments advanced by Aldo Leopold in *A Sand County Almanac,* Roderick Frazier Nash in *The Rights of Nature,* and Lawrence Buell in *The Environmental Imagination*. Later in this chapter, I take up this issue in more depth.

7. The scope widens, in a sense, as the focus of these studies narrows. For instance, in 1998 alone three books were published that pursue a particular line of life-writing (as I do here in *Refiguring the Map of Sorrow*), and by virtue of engaging new issues they take up noncanonical books. See Suzette Henke's *Shattered Subjects,* Diane Bjorklund's *Interpreting the Self,* and Carolyn A. Barros's *Autobiography: Narratives of Transformation*.

8. I recognize the inherent problems of the term *literary nonfiction* but think it the best available. Generally, literary nonfiction is distinguished in two ways: one, it often has the strategies and techniques we usually associate with fiction; and two, it does more than just present information: it values structure, language, and style and asserts their connection to the information. For a fuller discussion, see Weber's *The Literature of Fact* and the introduction to Anderson's *Literary Nonfiction: Theory, Criticism, Pedagogy*.

9. Walker Evans's famous photos of the sharecroppers open the book, of course, which does allow for Agee to "render" the sharecroppers in a medium that he believed more immediate and direct, though limited no less in its attempts to portray their lives.

10. For more on New Journalism, first consult Tom Wolfe's manifesto in his anthology *The New Journalism,* and then see Weber, Hollowell, Zavarzadeh, Hellman, Anderson, and Lounsberry.

11. These critics do not agree on these issues, of course. Zavarzadeh, by arguing that the thrust of the nonfiction novel is away from interpretation of any kind, toward a "zero degree of interpretation," disagrees with the others, who see in these nonfiction writers an attempt precisely to make significances and meanings within the confines of "facts." How significances are made is not agreed upon, certainly.

12. In his essay, Roth suggests that the fictive imagination is hardly necessary because contemporary events are more interesting than the novelist's inventions: "The American writer in the middle of the 20th century has his hands full in trying to understand, then describe, and then make *credible* much of the American reality. It stupefies, it sickens, it infuriates, and finally it is even a kind of embarrassment to one's own meager imagination. The actuality is continually outdoing our talents, and the culture tosses up figures almost daily that are the envy of any novelist" (224). This belief, and the corresponding truism it became for explaining the "rise" of literary nonfiction, is given a shrewd deconstruction by Phyllis Frus McCord in her essay "The Ideology of Form: The Nonfiction Novel." "Reality," she asserts, is not any more incredible in 1961 than it was at any other time—and perhaps less so than, for example, during the Holocaust. Roth confuses the events themselves with the way they are made images by popular media, she insists.

13. Certainly there is still literary criticism written about nonfiction texts, but the organizing "category" of those texts is no longer the rubric *literary nonfiction* but other rubrics that *include* literary nonfiction. For example, there has been great interest of late in books about the Vietnam War, fiction and nonfiction written by Americans and Vietnamese alike; among the fine critical studies are Philip M. Melling's *Vietnam in American Literature,* Philip D. Beidler's *Re-Writing America* and *American Literature and the Experience of Vietnam,* and Timothy J. Lomperis's *"Reading the Wind": The Literature of the Vietnam War.* Stewart O'Nan has recently edited an anthology, *The Vietnam Reader.* Some of the interest in literary nonfiction has moved toward composition studies, where occasional calls for criticism of the kinds of prose that fill writing anthologies have met with mixed results; see Dennis Rygiel's article, "On the Neglect of Twentieth Century Nonfiction: A Writing Teacher's View," and Anderson's introduction to *Literary Nonfiction.* Most importantly, there has emerged a strong interest in environmental literature, which would be the classification of most of the books in this study. I discuss such literature in the next section.

14. For more on this, see the essay by McCord and Eric Heyne's essay, "Toward a Theory of Literary Nonfiction."

15. Until a few years ago, and certainly when I left graduate school with a Ph.D. in American literature, I did not know this illustrious group of nature writers, though anyone who reads natural history can roll these names off the tongue as easily as I could say Whitman, Dickinson, Faulkner, and Morrison. Eco-critics regard Austin's *The Land of Little Rain* as highly as Americanists do any novel by Henry James. Despite all of the intense fighting in the last thirty years over the canon of American literature, it is ironic that few of those arguing for greater inclusiveness know much about environmental literature.

16. In this section and throughout the book, I use the term *nature writers* for writers of nonfiction whose subject seems "primarily" the nonhuman world. Landscape and nature have certainly been crucial in the texts of many fine American poets and novelists, from Twain, Cather, and Frost to Mary Oliver and Leslie Marmon Silko, though I would suggest that their works (and numerous others) should be classified in the larger category of environmental literature.

17. The quotation comes from David Abram's *The Spell of the Sensuous* (102).

18. Since the Industrial Revolution, there have been counterexamples of this position, of course, such as the Wordsworthian belief that nature is the soul's guide and nurse, or the American principles in the mid-nineteenth century about the "book of nature" being God's revelation. But learning through observation of and hands-on experience in the nonhuman world has been far less important than learning through books and about the human world. We are, in general I believe, mostly overwhelmed by the sheer quantity and physicality of the human-made world. "Nature" exists mostly for our entertainment, as evidenced by the way the natural world is portrayed on most "nature" shows on television, or by the success of mail-order firms and stores such as The Nature Company, or by the high television ratings for the reporting of "natural disasters" (an interesting label) such as hurricanes, tornadoes, and earthquakes.

19. My words echo those of Christopher Manes in his essay "Nature and Silence." For more on the subject, see this essay and Abram's *The Spell of the Sensuous,* particularly Abram's chapters 4 and 5.

20. The numbers, however, grew quickly in the 1990s, with numerous fine works of ecocriticism, including collections of essays and books by Cheryll Glotfelty and Harold Fromm, Peter Fritzell, Scott Slovic, Vera Norwood, John P. O'Grady, Don Scheese, Lawrence Buell, and others. For an overview of the history of ecocriticism, see Glotfelty's introduction to *The Ecocriticism Reader.* In addition to the rather rapid rise of ecocriticism, the 1990s has seen the publishing industry cranking up to respond to the large market for environmental literature. Not only countless books and essays and scores of

specialized nature anthologies, but numerous general anthologies were published in the 1990s, including Robert Finch's and John Elder's *The Norton Book of Nature Writing* and Thomas Lyons's *This Incomperable Lande: A Book of American Nature Writing.* A monumental research work edited by Elder, *American Nature Writers,* appeared in 1996.

21. I do not mean to suggest here that nature writers such as Annie Dillard or John McPhee are not writing literary nonfiction—they certainly are. These categories— *autobiography, literary nonfiction, nature writing*—often overlap and their borders are not by any means exact. But in general I would say that nature writing that aspires to a kind of literary performance is a subset of literary nonfiction; nature writing that has more in common with rather straightforward science writing is generally not literary nonfiction. I recognize the difficulties in the label *nature writing* but consider it the best available and the most common. Don Scheese, for example, in his fine overview of the genre, *Nature Writing: The Pastoral Impulse in America,* uses the term. For a lengthy discussion of this issue, see Lawrence Buell's introduction to *The Environmental Imagination.*

22. Two recent books have taken the fusion of these genres in an interesting direction by including literary criticism: In *Meeting the Tree of Life: A Teacher's Path,* John Tallmadge combines natural history, autobiography, and travel writing with interpretations of writers such as Thoreau, Leopold, and Abbey; John Elder, in his superbly written and wise book *Reading the Mountains of Home,* uses Frost's poem "Directive" as a guide to exploring the geological, geographical, and cultural region around Bristol, Vermont, where he lives.

2 Living the Questions, Writing the Story

1. Bly's words come from the cover of Paddock's *Handful of Thunder.*

2. In *Staying Put: Making a Home in a Restless World,* Sanders says that there is no need to go looking for home unless you have lost it, and certainly he has: the farm in Tennessee where he spent his early years was buried in asphalt; the military reservation where he lived next is now, to a civilian, inaccessible; and the farm in Ohio where he spent the rest of his childhood is under water, flooded by the building of a huge dam. "If I am to have a home," he writes, "it can only be a place I have come to as an adult, a place I have chosen" (xiv). For many Americans, including Hubbell, this is the case.

3. The term *historical truth* is Donald Pond Spence's, as is *narrative truth,* a term that I use later. Spence's critique of the psychoanalytic process is particularly helpful to me in that, rather than stressing the way in which free association digs into past memories, he emphasizes the therapeutic importance of making a story.

4. I agree, of course, with McEntyre's point that *A Country Year* combines

autobiography and nature writing, but the act of self-creation is more than some routine "self-reflections." Although Hubbell and this book are mentioned frequently in books and articles about nature writers, there is almost no scholarship on her—only McEntyre's piece and my early essay in the *Midwest Quarterly*—which suggests to me that as much as scholars have liked Hubbell's work, they are not sure what frameworks would allow them to discuss her in depth.

5. In her later books, among them *A Book of Bees, Broadsides from the Other Orders,* and *Far-Flung Hubbell,* she is not performing grief work or an act of self-creation; and so these books are astute and acute personal observations mixed with wide-ranging reading and self-reflections.

6. This remark comes from my personal interview with Hubbell, March 1990.

7. Hubbell interview, March 1990.

8. For more on the evolution of the historical kinship between humans and nature, see Buell's chapter "Nature's Personhood," in *The Environmental Imagination,* pp. 180–218.

9. The pastoral mode is difficult to define, of course, because "nature" has been used in a nearly infinite number of ways to oppose the human-made world. I mean to use the genre here in its most general sense, going back to Virgil's celebration of the bucolic life. For more on the pastoral, see Andrew V. Ettin's *Literature and the Pastoral* and Scheese's *Nature Writing: The Pastoral Impulse in America.*

10. Hubbell interview, March 1990.

11. For more on this subject, and solitude in general, see Anthony Storr's fine book, *Solitude: A Return to the Self.*

12. Though Skura is discussing the psychoanalytic process here, and not grieving in particular, her ideas resemble Bowlby's suggestions that one moves through the mourning process in general by creating order (explanatory stories) where disorganization reigned.

3 An Unnatural History Made Natural

1. Critical reception has been generally favorable, though responses to particular issues have been mixed, in large part guided by the critic's response to the implicit and explicit ideology. I will address these differences later in this chapter. Williams inscribes in *Refuge* a complex puzzle of grieving that has so many pieces that a critic can assemble nearly any interpretation by grouping some and ignoring others.

2. The chapters where there is relatively little on the particular bird species is not a fault of the text as much as a demonstration that an interesting structure for the book cannot always mesh with "reality." That is, Williams works from her journals, and the structural focus on the birds is a literary strategy, which simply works better at some times than others.

3. It is true that the deaths of the women in her family mean that Williams could hardly be out on this canoe except with a male family member. But she could have closed the book with a different scene. No literary criticism on *Refuge* acknowledges the role of Brooke, which is perhaps why I was struck by his active role in this final scene.

4. The irony in the quoted passage is that Williams, driving her friend to see the Bear River Migratory Bird Refuge, is explicitly worried that the rising waters have covered habitat, hardly an "unnatural" event.

5. Arnie Naess, in his 1973 article "The Shallow and the Deep, Long-Range Ecology Movements: A Summary," gave an enduring name to this ethical stance. Bill Devall and George Sessions, in their book *Deep Ecology*, define this new term as "a process of ever-deeper questioning of ourselves, the assumptions of the dominant worldview in our culture, and the meaning and truth of our reality" (8).

4 When All the World Is Cancerous

1. For readers who want a literary book about horse racing, who appreciate the style of sentences and Barich's references, out to the world and in to himself, *Laughing in the Hills* is considered a classic in this subject area; readers who desire a "how-to" book about thoroughbreds and horse racing would not be served as well, of course.

2. As quoted on the 1981 Penguin paperback edition of the book.

3. For more on tropes and their relation to human thought, see Kenneth Burke's *A Grammar of Motives* and Hayden White's *Tropics of Discourse*.

4. See, in particular, the anthology *Intimate Nature: The Bond between Women and Animals,* edited by Linda Hogan, Deena Metzger, and Brenda Peterson.

5. Hubbell and Williams conclude their books "in place," and so as readers we are imagining a life for them that is not that different than what they have described, except that their grief has ended. This is the projection that readers typically make with such autobiographies. In *Blue Highways, Laughing in the Hills,* and *The Snow Leopard*, however, the writer returns to a life only sketchily described.

5 Constructing a Self on the Road

1. For more on journeys and American literature, see Janis P. Stout's introductory chapter of her book *The Journey Narrative in American Literature,* which raises many of these issues and pursues them in depth.

2. Kris Lackey, in the introduction to his book *Road Frames: The American Highway Narrative,* sketches in detail the literary traditions of road literature. He concludes, however, that road books are unusual, compared with other genres, in that they draw so unsystematically on a variety of traditions:

romanticism, transcendentalism, naturalism, cultural criticism, the pastoral, the informational travel book, and so on. See *Road Frames* for interpretations of numerous books that blend these traditions.

3. Barich, likewise, might have gone to Golden Gate Fields knowing that he would write a book about his experiences there. But there is an obvious textual difference: Heat-Moon, who includes photographs of some of his subjects, as a traveler knowing that he would not return, would have to photograph them on the spot.

4. He told Alvin Sanoff, in an interview for *U.S. News and World Report*, that his writing in the book up until that time was hollow because he was "drawing only on the Anglo-Irish side of my existence" (58).

5. Kris Lackey, in *Road Frames*, argues that Heat-Moon's nostalgia for the "historical pastoral" helps him achieve a highly literary tone (one of the book's great accomplishments), even while it inhibits his ability to finally create a "transcendental self." See, particularly, pages 54–61.

6. The words nearly echo those of Williams and Barich at key moments in their narratives. It is interesting that all these writers in their grieving create a useless nostalgia for the past—useless, that is, except for their literary purposes. In order to have loss be compensated, they must transform their ideas and feelings about change, and this usually happens when the human is connected to animal life or something grand in the landscape such as mountains or rivers.

7. In this, *Blue Highways* is not unrelated to the other texts in this study. *Refuge,* for example, demonstrates the raw power that comes when Williams moves more directly toward family and her past by intertwining family history, personal history of her loss, and an "unnatural" history of place. And *Laughing in the Hills,* a book at first seemingly without any environmental context, dramatizes Barich coming to understand the therapeutic qualities of an animal totem.

8. Because *Blue Highways* was a bestseller, it was widely reviewed, as was *PrairyErth* and his recent book about traveling from coast to coast by rivers, *River-Horse.* There have been surprisingly few academic articles on him, however, given that he is included in the influential *American Nature Writers* reference series, edited by John Elder.

9. The information here comes from an interview with Heat-Moon by Daniel Bourne; as cited in David Teague's essay, the best critical article on Heat-Moon as a nature writer (514).

6 A Pilgrimage to Fashion a Zen Self

1. Matthiessen has a relatively small amount of serious literary criticism on his work, given that he is one of the few twentieth-century writers, and the only environmentalist, who has a substantial and critically praised

oeuvre in both fiction and nonfiction. Important novels include *At Play in the Fields of the Lord, Far Tortuga,* and his recent trilogy, *Killing Mister Watson, Lost Man's River,* and *Bone by Bone;* acclaimed nonfiction books, in addition to *The Snow Leopard* (which won the National Book Award), are *Wildlife in America, The Cloud Forest, Blue Meridian, In the Spirit of Crazy Horse,* and *The Tree Where Man Was Born.* Payne's essay in the *American Nature Writers* series is representative of the direction that ecocritics have gone with Matthiessen, in being descriptive and general, covering briefly all the major books, and praising Matthiessen's abilities to comprehend primitive cultures and to understand ecological issues (see also McKay Jenkins's introduction to the recent *Peter Matthiessen Reader*). Ross Winterowd concludes his book on literary nonfiction with a description and appreciation of *The Snow Leopard,* arguing that Matthiessen's book exemplifies the sophistication possible in literary nonfiction. Several critics have written about Matthiessen and Zen Buddhism; in particular, for more on Matthiessen's long-term involvement with Zen, which has continued up until the present day (Matthiessen became a Zen priest in 1981), consult William Dowie's useful *Peter Matthiessen.*

2. My summary here about the oxherding pictures is indebted to Lex Hixon's *Coming Home: The Experience of Enlightenment in Sacred Traditions.*

3. As quoted in *The Collected Works of Ralph Waldo Emerson,* with introductions and notes by Robert E. Spiller and text established by Alfred R. Ferguson, p. 10.

4. For a fuller discussion of de Man and these issues, see chapter 5.

5. The biographical information in this paragraph comes from chapter 8 of Dowie's *Peter Matthiessen.*

6. For more on Matthiessen's scrupulousness, see Dowie's chapter 3. *The Snow Leopard* itself is testimony to the high respect given to Matthiessen by such experts: the book came about because Schaller, one of the world's most eminent zoologists, invited Matthiessen to accompany him on his trip.

7 Making a Home on the Range

1. It was interesting to see the spate of new Hollywood westerns that began appearing in theaters in late 1993, movies about Geronimo, about Tombstone and Wyatt Earp, and so on. The "trend" largely evaporated, though a few westerns are still being made. It is difficult to tell, of course, whether Hollywood anticipates what the public wants or whether they know best how to do sequels and imitations, and were still spinning off the enormous popularity of *Dances with Wolves.*

2. For a delightfully spirited essay about this pact, see Barrett J. Mandel's essay "Full of Life Now."

3. I agree with Comer's assertion in general, though Kingsolver and

Williams did have articles written about their books by this date (see chapter 3 for more on Williams's critical reception). Comer's book has been a strong start toward reassessing these other writers, but she does not write on Ehrlich. The first and only article on *The Solace of Open Spaces*—Bonney MacDonald's "Desire of the Middle Ground"—appeared in the summer 1998 issue of *Western American Literature*.

4. For more on the hotly debated subject of cowboying, see Sharman Apt Russell's fine book, *Kill the Cowboy: A Battle of Mythology in the New West.* As Russell says, cowboys "have much to do with [Americans'] dreams of freedom and solitude. . . . In these dreams, we know the grandeur of an untrammeled continent. We are intimate with animals. We are intimate with the earth" (2); but, as she also points out, in reality "the cowboy's job is to transform the wild West into something that resembles, prosaically, a feedlot" (3).

5. MacDonald's essay is most interesting in its Bakhtinian-inspired description of how Ehrlich uses binaries to fashion a middle ground that constitutes the "open spaces" of the title. "In the sustained gap between oppositions, Ehrlich finds a home," MacDonald writes (146). She does not talk about grief work, however, or suggest that there is a narrative arc to the book, which is, of course, my emphasis here.

6. It is interesting that Ehrlich writes in a later book that she has been, for all her adult life, a "closet Buddhist."

7. I do not mean to suggest here that all the other books end in the exact same way. The authors conclude with varying degrees of hope, though all suggest that they have moved beyond feelings of being disabled by their grief. Ehrlich, however, goes along further in time, so to speak, than the other writers.

Bibliography

Abbey, Edward. *Desert Solitaire.* New York: Ballantine, 1968.

Abram, David. *The Spell of the Sensuous: Perception and Language in a More-than-Human World.* New York: Pantheon, 1996.

Adams, Henry. *The Education of Henry Adams.* Boston: Houghton Mifflin, 1973.

Agee, James. *Let Us Now Praise Famous Men.* Boston: Houghton Mifflin, 1941.

Anastoplo, Theodora. "Metaxa." *The Cresset* 61, no. 3 (1988):12–14.

Anderson, Chris, ed. *Literary Nonfiction: Theory, Criticism, Pedagogy.* Carbondale: Southern Illinois UP, 1989.

———. *Style as Argument: Contemporary American Nonfiction.* Carbondale: Southern Illinois UP, 1987.

Anzaldua, Gloria. *Borderlands/La Frontera: The New Mestiza.* San Francisco: Spinsters/Aunt Lute, 1987.

Armbruster, Karla. "Rewriting a Genealogy with the Earth: Women and Nature in the Works of Terry Tempest Williams." *Southwestern American Literature* 21, no. 1 (1995): 209–20.

Ashley, Kathleen, Leigh Gilmore, and Gerald Peters, eds. *Autobiography and Postmodernism.* Amherst: U of Massachusetts P, 1994.

Askins, Renee. "Shades of Gray." In *Intimate Nature,* ed. Linda Hogan, Deena Metzger, and Brenda Peterson. New York: Ballantine, 1998.

Augustine. *The Confessions of St. Augustine.* Trans. F. J. Sheed. New York: Sheed & Ward, 1943.

Austin, Mary. *The Land of Little Rain.* Albuquerque: U of New Mexico P, 1974.

Barich, Bill. *Laughing in the Hills.* New York: Penguin, 1981.

Barros, Carolyn A. *Autobiography: Narrative of Transformation.* Ann Arbor: U of Michigan P, 1998.

Barthes, Roland. "The Death of the Author." In *Image-Music-Text,* trans. S. Heath. New York: Hill & Wang, 1977.

Bartram, William. *The Travels.* Ed. Mark Van Doren. New York: Dover, 1928.

Beebe, William. *Half Mile Down.* New York: Harcourt, Brace, 1934.

Beidler, Philip D. *American Literature and the Experience of Vietnam.* Athens: U of Georgia P, 1982.

———. *Re-Writing America: Vietnam Authors in Their Generation.* Athens: U of Georgia P, 1991.

Benstock, Shari. ed. *The Private Self: Theory and Practice of Women's Autobiographical Writings.* Chapel Hill: U of North Carolina P, 1988.

Bergland, Betty. "Postmodernism and the Autobiographical Subject: Reconstructing the 'Other.'" In *Autobiography and Postmodernism,* ed. Kathleen Ashley, Leigh Gilmore, and Gerald Peters. Amherst: U of Massachusetts P, 1994.

Bernstein, Carl. *Loyalties.* New York: Simon & Schuster, 1990.

Berry, Wendell. "Preserving Wildness." In *Home Economics.* San Francisco: North Point, 1987.

Beston, Henry. *The Outermost House.* New York: Ballantine, 1971.

Blasing, Mutlu Konuk. *The Art of Life: Studies in American Autobiographical Literature.* Austin: U of Texas P, 1977.

Bly, Carol. "Bad Government and Silly Literature." Minneapolis: Milkweed, 1986.

———. "At the Edge of Town, Duluth, Minn." In *Townships,* ed. Michael Martone. Iowa City: U of Iowa P, 1992.

Bjorklund, Diane. *Interpreting the Self.* Chicago: U of Chicago P, 1998.

Bowlby, John. *Loss: Sadness and Depression,* vol. 3 of *Attachment and Loss.* New York: Basic, 1980.

Brodhead, Richard. "After the Opening: Problems and Prospects for a Reformed American Literature." *Yale Journal of Criticism* 5 (1992): 59–71.

Brodzki, Bella, and Celeste Schenk, eds. *Life/Lines: Theorizing Women's Autobiography.* Ithaca, N.Y.: Cornell UP, 1988.

Buell, Lawrence. *The Environmental Imagination.* Boston: Harvard UP, 1995.

Burke, Kenneth. *A Grammar of Motives.* New York: Prentice Hall, 1945.

Burroughs, John. *Wake-Robin.* Boston: Houghton, Mifflin, 1913.

Capote, Truman. *In Cold Blood.* New York: Random House, 1965.

Carson, Rachel. *The Sea Around Us.* New York: Oxford UP, 1951.

Chase, Richard. *The American Novel and Its Tradition.* Garden City, N.Y.: Doubleday Anchor, 1957.

Chernin, Kim. *In My Mother's House: A Daughter's Story.* New York: Harper & Row, 1983.

Chodorow, Nancy. *The Reproduction of Mothering: Psychoanalysis and the Sociology of Gender.* Berkeley: U of California P, 1978.

Claspell, Emily and Larry Cochran. *The Meaning of Grief.* New York: Greenwood P, 1987.

Comer, Krista. *Landscapes of the New West: Gender and Geography in Contemporary Women's Writing.* Chapel Hill: U of North Carolina P, 1999.

Conroy, Frank. *Stop-Time.* New York: Viking, 1967.

Couser, G. Thomas. *American Autobiography: The Prophetic Mode.* Amherst: U of Massachusetts P, 1979.

———. *Recovering Bodies: Illness, Disability, and Life Writing.* Madison: U of Wisconsin P, 1997.

Cox, James M. "Autobiography and America." *Virginia Quarterly Review* 47 (1971): 252–77.

De Man, Paul. "Autobiography as De-facement." *MLN* 94 (1979): 919–30.

De Quincey, Thomas. *Confessions of an English Opium Eater.* New York: A. L. Burt, 1856.

Derrida, Jacques. "Signature Event Context." *Glyph* 1 (1977), 172–97.

Devall, Bill and George Sessions. *Deep Ecology.* Salt Lake City: Gibbs Smith, 1985.

Didion, Joan. *The White Album.* New York: Simon & Schuster, 1979.

Dillard, Annie. *Pilgrim at Tinker Creek.* New York: Bantam, 1975.

Dodd, Philip. "The Views of Travellers: Travel Writing in the 1930s." *Prose Studies* 5 (May 1982): 127–38.

Dowie, William. *Peter Matthiessen.* Boston: Twayne, 1991.

Eakin, Paul John. *Fictions in Autobiography.* Princeton: Princeton UP, 1985.

———. "Toward a Theory of Relational Autobiography." Keynote address, 1994 National Conference on Autobiography, Hofstra, N.Y. Expanded and revised in *How Our Lives Become Stories.* Ithaca: Cornell UP, 1999.

Ehrlich, Gretel. *The Solace of Open Spaces.* New York: Penguin, 1985.

Eiseley, Loren. *The Immense Journey.* New York: Random House, 1957.

Elbow, Peter. "The Pleasures of Voice in the Literary Essay." In *Literary Nonfiction: Theory, Criticism, Pedagogy,* ed. Chris Anderson. Carbondale: Southern Illinois UP, 1989.

Elder, John, ed. *American Nature Writers.* 2 vols. New York: Scribner's, 1996.

———. *Reading the Mountains of Home.* Cambridge: Harvard UP, 1998.

Elder, John, and Robert Finch, eds. *The Norton Book of Nature Writing.* New York: Norton, 1990.

Ellison, Ralph. *Invisible Man.* New York: Random House, 1952.

Emerson, Ralph Waldo. *The Collected Works.* Intro. and notes by Robert E.

Spiller. Text established by Alfred R. Ferguson. Cambridge: Harvard UP, 1971.

Ettin, Andrew. *Literature and the Pastoral.* New Haven: Yale UP, 1984.

Feidelson, Charles, Jr. *Symbolism and American Literature.* Chicago: U of Chicago P, 1953.

Fiedler, Leslie. *Love and Death in the American Novel.* New York: Stein & Day, 1960.

Finch, Robert. "Into the Maze" and "Scratching." In *The Primal Place.* New York: Norton, 1983.

Foucault, Michel. "What Is an Author?" Trans. James Venit, *Partisan Review* 42 (1975): 603–14.

Freud, Sigmund. *Introductory Lectures on Psychoanalysis.* New York: Norton, 1966.

Friedman, Susan Stanford. "Women's Autobiographical Selves: Theory and Practice." In *The Private Self,* ed. Shari Benstock. Chapel Hill: U of North Carolina P, 1988.

Fritzell, Peter A. *Nature Writing and America: Essays upon a Cultural Type.* Ames: Iowa State UP, 1990.

George, Roger. "A Boat Filled with Abstractions: Reading Raban's River." In *Temperamental Journeys: Essays on the Modern Literature of Travel,* ed. Michael Kowalewski. Athens: U of Georgia P, 1992.

Gergen, Kenneth J. *The Saturated Self.* New York: Basic, 1991.

Gilligan, Carol. *In a Different Voice: Psychological Theory and Women's Development.* Cambridge: Harvard UP, 1982.

Gilmore, Leigh. *Autobiographics: A Feminist Theory of Women's Self-Representation.* Ithaca: Cornell UP, 1994.

Glotfelty, Cheryll. "Flooding the Boundaries of Form: Terry Tempest Williams's Ecofeminist *Unnatural History.*" In *Change in the American West,* ed. Stephen Tchudi. Reno: U of Nevada P, 1996.

Glotfelty, Cheryll, and Harold Fromm, eds. *The Ecocriticism Reader: Landmarks in Literary Ecology.* Athens: U of Georgia P, 1996.

Goffman, Erving. *Presentation of Self in Everyday Life.* Garden City, N.Y.: Doubleday, 1959.

Gornick, Vivian. *Fierce Attachments.* New York: Farrar, Straus & Giroux, 1987.

Gosse, Edmund. *Father and Son.* New York: Norton, 1963 [1907].

Gruchow, Paul. "Traveling Much in Concord: Regaining Our Sense of Place." Unpublished essay.

Gusdorf, Georges. "Conditions and Limits of Autobiography." In *Autobiography,* ed. James Olney. Princeton: Princeton UP, 1980.

Guthrie, A. B. *The Big Sky.* 1947. Reprint, New York: Houghton Mifflin, 1965.

Hamlyn, David W. "Self-Knowledge." In *The Self: Psychological and Philo-*

sophical Issues, ed. Theodore Mischel. Totowa, N.J.: Rowman & Little-field, 1977.

Hasselstrom, Linda. *Windbreak.* Berkeley: Barn Owl, 1987.

Hay, John. *The Run.* New York: Doubleday, 1959.

Heat-Moon, William Least. *Blue Highways.* Boston: Little, Brown, 1982.

———. "Journeys into Kansas." In *Temperamental Journeys: Essays on the Modern Literature of Travel,* ed. Michael Kowalewski. Athens: U of Georgia P, 1992.

———. *PrairyErth.* Boston: Houghton Mifflin, 1991.

Hellman, John. *Fables of Fact: The New Journalism as New Fiction.* Urbana: U of Illinois P, 1981.

Henke, Suzette A. *Trauma and Testimony in Women's Life-Writing.* New York: St. Martin's, 1998.

Hersey, John. *Hiroshima.* 1946. Reprint, New York: Knopf, 1985.

Heyne, Eric. "Toward a Theory of Literary Nonfiction." *Modern Fiction Studies* 33, no. 3 (1987): 479–90.

Hixon, Lex. *Coming Home: The Experience of Enlightenment in Sacred Traditions.* Los Angeles: Tarcher, 1989.

Hochschild, Adam. *Half the Way Home.* New York: Penguin, 1986.

Hogan, Linda, Deena Metzger, and Brenda Peterson, eds. *Intimate Nature: The Bond between Women and Animals.* New York: Ballantine, 1998.

Hollowell, John. *Fact and Fiction: The New Journalism and the Nonfiction Novel.* Chapel Hill: U of North Carolina P, 1977.

Hooten, Joy. "Individuation and Autobiography." In *Left, Right or Centre? Psychiatry and the Status Quo,* ed. Harry Heseltine. Occasional paper no. 19. Canberra: University College, U of New South Wales P, 1990.

Houston, Pam. *Cowboys Are My Weakness.* New York: Norton, 1992.

Howarth, William. "Some Principles of Autobiography." *New Literary History* 5 (1974): 363–81.

Hubbell, Sue. *A Book of Bees.* New York: Random House, 1988.

———. *A Country Year.* New York: Random House, 1986.

Jefferson, Thomas. *Notes on the State of Virginia.* Ed. Thomas Perkins Abernethy. New York: Harper & Row, 1964.

Jenkins, McKay. *The Peter Matthiessen Reader.* New York: Vintage, 1999.

Jenkins, Peter. *A Walk across America.* New York: Morrow, 1979.

Kaza, Stephanie. "Gretel Ehrlich." In *American Nature Writers,* ed. John Elder, vol. 1. New York: Scribner's, 1996.

Kerouac, Jack. *On the Road.* New York: Viking, 1958.

Kingston, Maxine Hong. *The Woman Warrior.* New York: Alfred A. Knopf, 1976.

Kircher, Cassandra. "Rethinking Dichotomies in Terry Tempest Williams's *Refuge.*" *ISLE* 3, no. 1 (1996): 97–113.

Kittredge, William. *Owning It All.* St. Paul, Minn.: Graywolf, 1987.

Koller, Alice. *An Unknown Woman.* New York: Holt, Rinehart & Winston, 1982.

Krutch, Joseph Wood. *The Desert Year.* New York: Sloane, 1952.

Lackey, Kris. *Road Frames: The American Highway Narrative.* Lincoln: U of Nebraska P, 1997.

Lakoff, George, and Mark Johnson. *Metaphors We Live By.* Chicago: U of Chicago P, 1980.

Langer, Ellen. *Mindfulness.* Reading, Mass.: Addison-Wesley, 1989.

Leopold, Aldo. *A Sand County Almanac.* New York: Oxford UP, 1949.

Lewis, C. S. *A Grief Observed.* New York: Bantam, 1976.

Lewis, R. W. B. *The American Adam.* Chicago: U of Chicago P, 1955.

Limerick, Patricia Nelson. "What on Earth Is the New Western History?" In *Trails,* ed. Patricia Nelson Limerick, Clyde A. Milner II, and Charles E. Rankin. Lawrence: UP of Kansas, 1991.

Lindbergh, Anne Morrow. *Gift from the Sea.* New York: Pantheon, 1955.

Lomperis, Timothy J. *"Reading the Wind": The Literature of the Vietnam War.* Durham, N.C.: Duke UP, 1987.

Lopez, Barry. "The American Geographies." In *Finding Home,* ed. Peter Sauer. Boston: Beacon, 1992.

———. *Arctic Dreams: Imagination and Desire in a Northern Landscape.* New York, Scribner's, 1986.

Love, Glen A. "Revaluing Nature: Toward an Ecological Criticism." *Western American Literature* 25, no. 3 (1990): 201–15.

Lyons, Thomas. *This Incomperable Lande: A Book of American Nature Writing.* Boston: Houghton Mifflin, 1989.

Lounsberry, Barbara. *The Art of Fact.* New York: Greenwood, 1990.

MacDonald, Bonney. "Desire of the Middle Ground: Opposition, Dialectics, and Dialogic Context in Gretel Ehrlich's *The Solace of Open Spaces.*" *Western American Literature* 33, no. 2 (1998): 127–48.

Maclean, Norman. *A River Runs Through It and Other Stories.* Chicago: U of Chicago P, 1976.

Mailer, Norman. *The Armies of the Night.* New York: New American Library, 1968.

Malcolm X. *The Autobiography of Malcolm X.* 1965. Reprint, New York: Ballantine, 1973.

Mandell, Barrett. "Full of Life Now." In *Autobiography,* ed. James Olney. Princeton: Princeton UP, 1980.

Manes, Christopher. "Nature and Silence." *Environmental Ethics* 14 (winter 1992): 339–50.

Marek, Elizabeth. *The Children at Santa Clara.* New York: Viking Penguin, 1987.

Mason, Mary G. "The Other Voice: Autobiographies of Women Writers."
    In *Autobiography*, ed. James Olney. Princeton: Princeton UP, 1980.
Matthiessen, F. O. *American Renaissance*. London: Oxford UP, 1941.
Matthiessen, Peter. *Nine-Headed Dragon River*. Boston: Shambhala, 1987.
———. *The Snow Leopard*. New York: Bantam, 1979.
McCall, George J. "The Social Looking-Glass: A Sociological Perspective on
    Self-Development." In *The Self: Psychological and Philosophical Issues*, ed.
    Theodore Mischel. Totowa, N.J.: Rowman & Littlefield, 1977.
McCarthy, Mary. *Memories of a Catholic Girlhood*. San Diego: Harcourt
    Brace Jovanovich, 1957.
McCord, Phyllis Frus. "The Ideology of Form: The Nonfiction Novel."
    Genre 19, no. 1 (1986): 59–79.
McEntyre, Marilyn Chandler. "Sue Hubbell." In *American Nature Writers*,
    ed. John Elder, vol. 1. New York: Scribner's, 1996.
McKibben, Bill. *The End of Nature*. New York: Random House, 1989.
McPhee, John. *Basin and Range*. Farrar, Straus & Giroux, 1981.
Melling, Philip M. *Vietnam in American Literature*. Boston: Twayne, 1990.
Metzger, Deena. "Coming Home." In *Intimate Nature*, ed. Linda Hogan,
    Deena Metzger, and Brenda Peterson. New York: Ballantine, 1998.
Morris, John N. *Versions of the Self: Studies in English Autobiography from
    John Bunyan to John Stuart Mill*. New York: Basic, 1966.
Muir, John. *My First Summer in the Sierra*. Boston: Houghton Mifflin, 1911.
Nabhan, Gary Paul. *The Desert Smells Like Rain*. San Francisco: North Point,
    1982.
Naess, Arnie. "The Shallow and the Deep, Long-Range Ecology Movements:
    A Summary." *Inquiry* 16 (1973): 95–100.
Nash, Roderick Frazier. *The Rights of Nature: A History of Environmental
    Ethics*. Madison: U of Wisconsin P, 1989.
Norris, Kathleen. *Dakota: A Spiritual Geography*. New York: Ticknor &
    Fields, 1993.
Norwood, Vera. *Made from This Earth: American Women and Nature*. Chapel
    Hill: U of North Carolina P, 1993.
O'Grady, John P. *Pilgrims to the Wild: Everett Ruess, Henry David Thoreau,
    John Muir, Clarence King, Mary Austin*. Salt Lake City: U of Utah P, 1993.
Oliver, Mary. *Dream Work*. Boston: Atlantic Monthly P, 1976.
Olney, James. "Autobiography and the Cultural Moment." In *Autobiogra-
    phy*, ed. James Olney. Princeton: Princeton UP, 1980.
———. *Metaphors of Self: The Meaning of Autobiography*. Princeton: Prince-
    ton UP, 1972.
Olney, James, ed. *Autobiography*. Princeton: Princeton UP, 1980.
O'Nan, Stewart, ed. *The Vietnam Reader*. New York: Doubleday, 1998.
Orwell, George. *The Road to Wigan Pier*. New York: Harcourt, Brace, 1958.

Paddock, Joe. *Handful of Thunder*. Millville, Minn.: Anvil, 1983.

Payne, Daniel G. "Peter Matthiessen." In *American Nature Writers*, ed. John Elder, vol. 2. New York: Scribner's, 1996.

Percy, Walker. "The Loss of the Creature." In *The Message in the Bottle*. New York: Farrar, Straus & Giroux, 1975.

Peterson, Brenda. *Living by Water*. New York: Ballantine, 1994.

Peterson, Roger Tory. *A Field Guide to the Birds*. Boston: Houghton Mifflin, 1947.

Pollock, George. "Process and Affect: Mourning and Grief." *International Journal of Psycho-Analysis* 59 (1978): 255–76.

Renza, Louis A. "The Veto of the Imagination: A Theory of Autobiography." *New Literary History* 9 (1977): 1–26.

Ricoeur, Paul. *The Rule of Metaphor*. Trans. Robert Czerny. Toronto: U of Toronto P, 1977.

Rose, Gilbert. *Trauma and Mastery in Life and Art*. New Haven: Yale UP, 1987.

Roth, Philip. *Patrimony*. New York: Simon & Schuster, 1991.

———. "Writing American Fiction." *Commentary* 31 (March 1961): 223–33.

Rousseau, Jean-Jacques. *The Confessions* [1781]. Trans. J. M. Cohen. Harmondsworth, U.K.: Penguin, 1953.

Russell, Sharman Apt. *Kill the Cowboy: A Battle of Mythology in the New West*. Reading, Mass: Addison-Wesley, 1993.

Rygiel, Dennis. "On the Neglect of Twentieth Century Nonfiction: A Writing Teacher's View." *College English* 46 (1984): 392–400.

Sanders, Scott Russell. *Staying Put*. Boston: Beacon, 1993.

Sanoff, Alvin P. "Whispers from the Kansas Tallgrass." *U. S. News & World Report*, Nov. 11, 1991.

Schafer, Roy. *Language and Insight*. New Haven: Yale UP, 1978.

Scheese, Don. *Nature Writing: The Pastoral Impulse in America*. New York: Twayne, 1996.

Schmidt, Maia Saj. "Literary Testimonies of Illness and the Reshaping of Social Memory." *a/b: Auto/Biography Studies* 6, no. 1 (1998): 71–91.

Shea, Daniel B., Jr. *Spiritual Autobiography in Early America*. Princeton: Princeton UP, 1968.

Skura, Meredith. *The Literary Use of the Psychoanalytic Process*. New Haven: Yale UP, 1981.

Slovic, Scott. *Seeking Awareness in American Nature Writing*. Salt Lake City: U of Utah P, 1992.

Smith, Barbara Herrnstein. *On the Margins of Discourse: The Relation of Literature to Language*. Chicago: U of Chicago P, 1978.

Smith, Sidonie. *A Poetics of Women's Autobiography*. Bloomington: Indiana UP, 1987.

———. "The (Female) Subject in Critical Venues: Poetics, Politics, Auto-biographical Practices." *a/b: Auto/Biography Studies* 6, no. 1 (1991): 109–30.

Smith, Sidonie, and Julia Watson, eds. *De/Colonizing the Subject: The Politics of Gender in Women's Autobiography.* Minneapolis: U of Minnesota P, 1992.

Sontag, Susan. *Illness as Metaphor.* New York: Farrar, Straus & Giroux, 1978.

Spence, Donald Pond. *Narrative Truth and Historical Truth.* New York: Norton, 1982.

Spengemann, William C. *The Forms of Autobiography: Episodes in the History of a Literary Genre.* New Haven: Yale UP, 1980.

Spiegelman, Art. *Maus I: A Survivor's Tale; My Father Bleeds History.* New York: Pantheon, 1986.

———. *Maus II: A Survivor's Tale; And Here My Troubles Began.* New York: Pantheon, 1991.

Sprinker, Michael. "Fictions of the Self: The End of Autobiography." In *Autobiography,* ed. James Olney. Princeton: Princeton UP, 1980.

Stanton, Domna C. "Autogynography: Is the Subject Different?" In *The Female Autograph,* ed. Domna C. Stanton. Chicago: U of Chicago P, 1987.

Steedman, Carolyn Kay. *Landscape for a Good Woman: A Story of Two Lives.* New Brunswick, N.J.: Rutgers UP, 1987.

Stein, Gertrude. *The Autobiography of Alice B. Toklas.* New York: Harcourt, Brace, 1933.

Steinbeck, John. *The Grapes of Wrath.* New York: Viking, 1939.

———. *Travels with Charley.* New York: Viking, 1963.

Stone, Albert E. *Autobiographical Occasions and Original Acts.* Philadelphia: U of Pennsylvania P, 1982.

Storr, Anthony. *Solitude: A Return to the Self.* New York: Ballantine, 1988.

Stout, Janis P. *The Journey Narrative in American Literature.* Westport, Conn.: Greenwood, 1983.

Tallmadge, John. "Beyond the Excursion: Initiatory Themes in Annie Dillard and Terry Tempest Williams." In *Reading the Earth,* ed. Michael P. Branch et al. Moscow, Idaho: U of Idaho P, 1998.

———. *Meeting the Tree of Life: A Teacher's Path.* Salt Lake City: U of Utah P, 1997.

Teague, David W. "William Least Heat-Moon." In *American Nature Writers,* ed. John Elder, vol. 1. New York: Scribner's, 1996.

Teale, Edwin Way. *North with the Spring.* New York: Dodd, Mead, 1951.

Thoreau, Henry David. *Walden and Other Writings.* Ed. William Howarth. New York: Random House, 1981.

———. *The Journal of Henry David Thoreau.* Ed. Bradford Torrey and Francis H. Allen. Salt Lake City: G. M. Smith, 1984.

Updike, John. "A Long Way Home." *New Yorker,* May 2, 1983.

Viorst, Judith. *Necessary Losses.* New York: Simon & Schuster, 1986.

Watson, Julia. "Toward an Anti-Metaphysics of Autobiography." In *Culture of Autobiography,* ed. Robert Folkenflick. Stanford: Stanford UP, 1993.

Weber, Ronald. *The Literature of Fact: Literary Nonfiction in American Writing.* Athens: Ohio UP, 1980.

White, Hayden. *Tropics of Discourse.* Baltimore: Johns Hopkins UP, 1978.

Wideman, John Edgar. *Brothers and Keepers.* New York: Holt, 1984.

Williams, Terry Tempest. *Refuge: An Unnatural History of Family and Place.* New York: Pantheon, 1991.

Winterowd, Ross. *The Rhetoric of the "Other" Literature.* Carbondale: Southern Illinois UP, 1990.

Wolfe, Tom. "The New Journalism." In *The New Journalism,* ed. Tom Wolfe and E. W. Johnson. New York: Harper & Row, 1973.

Wolff, Geoffrey. *Bad Debts.* New York: Simon & Schuster, 1969.

———. *The Duke of Deception.* New York: Random House. 1979.

———. "Minor Lives." In *Telling Lives,* ed. Marc Pachter. Washington, D.C.: New Republic, 1979.

Wright, Richard. *Black Boy.* New York: Harper & Bros., 1945.

Zavarzadeh, Mas'ud. *The Mythopoeic Reality: The Postwar American Nonfiction Novel.* Urbana: U of Illinois P, 1976.

Zwinger, Ann. *Run, River, Run.* Tucson: U of Arizona P, 1975.

Index

Under the Sign of Nature:
Explorations in Ecocriticism